RACIAL PROFILING IN CANADA:
CHALLENGING THE MYTH OF 'A FEW BAD APPLES'

In October 2002, the *Toronto Star* ran a series of feature articles on racial profiling in which it was indicated that Toronto police routinely target young Black men when making traffic stops. The series drew strong reactions from the community, and considerable protest from the media, politicians, law enforcement officials, and other public figures. Although the articles were supported by substantial documentation and statistical evidence, the Toronto Police Association sued the *Star*, claiming that no such evidence existed. The lawsuit was ultimately rejected in court. However, as a result, the issue of racial profiling – a practice in which certain criminal activities are attributed to individuals or groups on the basis of race or ethno-racial background – was thrust into the national spotlight.

In this comprehensive and thought-provoking work, Carol Tator and Frances Henry explore the meaning of racial profiling in Canada as it is practised not only by the police but also by many other social institutions. While providing a theoretical framework within which they examine racial profiling from a number of perspectives and in a variety of situations, the authors analyse the discourses of the media, policing officials, politicians, civil servants, judges, and other public authorities to demonstrate how those in power communicate and produce existing racialized ideologies and social relations of inequality through their common interactions. Chapter 3, by contributing author Charles Smith, provides a comparison of experiences of racial profiling and policing in Canada, the United States, and the United Kingdom. Chapter 7, by Maureen Brown, through a series of interviews, presents stories that demonstrate the realities of racial profiling in the everyday experiences of Afro-Canadians and ethno-racial minorities.

Informed by a wealth of research and theoretical approaches from a wide range of disciplines, *Racial Profiling in Canada* makes a major contribution to the literature and debates on a topic of growing concern. Together the authors present a compelling examination of the pervasiveness of racial profiling in daily life and its impact on our society, while suggesting directions for change.

CAROL TATOR is a course director in the Department of Anthropology at York University

FRANCES HENRY is a professor emerita in the Department of Anthropology at York University.

CAROL TATOR AND FRANCES HENRY
With Charles Smith and Maureen Brown

Racial Profiling in Canada

CHALLENGING THE MYTH OF
'A FEW BAD APPLES'

UNIVERSITY OF TORONTO PRESS
Toronto Buffalo London

© University of Toronto Press Incorporated 2006
Toronto Buffalo London
Printed in Canada

ISBN-13: 978-0-8020-8714-0 (cloth)
ISBN-10: 0-8020-8714-0 (cloth)

ISBN-13: 978-0-8020-8666-2 (paper)
ISBN-10: 0-8020-8666-7 (paper)

Printed on acid-free paper

Library and Archives Canada Cataloguing in Publication

Tator, Carol
Racial profiling in Canada : challenging the myth of 'a few bad
apples' / Carol Tator and Frances Henry ; with Charles Smith
and Maureen Brown.

Includes bibliographical references and index.
ISBN-13: 978-0-8020-8714-0 (bound)
ISBN-10: 0-8020-8714-0 (bound)
ISBN-13: 978-0-8020-8666-2 (pbk.)
ISBN-10: 0-8020-8666-7 (pbk.)

1. Racism – Canada.   2. Racial profiling in law enforcement –
Canada.   3. Minorities – Civil rights – Canada.
I. Henry, Frances, 1931–   II. Title.

HV7936.R3T38 2006   305.8'00971   C2006-900895-7

University of Toronto Press acknowledges the financial assistance to its
publishing program of the Canada Council for the Arts and the Ontario
Arts Council.

University of Toronto Press acknowledges the financial support for its
publishing activities of the Government of Canada through the Book
Publishing Industry Development Program (BPIDP).

This book is dedicated to all those who dared break the silence surrounding racial profiling in Canada: victims and their families; Black and Aboriginal communities; the publisher, editors, and journalists at the Toronto Star; *and those courageous members of law enforcement agencies who dared to challenge the official dominant narratives of denial, deflection, and oppression.*

Contents

Acknowledgments

Many people were instrumental in bringing this book to fruition. We wish to thank Dean Drummond of the Faculty of Arts at York University for providing support towards the publication of this book. We are also appreciative of the Canadian Race Relations Foundation for funding the initial phase of our study on racial profiling. Our first contributing author, Charles Smith's comparative study of racial profiling in the UK, the USA, and Canada provides a critical comparative perspective on racial profiling in those countries. Maureen Brown's chapter documents the findings of her study, 'In Their Own Voices,' and provides important insights into the impact of racial profiling on the everyday lives of young Black Canadians in the Greater Toronto Area. Both of these studies were commissioned by the African Canadian Community Coalition on Racial Profiling.

Racial Profiling in Canada: Challenging the Myth of 'a Few Bad Apples' is our third book to be published by the University of Toronto Press on the subject of racism in Canada. Over the past ten years, our work has benefited significantly from the support and expertise of many people at the press, especially Virgil Duff and Anne Laughlin.

Central to the issue of racial profiling are the costs and consequences to those individuals and communities that continue to experience this injustice in their everyday lives. We wish to acknowledge the courage and strength it took to share these stories and experiences in public forums and inquiries, in consultations with researchers, in interviews with the media, and in many other venues. We hope their voices will be heard and that actions will be taken across a wide range of public institutions.

The *Toronto Star* has also played a significant role in this book. The commitment by the *Star* to help uncover the 'real' story of racial profiling in Toronto was sustained over more than three years. We wish to recognize the contribution of all the columnists who worked on this story, especially Jim Rankin, who not only was part of the team of writers, but also produced the photograph that enhances the cover of this book.

Finally, we thank our husbands, Charles Tator and Jeff Henry, and our children Ira, Michael, and Julie Tator, and Terrence and Miriam Henry, for their love and support, which has enriched our lives and our work.

RACIAL PROFILING IN CANADA:
CHALLENGING THE MYTH OF 'A FEW BAD APPLES'

Introduction

Profiling is the inverse of law enforcement. In law enforcement, a crime is discovered and the police then look for a suspect who might possibly have committed it. Profiling means that a suspect is discovered and the police then look for a crime for the person to have possibly committed. (Martinot 2003, 168)

This book on racial profiling begins with a story. 'Peter Owusu-Ansah's Nightmare' by Carol Goar appeared in the *Toronto Star* on 15 August 2004. Peter's story is repeated daily on the streets of Toronto and in towns and cities across Canada. The victims are often Black, but racial profiling also affects other racialized minority populations, including Aboriginals, Asians, Muslims, Arabs, and Latinos. The following is an edited version of the *Star* article:

Peter Owusu-Ansah is young, Black, and hearing impaired. Over a four-year period he was stopped by the police while riding his bicycle to work, while sitting in coffee shops, while walking down the street ... a total of seventeen times. He had been ordered to empty his knapsack and pockets countless times. He had been pushed against walls. 'Now, every time I see them coming, I'm afraid,' he says. The first seventeen times the police stopped him for questioning, he was cooperative. The *eighteenth* time (in September 2002), he and a group of friends had finished a game of basketball at the Bob Rumball Centre for the Deaf in Toronto. Afterwards they stopped at McDonald's and walked to the bus stop. Along the way a police cruiser, lights flashing, stopped them for questioning. The two officers got out of their car and began asking questions. Owusu-Ansah, who can lip-read, explained that his friends were deaf and that he was hard of hearing. One of the officers demanded that he produce identification; he responded that he did not have any on him. She asked for his name, address, and date of birth. 'Why are you asking me all these questions?' he responded. Two more officers were summoned. Owusu-Ansah was then separated from his friends and interrogated by another constable. What happened next has become the subject of two legal actions and a complaint to the Ontario Human Rights Commission. The police say they questioned him in relation to a reported robbery at a nearby high school. He alleges that he was pushed into the police cruiser and taken to a spot behind a high school and there was punched in the head and in the groin repeatedly. He couldn't understand anything the officers were saying because he cannot lip-read in the dark. Finally, the police officers put him back in the car and dropped him off at a bus stop. Owusu-Ansah filed a complaint with the Ontario Human Rights Commission and also launched a suit against the two police officers for assault. Elizabeth Brückmann, the lawyer handling his human rights complaint, held out little hope that the two officers would be convicted, arguing that 'when you have the word of a young Black male against the word of two police officers, the young Black man is going to lose every time.'[1]

Stories like Peter Owusu-Ansah's inspired the *Toronto Star* to publish a series of articles on the racial profiling of African Canadians. The first of these ran on 19 October 2002. Racial profiling is an issue that resonates strongly in the Black community and in other racialized minority communities. It affects the daily lives of men, women, and youth of colour. The *Star*, a paper with a long history of in-depth reporting on

---

1 On 14 October 2004 the case was heard by Judge Paul Robertson. The court rejected most of the constable's evidence and found that his explanation for why he drove Peter Owusu-Ansah to the parking lot of a high school at 1 a.m. 'defies common sense.' But in his decision he concluded that the victim had a 'pre-existing animus to police.' Owusu-Ansah attributed this to the fact that he had often been singled out for racial profiling because he is deaf and a person of colour. The two officers were acquitted of assaulting Owusu-Ansah, who has since filed a complaint with the Ontario Human Rights Commission against the officers and the Toronto Police Services Board (Small 2004). Note well that Judge Robertson gave no indication that he ever considered the role played by deafness in the miscommunication between Owusu-Ansah and the police. Yet as noted by Lesli Bisgould, a staff lawyer with ARCH, a legal resource centre for people with disabilities, Owusu-Ansah used a sign-language interpreter in court, and his first language is neither English nor ASL (http://www.archlegalclinic.ca/publications/archAlert/2004/08_dec13).

social issues, based its new series on a two-year probe of race and crime statistics gathered from a Toronto police database that documents arrests and charges laid. The database detailed more than 480,000 incidents in which an individual was arrested or ticketed for an offence, along with nearly 800,000 criminal and other charges laid by police from late 1996 to early 2002. The data were accessed through the Freedom of Information Act after police denied the *Star* access.

During its investigations, the *Star* consulted a statistician from York University to ensure the validity of its methodology and analysis. The data revealed significant disparities in how Blacks and Whites are treated in law enforcement practices. Specifically, they showed that a disproportionate number of Black motorists are ticketed for violations that only surface following a traffic stop. Furthermore, Black people who are charged with simple drug possession are taken to police stations more often than Whites facing the same charge. And once at the station, Blacks are held overnight for a bail hearing at twice the rate of Whites.

The *Star* series on race and policing generated hundreds of news stories, opinion pieces, editorials, and letters to the editor. Although the coverage was mainly in the *Star*, the issue was also taken up in other print media – including alternative presses such as *Share*, the African-Canadian newspaper – and on television and radio news programs, both local and national. The *Star* series provoked an immediate and hostile reaction from the police chief, the Toronto Police Services Board, the Toronto Police Association, and the president of the Toronto Police Union. Many politicians, as well as journalists from other papers, adopted a common discursive position: categorical denial that racial profiling exists. On the other side of the divide, voices in the Black community affirmed the reality of racial profiling as a persistent and systemic problem in their lives. With near unanimity, they validated the *Star*'s findings.

The *Star* series provoked a discursive crisis that continues to reverberate. Here, a 'discursive crisis' refers to a set of reactions that profoundly affect society – specifically, the state of minority–majority relations. The crisis is sometimes of short duration, but this one was prolonged. Three years after the *Star* began publishing its series, the struggle against racial profiling continues, as does the Black community's battle against racism in policing and in the broader Canadian society.

The Theoretical Foundations of This Book

This book is informed by many disciplines, including cultural studies, critical criminology, and critical race theory. In the sometimes acrimonious debate over the efficacy of various theoretical models in academic and other forms of research, we concur with Cottle (2000), who suggests that the clash of frameworks with regard to questions of knowledge, methodology, and the role of politics in academic life can be a positive force when issues of vital concern to society are addressed. Such a clash can help push the boundaries of knowledge into new, productive, and creative areas. We believe that critical theory in the social sciences, criminology, and the law, and the critical analytical approach that forms the core of cultural studies, taken together provide an appropriate methodology for studying the volatile issue of racial profiling. Critical theory addresses the contested constructs of ideology and hegemony, power and powerlessness, domination and resistance, representation and misrepresentation, normality and abnormality. It acknowledges the dialectical nature of knowledge, truth, and 'commonsense' beliefs. A critical approach also underscores the importance of discourse and discursive analysis, and dominant and counter narratives. Concepts such as essentialism, difference, identity, subjectivity, meaning, and myth are vehicles for understanding the dynamics of racism in democratic liberal societies. Thus the many disciplines that have been influenced by critical theory offer both common and unique strategic tools for uncovering the nexus of race, racism, and crime; they also provide alternative approaches and insights for studies of how racial profiling has been injected into policing and other institutional systems.

We have used the discursive approach in much of our recent work (Henry and Tator 1998, 2002, 2005), which has been strongly influenced by many scholars, including Hall (1997), Hall and colleagues (1978), van Dijk (1988, 1991, 1993), Fiske (1994, 1999, 2000), and Fairclough (1992, 1995). This approach emphasizes the belief that in democratic liberal societies, discourse essentially reproduces the racialized beliefs, values, norms, and actions of the White majority. For that reason, we and our contributing authors, Charles Smith and Maureen Brown, have chosen to use the 'discursive event' as means of accessing the many complex and challenging issues that racial profiling raises in modern Canada.

Although this book is framed around a particular set of phenomena, the issues addressed by the *Star* series and the responses that series generated have their roots in the broader historical struggle of Black people to be treated as full and equal citizens of a democratic liberal society. The long and heated debate over racial profiling reflects the deep chasm between the White political, cultural, and social systems – which have long been dominant and rarely change – and the individuals and groups who suffer from the dis-enabling and marginalizing effects of those systems.

The crisis the *Star* series provoked took the form of a highly charged set of dominant discourses across a broad spectrum of public spaces, which included newsrooms, courtrooms, and government agencies. Also, several academic and government-sponsored conferences were convened. The issue of racial profiling was hotly contested in the meeting rooms of the Police Service Board and in forums organized by social agencies and community and youth agencies. Perhaps the most wrenching of these 'conversations' took place in the private spaces of Black families. Royson James, a columnist at the *Star*, wrote of how racial profiling was affecting his own family:

> Only some of us parents know the palpable, paralyzing fear that the car will be stopped by Toronto, Peel, Durham or York police, searched, have its passengers harassed and humiliated – simply because the driver is our black son ...
>
> Ask your black colleague and he or she will share DWB stories. That's Driving While Black. They have the scars, most emotional but some physical as well to prove it ... They know the stereotype of the angry young black male; that a significant number of police officers feel blacks are criminal beasts deserving attention from law enforcers; that some elements of society harbour such racist sentiments; that blacks don't have the same freedom to make mistakes like everyone else because the consequences could be harsher, the punishment more severe. (R. James 2002)

The *Star* series and the responses to it from White authorities offer critical insights into how racialized discourse is used to banish – or at the very least deflect attention away from – the general issue of racism in policing and the specific issue of the racial profiling of Blacks.

We argue in this book that racial profiling is a manifestation of 'democratic racism,' in which bias and discrimination 'cloak their presence' in liberal principles. Democratic racism is an ideology in which two conflicting sets of values are made congruent. The consequences of this tension ensure that commitments to justice, fairness, and equality conflict with, but at the same time coexist with, negative feelings about people of colour and differential treatment of them (see Henry and Tator 2005).

The term racial profiling is of rather recent origin (see Harris 2002, 11). It is usually confined to discussions of the policing of racially diverse communities. In chapter 3 of this book, by Charles Smith, these practices are described in relation to the Black community. However, our use of this term is broader and deeper; it includes the various discourses that are articulated by the police, governments, and other authorities, *and* by the media, in their efforts to rationalize and justify racialized behaviours and practices. In our view, racial profiling is another word for racism or racialization; for that reason, we give it a discursive meaning, one that applies to all social institutions and aspects of everyday life within systems of social control and representation. Like Hall (1978, 1997) and Foucault (1977, 1980), we analyse the ideological foundations of racial profiling as they are revealed in the everyday dominant discourses of elite public authorities, including the police.

This approach, which draws from both Hall and Foucault, facilitates our understanding of White dominant beliefs and value systems. An exploration of the ideological underpinnings of racial profiling reveals how the 'the body of the criminal is produced and disciplined' within discourse according to various discursive formations, such as the state of knowledge about crime and the criminal and what counts as 'true' about how to change criminal behaviour (Foucault 1977, 63).

Our approach to the issue and practice of racial profiling is to deconstruct the hegemonic force that shapes the lives of Black people and other minoritized communities by identifying the markers of meaning that underlie the everyday text, talk, and actions of the policing community and of other White elites, including politicians and journalists (Hall 1980; van Dijk 1993).

The first crucial element in racial profiling is its link to the practices of racialization – practices that can be seen to operate in virtually every sector of society. Racialization is part of a broader process that inferiorizes and excludes groups in the population. It refers to 'both the cultural or political processes or situations where race is involved as an explanation' (Murji and Solomos 2004). It categorizes people and their social relations in terms of their biological characteristics.

Racialization begins with ideology, which is then filtered through the everyday micro-interactions and discourses of police, security officers, judges, journalists and editors, educators, politicians, and bureaucrats, among others. The processes of racialization are visible in the negative representations (in language, images, and ideas) of people of colour and Aboriginals, who are constructed as 'problem people.' Monolithic and persistent stereotypes of these groups are found in popular culture – in films, TV and print news stories, literature, advertising, and music.

Racialization is embedded in authoritative texts such as law books, government documents, and parliamentary debates. Racialization is supported by polls and surveys that repeatedly frame questions in ways that highlight the dominant culture's perceptions, beliefs, and norms. The racialization of minority groups is obvious in the economic, social, political, and cultural structures of society – structures that ensure an unequal distribution of resources and that preserve power for the hegemonic White culture (Anthias 1998; Small 1999).

Racism can also be understood as the racialization of the White race. Here, Whiteness becomes a socially constructed identity, a force that both compels and underpins the maintenance of systems of Eurocentric and Anglocentric power and privilege. Whiteness can be viewed *as* an *essentializing* strategy (often unconscious) for defending and maintaining the established social order and for preserving White cultural hegemony (Gabriel 1998). In this book we shall demonstrate that Whiteness plays a significant role in racial profiling, just as it does in all other forms of racism.

In deconstructing racial profiling, it is also important to draw attention to the role played by culture.[2] Scholars of Whiteness studies – especially those who focus on the relationship between race and crime (Razack 1998; Visano 2002; Jiwani 2002; Barnes 2002) – maintain that the discourses of race and racism often use culture to reinforce the distance between 'our' superior (that is, Eurocentric and Anglocentric) cultural values and norms and 'their' inferior (that is, non-Western) ones. For example, the discourses around criminal acts by particular minority groups depend on essentialized and stereotypical thinking. Thus, Jamaican culture becomes a signifier of deviant cultural behaviour, especially with regard to drug-related crimes (Barnes 2002; Benjamin 2002; Henry and Tator 2002; James 2002). In the same way, Asian

---

2 Lawrence (1982), working in the United Kingdom, many years ago emphasized the cultural underpinnings of racist ideology.

cultural groups are commonly depicted by police (and the media) as predisposed to gang-related activities. The categorization of minority gangs by 'ethnicity' and of majority gangs by 'activity' is contributing to the racialization of the street gang issue. In 1996 the Montreal Police Department declared that it would be making street gangs a priority issue for the next five years. It then identified five racial groups from which street gangs originate: Jamaican, Haitian, Asiatic, extreme right, and Latino (Symons 2002). More recently, Muslims and Arabs have been subjected to increased scrutiny and surveillance. Muslim and Arab cultural norms have been linked consistently with deviant (terrorist) acts.

Aboriginal peoples are constantly inferiorized, racialized, and racially profiled. Race-based inequality characterizes both the current realities of Aboriginal life and the long history of colonialist and racialized policies that have systematically undermined Aboriginal economic, social, and political self-sufficiency. This is dramatically demonstrated by the incarceration rates of Aboriginal people in Canada's prison system (Royal Commission on Aboriginal People 1996). It is also demonstrated by the growing evidence of the racial profiling of First Nations men in Saskatoon, Saskatchewan, and elsewhere in the West; some of these men have been found dead after encounters with police (see chapter 3). While we were writing this book, two public inquiries were in progress, investigating the role of the police in the deaths of Neil Stonechild in Saskatoon and Dudley George in Forest, Ontario.

Social class is closely related to processes of racialization and criminalization. Those identified as at the bottom of the social and economic hierarchy are perceived as the most prone to crime and also as less credible and deserving. This form of marginalization and stigmatization is embedded in the everyday discourses of police, judges, and other public authorities. Poor people are seen and described by the dominant discourse as dispossessed; furthermore, they are characterized in ways that suggest they are disposable (Jiwani 2002; Dulude 2000). The emphasis on Black crime and crime associated with other minority groups, rather than on white-collar crime, reflects the capitalistic nature of Canadian society, in which social stratification is based on wealth and White privilege and which simultaneously constructs people of colour as inferior (Russell 1998). Criminalization and racialization can be understood as a multidimensional process shaped by dominant narratives whose central theme is the so-called 'other.'

Problematizing Language in Writing about Racism

One of the first challenges in analysing racism is establishing an appropriate terminology. One must search for words that themselves are not perceived as racialized; at the same time, one must clearly and accurately communicate what racism means. However, as the phenomenon of racism continues to take on new forms and manifestations, so too does the language modify. Words change; and as well, their historical context affects how they are used. Furthermore, the sometimes fundamental changes that words undergo imply that there is no fixed or correct meaning for any term.

Apple (1993, 25) expresses the challenge of language in this way: 'Concepts do not remain still very long. They have wings so to speak, and can be induced to fly from place to place.' So in identifying the meaning of terms, one must consider the specific context in which they are used. We caution the reader that terms such as culture, race, truth, Black, White, Native, and immigrant, for example, are not neutral; they exist in many different social and interpretative frameworks. Powerful currents alter interpretations depending on the situation, location, and social context (Lentricchia and McLaughlin 1990; Fiske 1994).

Colour remains the nucleus of the race classification system, yet paradoxically, it bears little relation to the actual skin tones of human beings. No White person is truly white, nor is any Black individual completely Black. Whites do not consider themselves part of the colour spectrum; indeed, they identify their group as constituting the universal norm. However, the gradations of colour from white to black associated with various racial groups have economic, social, and cultural consequences. The ideology that defines Whites as superior renders people of different colours inferior.

As will be demonstrated throughout this book, skin colour has an important relationship to status and position in Canadian society. The language of colour delineates the politics of domination and subordination; it has been noted that 'White ... is the colour of domination' (Razack 1998, 11). Making this point in terms of her personal experience as a person of colour, Joanne St Lewis (1996, 28) observes: 'In conversations about race, all of my being is telescoped to my skin. The colour of my skin drives the engine of my public life.'

When we use the terms 'racial minorities,' 'people of colour,' and 'racialized communities,' we will be referring to groups of people who because of their physical characteristics are subjected to differential and unequal treatment in Canada. Their minority status is the result of a lack of access to power, privilege, and prestige in relation to the White majority. Although there are significant differences among racial minorities or people of colour, just as there are within any ethno-racial group, the members of these diverse communities share a history of discriminatory barriers and exposure to racial bias based on the colour of their skin. So for the purposes of this book, we will be grouping them together.

Also, references to colour in this book will be used in their political sense, and the terms "Black" and "White" will be capitalized to reflect this. The reader will note that some references citing British literature or experiences use the term 'Black' inclusively, to refer to all people of colour. American scholars, on the other hand, use 'black' to refer specifically to people of African descent.[3]

Finally, it is important to note the colour-coded nature of the language used to categorize different forms of criminal activities, as in 'Black-on-Black crime,' 'driving while Black,' and 'White-collar crime.' Throughout this book we will be using discourse analysis as an analytical tool for decoding the cultural symbols and representations that underlie the articulated plurality of discourses that frame the issues of racial profiling and criminality.

Chapter Outline

Chapter 1 sets out the theoretical approach, developed from several sources. We draw from some of the approaches utilized by other scholars to establish how race is used as a proxy for criminality. Applying methods of analysis and interpretation derived from a Foucauldian model and incorporated into the work, for example, of Rose (2002), Fiske (2002), Visano (2002), and Hall (1978), we show that racial profiling arises from the need to identify and manage 'risky' minority populations. Blackness becomes a racial signifier for crime and a threat to law and the social order. The Black body seen through the 'White gaze' requires racially differentiated forms of surveillance, containment, and control (Fiske 2000). The theoretical perspective includes the notion that racialization can also be analysed from the perspective of White-

---

3 Fiske employs the convention of capitalizing 'Black' to signify the positive reclaiming of that word. He suggests that the spelling 'black' in White racist discourse is derogatory.

ness – that is, the process whereby White culture comes to be interpreted as normative and natural, truthful and meritorious, civil and law abiding, tolerant and accommodating difference.

In chapter 2 we explore the processes of racialization and cultural hegemony that occur across public institutions such as the justice system, the immigration system, and the media. In this way an overview of how African Canadians are marginalized in each of these sectors is demonstrated. Our analysis explores the diverse ways in which the Black male body becomes culturally marked as 'different,' 'deviant,' and dangerous. At the intersections of diverse systems such as government, courtrooms, schools, newsrooms, television studios, radio talk shows, videos, and films, the images and discourses of Blackness become charged with the notion of the undesirable, alien other, who represents a threat to the moral and social order.

In chapter 3 the first contributing author, Charles Smith, analyses racial profiling and the practices the police in three different countries with racially diverse (and especially Black) communities. Smith provides an important historical overview as well as a contemporary critical approach to the issue of racial profiling as it has unfolded in the United States, the United Kingdom, and Canada. Drawing from an accumulated body of evidence that the police have long been racist towards Blacks, he explores how police forces have responded to the challenge of creating more just and equitable law enforcement systems. In the Canadian section of his chapter, he analyses racial profiling as it has affected Blacks in Ontario and Quebec. He ends his contribution by considering the racial profiling of Aboriginal people in Saskatchewan, Manitoba, British Columbia, and Ontario.

Chapter 4 focuses on police culture. The authors analyse some of the core values and norms of that culture. We then critically examine the tensions between the core culture – its everyday assumptions, values, beliefs, and practices – and the more macrolevel structure in which policies are developed, implemented, or ignored. The police culture exhibits numerous cultural traits, including social isolation, solidarity, a siege mentality, militaristic modes and structures, codes of secrecy and silence, and tensions between the top brass and the cops on the beat. All of these traits strongly shape the relationship between the police and the diverse publics they serve. The chapter discusses how these elements influence the police in their everyday interactions with people of colour, especially Blacks, and how police culture itself reinforces racism.

Chapter 5 begins with a theoretical introduction to the subject of narrative inquiry and its importance to the themes of this book. Dominant and oppositional narratives and discourses are powerful tools for examining human experience, especially racism. Deconstructing the discourses surrounding social issues such as racial profiling offers powerful insights into the processes of racialization. We suggest that conflicting dominant and oppositional narratives help expose the complex ruptures beneath the surface of institutional practices of policing.

Chapter 6 takes a case study approach to explore some of the discursive strategies that were followed by the police and other public authorities in their response to the *Star* series on race, crime, and policing. The White elites – including police officials and highly placed political figures – spoke with almost a single voice. The messages embedded in their communications with the public were contextualized in the discourses of deflection and denial – in the discourse of 'Otherness' and the discourse of moral panic, among others. We apply discourse analysis to deconstruct the dominant narratives of police officials, politicians, and other influential figures. We then study the texts of several journalists from Toronto newspapers and their responses to the issue of the racial profiling of Blacks. The chapter concludes with some startling revelations by a group of Black officers on the Toronto Police Service, who decided to share their own experiences with being racially profiled by their fellow officers. The focus group of Black officers was held in 2003, but became public only in March 2005.

Chapter 7, by our second contributing author, Maureen Brown, considers the role of counter-narratives – that is, stories that demonstrate the realities of racial profiling in the everyday experiences of African Canadians and other ethno-racial minorities. On the basis of extensive interviews across the Greater Toronto Area, Brown identifies some of the key feelings and experiences shared by young Blacks in relation to racial profiling. Some of her respondents were African-Canadian police officers. Her chapter offers a probing analysis of what racial profiling looks like and feels like to those who experience it. As well, the interviews offer constructive perspectives on how to address the problem of racial profiling.

Chapter 8 identifies some of the main findings of our analysis. A key premise of this book is that certain events require narration; the discursive crisis that flowed out of the *Star* series was one of those of events. The after-effects of the *Star* series and the lived experiences of racial profiling – which are ongoing – provide an opportunity to deconstruct the dynamics of discursive racism and, at the same time, to challenge widely accepted stereotypical assumptions about the alleged relationship between race and crime.

The controversy the *Star* series inspired had deep roots and was intrinsically linked to the struggles of Black people to be treated as full and equal citizens and to be freed from more than three decades of racialized police practices. The findings of this book also emphasize the powerful link between racism in policing and the racism that crosses all institutional sectors and spaces – racism that inferiorizes and marginalizes Blacks and other people of colour.

The personal accounts of racial profiling and other forms of racism documented throughout this book challenge the ideological framework of a democratic liberal society. The polarization between Whiteness and Blackness, and between "Aboriginalness" and Anglocentrism, raises questions about whether Canada should really be seen as a multicultural model by the rest of the world. However, in the concluding section of this book we point to some recent events that suggest change is possible.

1 Theoretical Perspectives

White people create the dominant images of the world and don't quite see that they thus construct the world in their image. (Dyer 1997, 9)

The relations between Black communities and law enforcement agencies have a long and troubled history in several countries, including Canada. We believe that the nexus between race and crime is rooted in racist ideologies as well as in the processes of racialization, culturalization, and criminalization that form the basis for racism in democratic liberal societies. These same processes provide a strong theoretical framework for a critical analysis of racial profiling.

This book draws from the work of many scholars (Rose 2002; Garland 1996; Visano 2002; Fiske 2000) and is informed by several theoretical perspectives on how postmodern societies marginalize and disadvantage certain groups, especially Blacks. Four distinct albeit related theoretical approaches have most influenced this book: (1) *Whiteness studies* examine the racialization of Whiteness and its role in sustaining systems of power and privilege. This approach focuses on Whites as a racial group in hegemonic control of marginalized subgroups in society. (2) *Blackness studies* focus on the abnormalization of Blackness and the Black body image. (3) *Danger and racialization theory* refers to the idea that people of colour – and especially Blacks – pose a danger to predominantly White societies. (4) *Discursive analysis theories* explore how White hegemonic discourse produces, reinforces, and disseminates racism in democratic liberal societies. Discursive analysis also examines the role of oppositional and counter discourses in challenging hegemonic ideologies and discourses as well as racialized practices.

One purpose of this book is to uncover and deconstruct racial profiling practices in Canadian society. We shall be concentrating on police activity but shall also be connecting that activity to the ways in which politicians, the media, and other White elites reinforce processes of racialization. To put it in Foucauldian terms, racial profiling has become a 'regime of truth' the purpose of which is to preserve and reinforce systems of White privilege and social control – systems that are rooted in structures of dominance.

The term 'racial profiling' has undergone some changes since it was coined in the United States. In its original sense, it referred to the compiling of race-based criminal profiles for use by the police. Nowadays the term is used in the United States and Canada to refer to the police use of discretionary authority to pull over Black drivers (Engel, Calnon, and Bernard 2002). It is also used by immigration authorities and other government agencies to describe an approach to controlling racialized minorities, including Arabs, Muslims, Aboriginals, and Latinos. However, it is used most often in the context of police behaviour – specifically, discriminatory behaviour rooted in stereotypes and prejudices held by individual police officers.

Racism within police forces has often been dismissed as nothing more than the rogue actions of a limited number of isolated and bigoted individuals. This is the 'few bad apples' thesis. Encoded in this discourse is the denial of racism as a set of institutional practices and patterned cultural behaviours that collectively support and reinforce racially different systemic outcomes. The implication of the 'bad apples' perspective is that all we need to do to solve the problem of racial profiling is provide police officers with more training in race relations and cultural sensitivity, or recruit a limited number of people of colour. This, of course, leaves unchanged the structure of policing as well as the core ideology of police officers – their beliefs, values, and norms.

To describe individual police as racist, or even to blame general systems of social control in society, is to evade the real question: Why does racial profiling occur in modern, industrialized nation-states such as Canada? In this book we will be applying various theories to the question of how prevalent racial profiling is in this country, and why. Our emphasis will be on investigating police profiling as a striking manifestation of the cultural and structural racism that is deeply embedded not just in the criminal justice system but in many other institutions in Canadian society. But in order to succeed at our task, we will have to investigate racial bias and the discriminatory treatment of people of colour across *all* sectors and institutions in Canadian society (see chapter 2).

Studies of racial profiling quickly encounter methodological problems. This chapter is concerned mainly with the theoretical perspectives that have influenced our work; but before we go into that, it is important that we sketch some of the research biases and thorny methodological issues that have characterized both studies of racial profiling and, more generally, the broader topic of the relationship between race and crime.

Research Issues in the Study of Race, Crime, and Racial Profiling

Social science research, most of which has been conducted in the United States and the United Kingdom, has not been especially useful in providing accurate data on police stops of Black drivers. The main methodological problem here is that it is difficult to establish accurate baseline rates of stops of Black drivers. Once the stops, searches, charges, and so on have been quantified, the figures for Black drivers must be compared with those for some other population group – typically, White drivers. Yet it is often difficult to decide which baseline rate of White drivers should be used for comparison. Should it be the rate for Whites overall, relative to that for 'non-Whites'? or the numbers who engage in traffic offences? or some other rate? Without a accurate, standardized indicator of comparison it cannot be determined that Black drivers have been subjected to more police stops. According to Engel and colleagues (2002), most researchers have relied on 'demographic proxies' – that is, they have used the numbers of Whites and non-Whites in the overall population. The problem with this approach is that it is a gross overall indicator and subsumes finer distinctions such as the number of drivers in each population group, their ages, their prior driving charges and convictions, and the like. In Canada, the *Toronto Star* study used overall population statistics.

As Engel and colleagues (2000) observed, most studies of police stops of Black drivers have compared those drivers to a sample of White drivers. In fact, nearly all studies of Black crime in the United States have compared Black and White crime rates either for particular crimes or in order to generate overall rates of crime.

Engel and colleagues (ibid.) analysed a number of American studies on racial profiling. They found six that showed differences by race, which 'likely reflected racial discrimination by police officers.' In a few other studies, the data collected could not 'rule out alternative and legitimate, race-neutral explanations for disparity' (ibid., 259). Generally speaking, though, progressive legal opinion in the United States, the United Kingdom, and Canada generally posits that the police do conduct racial profiling, especially of people of African descent but also of other racialized groups. Very often, stops and searches are conducted for no other reason than that the driver is Black, under thirty-five, and driving a late-model vehicle. This is how the phrase 'driving while Black' has achieved the status of folklore. The studies as a whole, whatever their methodological weaknesses, tend to show disparities in stops. These findings, combined with those from studies that report personal accounts from within Black communities, make it clear that the police do stop Blacks more often than others. Thus the 'few rotten apples' theory is grossly inadequate to answer the central question: Why does racial profiling against Blacks arise so consistently in so many countries?

Setting aside police stops for a moment, a great deal of social science research reflects a much broader concern with Black crime rates in the United States and elsewhere. Specifically, research has concentrated on how high or low the rates actually are, and on how to explain Black crime rates. Covington (1999, 560) has challenged the basic methodological premises that underlie such studies: 'The notion that Black crime rates are high and thus the desire to theorize about that excess stems solely from a comparison of Black and White crime rates.' This results in the racialization of the Black crime rate: 'Between-race analyses, which compare Blacks and Whites, are able to racialize, in part, because they impose a uniform response on Blacks: this means that all Blacks are believed to react in like manner (racial response) or to be motivated by similar concerns (racial motives)' (ibid., 560). Covington argues compellingly that the construct of the 'high Black crime rate' – which has been generated solely in comparison to Whites – has tarred an entire population as prone to crime. It ignores the fact that the vast majority of Blacks are not criminals. Using murder rates in the United States as an example, she notes that even among the urban Black 'underclass' – from which the majority of Black murderers come – murder rates are high only relative to those in White communities. Even so, the vast majority of similarly placed 'underclass' Black citizens who do not commit murder are assigned 'criminal propensities.'

Delgado writes on the same point: 'No one focuses on White crime or sees it as a problem. In fact the very category "White crime" sounds funny, like some sort of debater's trick' (in Russell 1998, 110). Russell notes that a language has been developed for describing and studying black crime – a language that includes terms such as 'Black-on-Black crime,' 'Black criminality,' and 'Black crime.' This language does *not* include terms such as 'White crime' or 'White-on-White crime' (ibid.). There is a widespread belief – largely fostered by sensationalist reporting in the news media – that Blacks commit more crimes than Whites. Yet in the United States, the majority of those arrested are White, and 49 percent of the total incarcerated population is White (ibid.). Blacks commit more crimes in proportion to their overall numbers in the population; that said, the majority of crimes are committed by Whites.

The overemphasis on Black crime and the general perceptions of Black criminality are also reflected in analyses of these issues in criminology and the social sciences. For example, Russell (ibid.) examined thousands of articles in the Lexus Nexus database and found only a handful that discussed White crime or 'White-on-White' crime. Along with journalists and law professors, criminologists have avoided explicitly recognizing White crime. Russell reviewed four influential criminology journals and found that between 1992 and 1996 they published few articles devoted specifically to 'White crime.'

White crime *is* being studied – it just isn't called White crime. The many academic articles that focus on the deviance of White adults and White youths avoid terms such as 'White criminality.' The non-labelling of White crime contrasts sharply with the pervasive labelling of Black crime. Moreover, social scientists use a number of supposedly 'race neutral' terms, such as 'inner city,' 'truly disadvantaged,' 'underclass,' 'poverty ghetto,' and 'urban.' Often these are code words for 'Black crime.' Russell suggests that the unequal focus on Black crime may be related the attention paid by the media and the social sciences to street crime, which is disproportionately committed by Blacks. This, however, does not explain the lack of attention to White crime. Researchers have observed that Whites commit more white-collar crimes because they have a disproportionate opportunity to commit high-status offences, since they are more likely to hold high-status jobs.

It has been suggested that the amount of attention focused on Black crime relative to White crime is also related to the relatively small numbers of Black professional criminologists and to the underrepresentation of Blacks in the legal professions and the justice system (ibid.). Thus one of the central methodological issues in race/crime studies relates to the tendency of not only the media but also the social sciences and traditional criminology to focus on the study of Black criminality while generally ignoring White crime. Schissel and Brooks (2002) also point to the role of conventional criminology in framing how we think about (a) issues of 'badness and goodness,' (b) what should be defined as criminality, and (c) the role of 'criminogenic cultures that produce the values and norms of criminality in its members – values and norms that run counter to the norms of greater society' (ibid., 51).

The Four Theoretical Perspectives

Whiteness Studies

The emerging field of 'Whiteness studies' focuses on racialization – a process that is normally understood as making race a relevant factor to people or situations when it is, in fact, totally irrelevant. In this context, we are reversing the term to refer to the racialization of the 'White' race. Whiteness scholars accept – as do all critical scholars today – that race as a biological construct is no longer important or relevant to the understanding of human differences. Yet social racism continues to emphasize race as a visible trait for use in practising racial discrimination. Whiteness studies maintain that if people of colour are racialized, then so should Whites be recognized and identified as members of the White or Caucasian race. White identity is based on the concept that those who have traditionally held hegemonic positions of power over all other groups have done so by constructing hierarchical structures of exclusion and marginality. White studies scholars contend that Whites must accept a race category for themselves, but one which does not include the assumption that they are biologically superior to other 'races.' Whiteness studies will help answer a question we will be raising throughout this work: Why is the discourse of denial of racism still so powerful and persistent in Canadian society and especially among White power elites?

A bedrock truth in many postmodern societies is that Whiteness is hegemonic over Blackness. This 'truth' is believed not only by those who are strongly prejudiced but also by those who do not perceive themselves as prejudiced, and who are not generally viewed as prejudiced, yet who exercise control over society's structures and systems. The beliefs, values, and norms of the White elite operate in the law, the media, and the educational and criminal justice systems, as well as in other systems of social control and representation. The hegemonic concept has attained its own, largely unconscious reality, which manifests itself in terms of the meaning of 'Whiteness,' especially in contrast to the meaning of 'Blackness.' Whiteness has thus become another socially constructed identity – an identity that has long held the dominant position in perpetuating social inequities.

The field of White studies owes much to literary figures and other scholars such Toni Morrison, bell hooks, Richard Dyer, and Ruth Frankenberg, whose seminal work *White Women, Race Matters: The Social Construction of Whiteness* (1993) succinctly defined the field of study. Whiteness, according to her, has three interlinked dimensions: it is 'a location of structural advantage'; it is a 'standpoint or place from which White people look at ourselves, at others and at society'; and it refers to a set of cultural practices that are usually unmarked and unnamed. Morrison (1992) further advances the field by placing the onus of responsibility on the 'racial subject' – namely, White people: 'My project is an effort to avert the critical gaze from the racial object to the racial subject; from the described and imagined to the describers and imaginers; from the serving to the served' (ibid., 90). This shifts the onus in studies of institutionalized racism, of racism in popular culture, and of racism deeply embedded in society, from the disadvantaged groups of colour to those who are White and privileged and whose views are considered natural, normative, and basically raceless.

Whiteness studies reverse the focus on 'Blackness' and 'Otherness' to critically examine the role of Whites in preserving and reinforcing racial bias and exclusion. Whiteness studies offers 'the possibility of destabilizing whiteness as an identity and an ideology to gain a different vision of society. The problem of race now includes those who are raced white' (Johnson 1999, 5).

Whiteness studies analyse the link between white skin and the position of privilege operating in most societies, including those which have been subjected to European colonialism. White privilege confers benefits, whereas people of colour are often disadvantaged, excluded, and marginalized because of their skin colour and its associated stereotypic constructs. Whiteness contests the common notion of colour-blindness – the notion that one does not see skin colour – as untrue and inaccurate. Whites see the 'colour' in others in the same manner that they are seen as 'White.' Most White people do not, however, recognize themselves as a racial category, and their self-identification rarely includes the descriptor 'White.' White people are often not even aware they are White; and without that essential self-recognition they find it difficult to recognize and accept their role as perpetrators of racial discrimination and exclusion. Many Whites do not recognize their own identity as based on race; thus they do not participate in conversations in which race is discussed.

It is crucial to remember that 'Whiteness,' like 'colour' or 'Blackness,' is essentially a social construct applied to human beings rather than a truth of universal validity. The power of Whiteness manifests itself in the ways in which racialized Whiteness becomes transformed into social, political, economic, and cultural behaviour. White culture, norms, and values in all these areas become normative and natural. They become the standard against which all other cultures, groups, and individuals are measured – and usually found wanting. Whiteness comes to mean truth, objectivity, and merit. Against this background, scholars of Whiteness such as Richard Delgado (1995), Patricia Williams (1991), and Derrick Bell (1987) are now attempting to gain insight into these dynamics; their goal is to expose the power of Whiteness in order to dismantle some of its overwhelming hegemony over those who are 'non-White.'

Blackness Studies: Black Body Imagery and Definitions of Masculinity

We will have to racialize Whiteness in order to understand the hegemonic role it plays – often inadvertently – in modern societies. Similarly, we will have to understand Blackness – which has long been racialized – as the other side of that coin. Blackness is contextualized in images of the Black male heterosexual body as represented in a broad spectrum of systems, including in public, social, and cultural spaces. These images serve an important function: they define not only skin colour but also constructions of masculinity.[1] More specifically, ideas of Black heterosexual masculinity are found in

---

1 Because racial profiling is directed primarily against men, we exclude from our study discussion of racialized female body imagery. However, we recognize the importance of such imagery, especially in regard to the Black woman as sexual object in history and in contemporary society. We also note that there are issues surrounding Black homosexual men, although we do not deal with this added dimension (see Chapman and Rutherford 1988; Mercer and Julien 1988).

the popular imagination as the basis of masculine hero worship in the case of the rappers; as naturalized and commodified bodies in the case of athletes; as symbols of menace and threat in the case of black gang members; and as noble warriors in the case of Afrocentric nationalists and Fruit of Islam. While these varied images travel across different fields of electronic representation and social discourse, it is nevertheless the same black body – super star athlete, indignant rapper, 'menacing' gang member, and pitch-man, appropriate middle class professional, movie star – onto which competing and conflicting claims about (and for) black masculinity are waged. (Gray 1995, 402)

Negative and disturbing concepts of the Black male body were constructed under colonialism, which defined Blackness as 'the other' and in doing so confirmed the supremacy of Whites as well as the discursive power of the colonizers. Black men thus became subordinate and powerless, robbed of their cultural identities and reduced to stereotypic images based on White men's fantasies (Fanon 1967). These fantasies were mainly sexual and erotic and based on the imagery of the Black primitive. But those images projected a menace. Colonialism had eroticized Black men and at the same time denied them power; yet their images were threatening because of their potential to attract White women and thereby undermine the confidence and self-esteem of White men. Many of the constructs of the Black man that have evolved throughout history are still pervasive, albeit in a altered form. What has remained consistent, however, according to writers on this subject (most of them Black), is the image of the Black male body (Mercer 1994; Gray 1995; Carrington 2002; Chapman and Rutherford 1988).

According to these scholars the Black male body is a construct created largely by White men; moreover, Black men do not own their own bodies because they have been subjected to slavery and colonialism by Whites. Blackness is a visible sign of racial difference that leaves Black people vulnerable to societal and individual racism; yet at the same time, the image of the Black male body carries a set of highly ambivalent meanings. It is the one thing that White men allow Black men to have; they have no choice in this, for after all, one cannot be deprived of one's body except through death. As Chapman and Rutherford (1988) note: 'But it is a body filled with white fantasy and foreboding. For the white man the black man's physicality is what defines his presence. For the white man the black man is more violent, more of a rapist, more misogynist than himself ... He becomes the constructed image of white men's repressed lust; imbued with an animal-like sexuality and a huge penis; a body closer to nature than the "cultured white man"' (1988, 63).

The supposedly animalistic Black male body is still represented strongly today in the arena of sports. Sport is a naturally competitive activity, and the competition between White men and Black men is highlighted especially in track and field, where Blacks are alleged to have a natural superiority. The media play a key role in perpetuating these images, in that sports reporting is how most people learn about and follow sports (see, for example, Wilson 1997; Carrington 2002). In reporting on sports, journalists indirectly strengthen racist ideologies – for example, they refer to the 'natural' athletic ability of athletes who happen to be African Americans, they disseminate stereotypes about 'dumb jocks'; they demonize Black males, and they generally categorize Blacks as 'good' or 'bad.' This is especially true in the American media, though Canadian sports reporters tend towards it as well (Wilson 1997).

Carrington (2002, 3) notes that the 'facts of Blackness, or the lived experiences of being Black in the new century are no longer marked by an invisibility within the public sphere' as markers of social inequality. Indeed, Blackness is promoted through 'mantras of equal opportunities, diversity and multiculturalism.' Mainstream media culture is 'dominated by Black faces and bodies, from the sports fields and fashion catwalks, to our cinematic screens and music video channels.' Carrington observes that Blackness can now be enjoyed '24–7 in a way which is no longer threatening by its mere presence.' However, the effects of discrimination and inequality are still present in Western liberal democracies. This 'spectacle of hyperblackness' is a mechanism for continuing historically derived racialized images and ideologies. Blackness is represented to this day by these images, and the Black male body 'has come to occupy a central metronymic site through which notions of "athleticism" and "animalism" operate ... These tropes of Blackness provide the discursive boundaries within which the black subject is still framed' (ibid., 4). Black participation in sports, Black presence in media reporting, and the growing use of Black bodies in advertisements in which their strength, power, and virility are highlighted, all point to a paradoxical contradiction between these images and the reality of the lived experiences of most Black people.

Thus the image of the Black male body, in earlier times as well as in contemporary society, creates fear and apprehension and is probably one important factor in the continued oppression of Blacks, and especially men, by dominant hegemonic forces – primarily White men. Images of Black men and their bodies are disseminated today largely through those sports in which they are alleged to have natural ability; through the media, which highlight their supposed propensity for criminal activity (mugging, rape, homicide); and through the spectre of racialized crime.

Gray (1995a) is also concerned about these images; however, his focus is more on representations of Black masculinity in recent times. He begins by noting that the great jazz figures of the mid-twentieth century – exemplified by John Coltrane and Miles Davis – used themselves and their music to create a new and powerful image of Black masculinity. However, their strong images of Black masculinity were also contradictory; although the Black man was prized and celebrated by White society, he was also 'policed as a social threat because he transgressed the social role assigned to him by the dominant culture and celebrated as the "modern primitive" because he embodied and expressed a masculinity that explicitly rejected the reigning codes of propriety and place. Drugs, sexism, pleasure, excess, nihilism, defiance, pride, and the cool posse of disengagement were all a part of the style, personality, vision and practices of an assertive heterosexual black masculinity that could not be confined within the dominant cultural logic' (1995, 402).

Today, similar contradictory images are being produced and disseminated that require 'new contextualizations and different reading strategies.' An example is young Blacks' hero worship of gangsta rap, which also generates powerful images of Black masculinity. Another example is the commodification and naturalization of Black athletes, who are deemed to have natural prowess, and whose talents are then commodified in advertisements. The menace presented by Black gang members and the construct of the 'noble warrior' presented by Afrocentric nationalists and the Fruit of Islam are further examples. These images are found on television and in films and are often cited in social discourse. And they all branch out from the same trunk: 'It is nevertheless the same black body – super star athlete, indignant rapper, "menacing" gang member, ad pitch-man, appropriate middle class professional, movie star – onto to which competing and conflicting claims about (and for) black masculinity are waged' (ibid., 402).

Gray (1995a) argues that the negative and disturbing images emanating from rappers and gang members represent the oppositional and resistive forces that have created a new and menacing construction of the Black male. These forces are contested not only by Whites but also by the middle-class and civil rights elements within the Black community itself.

Evident in the discourse of the new Blackness – as represented by these many and contested images that are emerging from the contemporary cultural life of Black Americans – is that racial profiling is by and large simply another approach to the social control of Blacks (and other ethno-racial communities, in Canada and elsewhere). Racial profiling is mostly about how the White gaze filters notions and images of Blackness.

Moving towards Racial Profiling: Danger and Racialization Theory

Whiteness has become normalized; it follows that non-Whiteness has become 'abnormalized.' It is easy to notice the abnormal because of their skin colour. Thus Black drivers are immediately perceived in terms of a particular body and colour image associated almost subliminally with a criminal disposition. Skin colour is the basic marker; agents of social control such as the U.S. Drug Enforcement Agency (DEA) then draw from a set of visible cultural behaviours associated with that 'abnormal' skin colour. Examples of these behaviours: wearing gold chains; wearing a black jump suit; carrying a gym bag; being a member of an 'ethnic group associated with the drug trade'; and travelling from 'a source city' such as Los Angeles, Miami, or Detroit, or in a car bearing licence plates from a state in which there are source cities (Ehrenreich 1990). These features are also observable through surveillance techniques such as CCTV. Individuals demonstrating these features are then stopped and searched for no other reason than that they fit a profile.

To be preventive, to be proactive, surveillance must be able to identify the abnormal by what it *looks like* rather than by what it *does:* it needs to abnormalize – or criminalize – by visible social category, not by social behaviour (Fiske 2000). Black men are the first group to be abnormalized; in this sense, racism is the ultimate source of their 'abnormalization by surveillance.' The abnormalization of the racial 'other' is what enables the DEA to identify drug runners by what they look like. The same process manifests itself in other arenas. Banks employ it to identify users of stolen credit cards; stores employ it to identify shoplifters by their appearance (that is, rather than by their behaviour). As Fiske (2000, 53) notes: 'Surveillance is a technology of Whiteness that racially zones both the city space that exists as a matter of physical geography, and the social space ... In both spaces, surveillance draws lines that Blacks cannot cross and Whites cannot see.' This abnormalization and criminalization of the racial 'other' through widespread forms of surveillance, whether by CCTV or by police in their scout cars, relies heavily on processes for identifying deviancy based on appearance rather than behaviour. This processing is central to modern-day forms of racism. Fiske (ibid., 62) states that 'at the core of this process is the way that Whiteness normalizes itself, and excludes itself both from categorizing and being categorizable: it thus ensures its invisibility.'

At the same time, many Blacks and other people of colour not only feel the oppressive application of norms, but also notice how Whites are largely free from the constraints of normalization. This difference that people of colour notice is part of the experience of discrimination. The racialization of the 'other' is part of the White process of abnormalization; it follows that the classification of non-Whiteness may – in different historic and social contexts – include diverse groups: 'Blackness is a product of whiteness, not of melanin' (ibid., 64).

The abnormalization of the Black male has also been noted in the processes whereby the notions of *race* and *danger* are brought together. The idea behind this is that people of colour – especially Blacks – pose a threat to predominantly White societies (Rose 2002; Garland 1996; Visano 2002; Hall et al. 1978; Jiwani 2002).

A highly provocative article by William Rose (2002) provides some compelling answers to the question of why racial profiling against people of colour happens. Rose discusses what he calls the 'risk society' or the 'return of dangerous classes.' He notes that the use of race and especially Blackness as a 'proxy for criminal dangerousness' is embedded deep in American history: 'Black bodies have [been] supersaturated with meaning ...   The narrative attached to Black men in particular, has been one of criminal danger' (ibid., 182).

Drawing from Garland (1996), a British criminologist, Rose notes that penology has moved away from the rehabilitative model towards one wherein society must be protected from rising criminality. Garland notes that high crime rates have become a normal social fact in the United Kingdom and in many other countries as well. The fear of crime (and criminality) has reached epic proportions. It has become yet another modern danger 'which has been routinized and normalized over time.' As a consequence, the emphasis has shifted from rehabilitating criminals to managing crime in the most efficient manner possible given the state's limited resources. In the United States this has resulted in a bureaucratic approach to crime, one that involves more and more punitive measures. State after state has undertaken 'legislative efforts to stiffen criminal penalties, introduce mandatory minimum sentences, revitalize the death penalty.' Garland further notes that since the late 1970s there has been a 'new and urgent emphasis upon the need for security, the containment of danger, and the identification and management of any kind of risk.' He goes on to argue that an important effect of all this has been the 'emergence of a criminological discourse of the "alien other." [This approach] represents criminals as dangerous members of distinct racial and social groups which bear little resemblance to "us" ... [It is] a criminology which trades in images, archetypes and anxieties, rather than in careful analyses and research findings' (ibid., 459–63).

Rose maintains that racial profiling is driven by two factors: an adaptive or managerial approach to crime, and a new emphasis on punitive responses to it. He believes that racial profiling 'results from the politicization of danger. That is, "profiling" would seem to be grounded in some sort of precise actuarial calculation, but it is not. Rather, it is a new way of talking about danger' (Rose 2002, 185). He cites Feeley and Simon (1994), who maintain that there is a 'new penology' that deals less with morality, diagnosis, or intervention than with regulating levels of deviance. This new penology is concerned with 'techniques to identify, classify and manage groupings sorted by dangerousness.' The objective is not to identify a dangerous offender but to 'identify and manage "risky" population subgroups sorted by danger' (Rose 2002, 185–6).

Reinforcing this point, Rose points to the work of an influential American criminologist, James Q. Wilson (1995), who described the new 'predator' as relatively young and who noted that 6 per cent of boys of a given age commit half or more of all crimes perpetrated by boys of that age. That 6 per cent come from dysfunctional homes, have criminal parents, do poorly in school, are emotionally cold, and so on. Although Wilson does not identify this group of boys by race, Rose (2002, 190) tells us: 'We can almost hear him say as well that, more often than not, the faces of this relatively small but dangerous class are black.' Wilson states that even though American research tells us that

Blacks commit more criminal offences than Whites, a reactive police strategy is no longer effective. He calls instead for a proactive strategy that would involve police in directed, 'not random, patrol, and should make the following the goal of that direction: to reduce ... the opportunity for high-risk persons to do those things that increase the likelihood of their victimizing others' (in ibid., 190). In commenting on Wilson's thesis, Rose observes that following this line of reasoning, policing and other mechanisms of social control in modernizing or postmodern societies would have to manage criminal activity through 'preemptive targeting, containment and exclusion of risky population subgroups' (ibid., 191).

Racial profiling, and police stops and searches of Black drivers undertaken not because of traffic violations but because they are 'driving while Black,' have become endemic in these societies. Similarly, police stops and searches of Blacks on street corners, in Black neighbourhoods, and in shopping malls are conducted on suspicion of criminal activity even when there is no observable evidence that any law is being violated. Russell-Brown (2004, 66) suggests that the profiling of young Black men takes place 'whether they are driving while Black, walking while Black, sitting while Black, bicycling while Black, or breathing while Black.'

Citing Rodney King, Mike Tyson, and O.J. Simpson as examples, Fiske (2000, 60) maintains that in White America, Blacks – and especially Black men – must be watched because they demonstrate an ever present danger to the social order of White society: 'In the contemporary U.S. city the image of a Black man "out of place" is immediately moved from information to knowledge, from the seen to the known. In these conditions being seen is in itself oppressive. To be seen to be Black or Brown, in all but a few places in the U.S., is to be known, to be out of place, beyond the norm that someone else has set, and thus to be the subject of white power.'

It is not only that such persons are *seen* in places, but also that this seeing becomes transformed quickly into the notion of *danger*. An example of this – one often encountered by individuals of African descent – involves being stopped by the police for being present in a White neighborhood. A Black man in a predominantly White geographic space is immediately suspect because he is out of place and perceived as acting abnormally.

The need to see and monitor the 'other' has led, at least in the United States, to the widespread use of video surveillance. This technology 'functions as a control mechanism directed particularly upon the Black male as he moves through its so-called public spaces from the neighborhood store to the suburb, from the shopping mall, the office building or the airport to the public street' (ibid., 53). Fiske argues that the surveillance that both Orwell and Foucault saw as crucial to the modern social order has been racialized in a manner unforeseen by those forward-looking writers: 'Today's seeing eye is white, and its object colored' (ibid.).

Moreover, White people need to engage in critical self-reflection to find the 'traces of a deeply sedimented white knowledge that the Black man is always, potentially at least, the source of social disorder, and that this disorderliness can be all too easily imagined in terms of excessive sexuality or criminal drug use' (ibid., 54). The Black man has been made to symbolize the internal threat to law and order, which is implicitly framed in the discourse of Whiteness. Threats of Blackness that cannot be eliminated must be contained. Surveillance must therefore be directed constantly at the male Black body to ensure that he is contained in his place (both geographically and socially). When he is allowed outside of his place, he must be watched to ensure that his behaviour is 'normal,' as measured by White standards. In this way, not only surveillance but also constant monitoring in the form of police stops and searches and other forms of racial profiling become essential to what is a highly segmented and racialized postmodern society. These dynamics are more deeply entrenched in the United States and United Kingdom; however, the signs of surveillance, control, and containment are also present in Canada, especially in large urban centres such as Toronto.

Visano (2002) embraces a similar analytical framework in his examination of racial profiling and criminalization in the criminal justice system – specifically in policing. He asserts that the qualitatively different policing of Black and White communities reflects historical and colonial hegemonic systems of racism. Approaches to policing that view Blacks as intrinsically criminal and as potential threats to law and order open the gates for more strongly racialized practices, including racial profiling. He suggests that criminalization can be understood as a 'staged process that manipulates sanctions by defining disturbances … as totalizing narratives of trouble that warrant closure, containment, and coercion' (ibid., 212). One of the dominant narratives on which the criminal justice system builds is 'the criminal subject as the essentialized and inferior other.' When layered with colour, class, and gender, the criminalized 'other' constitutes a serious threat to the dominant White society, its social institutions, and the state as a whole.

The criminal justice system and other institutions – including the media and other vehicles of cultural and knowledge production – perpetuate a pathology of deviance by problematizing race and thereby generating a 'climate of mutual threat' (Russell-Brown 2004, 67). The resulting relationship between minority citizens and the police is characterized by what Russell-Brown describes as underground codes. These codes, which focus on the nexus between race and crime, make it possible for society to ignore and dismiss the concerns of minority communities. Thus the dominant White culture does not perceive racial profiling as a threat to the public. At the same time, these codes or myths reinforce stereotypes of crime and criminality as 'a Black problem' or 'an Aboriginal issue.'

As we will demonstrate throughout this book, myths play a powerful role in racialization processes – specifically, in processes of constructing the deviant and alien 'other.' Criminal mythologies form part of those master narratives, which serve to amplify moral panics as well as perceptions of fear and threat (Hall et al. 1978; Solomos 1988). We will examine many of these myths in chapter 6, which analyses the role of dominant/elite discourses in reinforcing cultural and systemic racism in the context of racial profiling.

In their pioneering work *Policing the Crisis* (1978), Hall and his colleagues probed beneath the surface – as expressed in newspaper coverage of the problem of mugging – to outline the 'deep structure' of what mugging had come to mean in British society in the 1970s. In doing so, they documented the emergence of a particular 'moral panic' about youth. The press and the police and even some sectors of the public wove together various threads – street crime, sexuality, unemployment, 'strange' religions, the foreign ways of primarily Caribbean youths, and so on – to develop the image of the black mugger, who soon emerged as a symbol of crime, urbanism, and other undesired social and political changes. The dangerous black mugger thus became a metaphor for all that was wrong with Britain in the 1970s, as well as a main plank in the turn towards the 'law and order' discourse that ushered in the Thatcher era. The image of the black mugger as responsible for crime and other social ills became a dominant discourse in Britain during those years, and this led to harsher laws to control this racialized crime. The media focused a great deal of attention on the courts, which issued stiff sentences in the name of the public interest and public safety and which justified doing so on the basis that violent crime was rising. Police activity increased as a response, and a number of prominent figures intervened, including the home secretary and Prince Philip. Substantial numbers of people supported the view that crime – and especially muggings by Blacks – needed to be controlled. The campaign took on racial tones to the point that mugging became synonymous with street crimes committed by Black youths. As a result, 'police versus blacks' soon became the 'paradigmatic relation' to the mugging phenomenon (ibid., 51). This tapped into a long history of difficult race relations. The media did much to promote the public's change in perspective by sensationalizing and overemphasizing Black mugging and crime. As a consequence, the relationship between crime and the marginalization of the racialized 'other' became part of the dominant discourse.

The three approaches outlined above are all aimed at explaining the prevalence of racial profiling, especially as the police direct it against Blacks. All three set out to explain how Blacks have become a visible and observable symbol of danger. This construct is rooted in perceptions not only that Blacks are socially, culturally, and physiologically different from Whites, but also that they are at variance with the White-defined norms that regulate modern societies. As a consequence, Blacks (and other people of colour) are inferiorized as human beings, their cultures are stigmatized, and they are cast to society's margins. This White perception that Blacks are dangerous to White society leads to an acceptance of strategies such as racial profiling as mechanisms of social control.

Discourse and Discursive Practices

Another important influence on this book is the theory that racism manifests itself in the everyday discourses of the White elite. Attention therefore will be paid to the power of discourse – in particular, to race, crime, and racial profiling as these are communicated through public and official discourses.

The ideologies of Whiteness and Blackness, and of danger, racialization, and criminalization, rely on complex sets of discourses framed by untested assumptions, unexamined beliefs, and biases rooted in structures of dominance and articulated by White elite authorities and officials (van Dijk 1993; Hall 1997; Visano 2002). The criminalization of Blackness – of the Black face, of the Black body – is a discursive practice that quickly becomes translated into law enforcement norms. A discursive approach is a tool not only for exploring the ideological meaning of racial profiling but also for decoding the discourses that flow from it. These discourses are articulated in the 'talk and text' of the media, academe, legislatures, the criminal justice system, the bureaucracies ... everywhere members of the White elite occupy positions of authority and control.

Discourse is most closely associated with language and the written or oral text. At this level it challenges the concept of 'language' as an abstract system and relocates the entire process of making and using meanings from abstracted structural systems into particular historical, social, and political conditions (Fiske 1994). Discourse is how language is used socially to convey broad historical meanings. It is language identified by the social conditions of its use, by who is using it, and by the conditions under which it is used. Language can never be 'neutral,' for it serves as a bridge between our personal and social worlds (van Dijk 1988). It can never be 'objective' or 'detached' because it draws from myth and fantasy (Hall 1997). It can never be entirely free of the socio-cultural influences and economic interests in which it was produced and disseminated.

Discourse thus comes with a set of social meanings that typically are politicized in the sense that they carry with them a concept of power that reflects the interests of the power elite who use them. Opinion leaders, including politicians, senior bureaucrats, lawyers and judges, editors and journalists, academics, and business leaders, play a vital role in shaping the issues as well as in identifying the boundaries of 'legitimate' discourse. These people can marginalize and even silence opponents by defining them as 'radicals,' 'special interest groups,' or, 'spokespeople who do not represent anyone but themselves.'

Discourses are ways of referring to or constructing knowledge about a particular topic; they are clusters or formations of ideas, images, and practices that provide ways of talking about forms of knowledge and conduct associated with a particular topic, social activity, or institutional site in society. These *discursive formulations* define what is and is not appropriate in our formulations of – and in our practices in relation to – particular subjects or sites of social activity. They also tell us which knowledge is useful, relevant, and true in which context, as well as which sorts of people or subjects embody its characteristics. Discourses can also be understood in terms of their capacity to identify, regulate, and construct social groups; their ability to provide resources for making evaluations and constructing 'factual' versions; their success in creating the impetus and motivation to act; and their capacity to constitute 'truth' and to maintain social relations and disadvantage (Wetherell and Potter 1992, 90ff).

Dominant discourse can be understood as the collection of expectations we take for granted. It embodies socialization by the dominant or decision-making group. Dominant discourse gives us the prevailing normative rules of everyday living as practiced by decision-makers. Dominant discourse rarely includes the perspective of the Other. One of the key attributes of a dominant discourse is its power to interpret major social, political, and economic issues and events – such as the crisis that followed the publication of the *Star* series on racial profiling.

Note also that discourses are articulated not only through the spoken word but also through texts, including media stories and editorials, academic texts, government studies, conference and commission reports, and institutional and organizational policies – and perhaps most significantly the law itself. Embedded in law enforcement discourses are procedural conventions, administrative and bureaucratic rules, professional standards, and cultural norms and rituals. Each of these texts – and the spoken word as well – can be viewed as an ideological expression of Whiteness. Collectively they represent vehicles for producing, distributing, and consuming the meanings that underpin racism. They confer legitimacy and authority on the existing dominant White culture.

The discursive crisis generated by the *Star* series on racial profiling, which began running in October 2002 and was still being published while this book was being written, led to the construction of a number of dominant discourses by police authorities, political figures, police union leaders, journalists, and others. Their reactions to the series reflected some of the core elements of racialized elite discourses that allegations of racism have traditionally generated (see chapter 6). Here we briefly note that dominant among all these discourses as it relates to racial profiling is *total and pervasive denial that racism exists in the structures and cultures of policing or in the everyday practices of law enforcement agencies.* These discourses are of course not unique to the Toronto Police Service; they form a common set of rhetorical strategies utilized by law enforcement agencies in other jurisdictions as well. Following Ewick and Silbey (1995), we argue in this work that these hegemonic narratives articulated by White policing officials and White public figures were not merely *reflective* of the dominant meanings and power relations that form the basis of these discourses, but in fact *contributed* to the very *production* of those meanings and power relations. The mere act of telling dominant narratives constitutes the hegemony that shapes the social lives and well-being of people of colour.

As Hall (1978) maintains, discursive events by their very nature can become catalysts for social change. Even while the *Star* series was unfolding, the dominant and hegemonic narratives of Whiteness were being made to confront counter-narratives emerging from the Black community. Editorials and opinion columns in the *Star* provided a vehicle for minority communities – and the Black community in particular – to confirm their experiences by telling their own stories. These counter-narratives enabled those who were being racialized and criminalized to bear witness to their lived experience in the face of a dominant culture that was distorting, stereotyping, and marginalizing them (Bell 2003, 6; Delgado 1995). In chapter 7, Maureen Brown provides a powerful analysis of how the oppositional narratives she collected from Black youth and adults across the GTA challenged the dominant narratives. These kinds of oppositional stories have been described as a form of 'cultural activism' (Morales 1998).

Conclusion

Much of the theoretical and empirical work on racial profiling comes from the United States and United Kingdom. These attempts to explain racial profiling work equally well for Canadian society, and much of the work on profiling has crossed the border through the public media and academic scholarship.

Black subculture is growing in Toronto, along with the assumption that Black men are heavily involved in drug trafficking and other deviant behaviours. This has strongly reinforced the practice of police stops and surveillance in Canadian communities. Approaches to policing the 'crisis' focus on containing and controlling a racialized and essentialized Black population. The 'moral panic' that flowed from the *Star* articles on racial profiling was evidence not only of the actuarial incidence of racial profiling but also of the discourses that resulted from it. These discourses exist as mechanisms of (a) representation/misrepresentation and (b) social control and White domination. As this book will demonstrate, these mechanisms have resulted in an extraordinarily diverse community being portrayed as 'needing correction, incarceration, censoring, silencing ... This is the consequence and function of official stories: to impose the will of the dominant culture' (Morrison 1997, xxviii).

Finally, in terms of the theoretical approaches that have influenced this work, it is important for us to emphasize that we cannot be satisfied with merely recording the quantitative findings of empirically oriented studies. We accept a priori the idea that the police (and other institutions such as the courts, the schools, the media, and social services) do practise differential behaviour towards Aboriginal peoples, people of colour, and especially people of African origin (Henry and Tator 2005; Razack 1998; Calliste and Dei 2000). Thus we are less interested in determining the numbers involved in racial profiling practices – in what constitutes an 'actuarial' approach - and more concerned with analysing why these kinds of differential behaviours are targeted towards racialized groups. What does the new concern with racial profiling tell us about the subtler values, beliefs and norms that underlie the social construction of Black and other people of colour as the 'other'?

2 The Interlocking Web of Racism across Institutions, Systems, and Structures

> We are not suggesting that the police invent racialized categories. Rather, they draw upon and sometimes modify or reinforce those racialized categories already constructed and firmly embedded in society at large. (Holdaway 1997, 85)

The questions and controversies surrounding the issue of race, crime, and racial profiling cannot be answered in isolation from other institutional and societal contexts. The production and reproduction of racism does not happen within the hermetically sealed walls of law enforcement agencies, nor is it confined to the specific organizational norms and decision-making processes of particular structures. Policing culture and its structures are a composite of ideologies, values, norms, and practices that are deeply connected to and embedded in diverse societal systems.

In this chapter we look more closely at how the processes of racialization and Whiteness operate and intersect across institutional and discursive spaces; and at how these processes have categorized, inferiorized, marginalized, and criminalized people of colour and First Nations people as individuals and as communities. We also explore how otherness is 'marked' in the law, the justice system, and systems of governance. Vehicles of cultural production, including education and the media, are also discussed. White elites in these public spheres heavily influence and strongly control many ideological beliefs, which in turn affect public discourse and public responses to the critical issue of race and racism in democratic liberal societies (Razack 1998; Henry and Tator 2002; van Dijk 1993).

An important dimension of the racialization process is what Frantz Fanon (1967) called the 'white gaze.' His famous book *Black Skin, White Masks* offers critical insights into the nature of racialization and the ideological construction of Blacks and other racialized groups. In it he describes how a young boy once fixed him with his white gaze and, turning to his mother, said 'Look, a Negro [*négre*].' The child saw and commented on his skin colour rather than on his build or the scar on his face. Moreover, he did not refer to him as a 'black' or 'a man of colour.'

The importance of the White gaze – the way White people and especially White elites perceive people of colour – is that it allows a dominant group to control the social spaces and social interactions of all other groups. In this way Blacks, for example, can be rendered visible and invisible at the same time under the gaze of a White police officer, lawmaker, judge, journalist, educator, or filmmaker.

The Law, or Legalized Racism

Throughout Canadian history the state has used the law as an instrument for explaining racial differences, for reinforcing commonsense notions embedded in a dominant cultural system, and for establishing new social constructions of 'otherness' (Kobayashi 1990; Backhouse 1999; Aylward 2002; Visano 2002). Legislation has neither eliminated nor controlled racism: the legacy of racism is too intertwined with the national White culture and its core myths, values, ideals, and norms. The racial profiling or racialization of Aboriginals, Blacks, Japanese, Chinese, South Asians, and other people of colour has a long history and legacy.

We encounter Canada's racist legacy in some of its earliest laws. The Canadian government, through the Indian Act of 1876 and subsequent legislation and treaties, introduced institutionalized racism to the relationship between Canada and its Aboriginal peoples. Racism has flourished to this day. First Nations peoples have been subjugated, segregated, and in some instances annihilated by racist policies and assumptions. They have been subjected to overtly racist and assimilationist policies that have led to their segregation and degradation and to never-ending poverty. Specific manifestations of racist policies include the denial of the right to vote, the prohibition on purchasing land, the outlawing of spiritual ceremonies, forced relocation to and segregation on reserves, restrictions of civil and political rights, and the expropriation of land (Ponting 1997; Frideres and Gadacz 2001; Satzewich and Wotherspoon 1993).

It has long and often been alleged that the law is neutral, yet it was in fact the main instrument for maintaining slavery. It was laws that made it illegal for Blacks to learn to read and write and to participate in public life as citizens. It was laws that during the Second World War forcibly removed Japanese Canadians from their homes and incarcerated them in jails and internment camps. All of their property, including their homes, their businesses, and their boats, was expropriated. Those who were interned were not released until two years after the war was over. The government justified all this on the basis of national security, yet no Japanese Canadian was ever charged with any kind of disloyalty (Sunahara 1981). The law has long ignored or omitted racism in its deliberations; not only that, but racialized laws have in the past denied the franchise to First Nations peoples, Japanese, Chinese, and African Canadians. Thus the law cannot be understood as a neutral construct. Both the common law and statute laws are inherently political.

Kobayashi (1990, 449) maintains that the culpability of the law can be examined in many ways: 'The law has been used through direct action, interpretation, silence and complicity. The law has been wielded as an instrument to create a common sense justification of racial differences, to reinforce common sense notions already deeply embedded within a cultural system of values.'

Recent work in critical legal theory posits the need to establish a connection between law and culture, 'situating legal theory within social, political, and economic conditions, and interpreting juridical procedures according to dominant ideologies' (ibid., 449). None of this was evident in traditional legal discourse because the law, like other disciplines, did not 'address the meaning of law outside [its] own terms.' The study of law in abstraction from social relations and the social system it purports to regulate will always be idealistic, artificial, and inherently biased. The legal system produces and reproduces the essential character of law as a means of rationalizing, normalizing, and legitimizing social control on behalf of those who hold power and the interests they represent (Aylward 2002; Razack 1998; Delgado 2000; Backhouse 1999).

Immigration: Policing the Borders of Canada

Legalized racism and racial profiling are easy to discern in Canada's immigration policies, both past and present. Laws have been used throughout Canadian history to restrict the entry of racial minorities into Canada and to prevent immigrants of colour from participating fully in Canadian society. Until 1967, when Canada's immigration legislation was liberalized, this country's policies divided the world's peoples into two broad groups: preferred immigrants, who were of British and European ancestry and White; and the rest of the world, largely composed of people of colour. The Canadian government's immigration policy was based on the premise that Blacks, Asians, and other people of colour were 'inassimilable' – that is, they had genetic, cultural, and social traits that made them both inferior and inadaptable (Bolaria and Li 1988).

Included in this category of unacceptable groups were people of African descent, who were deemed to be mentally, physically, and socially inferior and to have the potential to create a permanent social problem in Canada (Williams, in Smith 1993). The enslavement of African Canadians and the segregation of and discrimination against 'free' Black people is a part of the racialized history of immigration policies and practices in Canada (Alexander and Glaze 1996). Black Canadians were subject to legislation that enforced segregated schools and communities in Nova Scotia, New Brunswick, and Ontario. Residential segregation was widespread and legally enforced. The separation and refusal of service was commonplace in restaurants, theatres, and recreational centres. Black Canadians launched several court challenges against these practices. The most celebrated case began in 1931 with a Montreal tavern's refusal to serve a Black customer. It ended in 1940, when the Supreme Court of Canada ruled that racial discrimination was legally enforceable. That is, racial discrimination could not be used to bring forward a court action (*Christie v. York* 1940).

Chinese immigration has been marked just as deeply by racism. Chinese labourers in Canada were subjected to an escalating head tax for entry into Canada from the late 1880s until 1903, by which time the tax had reached $500. Chinese male labourers were paid one-quarter to one-half less than their White counterparts. Bolaria and Li (1988) state that Chinese immigration was encouraged solely for the purpose of exploiting their labour. As soon as there was a labour surplus, the Chinese were considered a threat to Canadian society and were subject to intense racial bias and discrimination. Between 1923 and 1947 the Chinese Exclusion Act closed Canada's border to Chinese immigrants.

Immigration legislation in the 1960s presented a new approach to people of colour. Desperate for skilled labour, Canada turned to 'non-traditional' (that is, non-White) source countries to meet its labour needs. The new system awarded points to prospective immigrants based on skills, experience, language ability, and the like. It was argued that under this system, those with the most points would have a better chance of integrating themselves into Canadian society. This opened the door to immigrants from regions — Asia, the Caribbean, Latin America, the Middle East, and Africa – that for two hundred years had been largely excluded. However, discrimination did not vanish from Canada's immigration policy. Buried in the fine print of the new selection process were a myriad of seemingly neutral administrative procedures that amounted to preferential treatment for White immigrants and racial discrimination against minority immigrants.

Legislation introduced in June 2002 – the Immigration and Refugee Protection Act (IRPA) – provided for three classes of immigrants: economic, family class, and refugee. Critics of the present system maintain that it discriminates against immigrants because the economic class of immigrants is the one most promoted – in fact, it accounted for 61 per cent of all immigrants in the year preceding the new act. The family class accounted for 27 per cent, and refugees for 11 per cent (Li 2003). Other critics were more concerned about the sheer numbers being admitted to the country, and questioned the official position that Canada's aging population and low birthrates were making substantial immigration necessary. Critics such as Stoffman (2002), Collacott (2002), and Francis (2002) contend that 200,000 or more immigrants per year is excessive.

During the 1990s a new era of policing the border was inaugurated (Razack 1999). A wide range of legislative initiatives were introduced to regulate more tightly the flow of immigrants and refugees into Canada. Embedded in these new policies and procedures was the racialized construct of 'the criminal attempting to cross our borders' (ibid., 60) The emphasis was now on classifying and identifying the types of individuals who needed to be monitored, managed, and kept out of Canada.

Jakubowski (1997, 115) contends that other pieces of immigration legislation, such as Bill C-86 (1992), reflect an interplay among class, ethnicity, and race – an interplay that has created a preferential category of immigrants, one that most *White* (our italics) Canadians can accept and feel comfortable with (ibid., 115). Bill C-86 was an effort to prevent Canada from becoming a safe haven for terrorists and international crime syndicates.

In 1995 the Canadian government enacted Bill C-44, largely as a response to the murder of a young White woman in a Toronto cafe committed by three Black men, one of whom was an immigrant whose deportation had been stayed. This was the now famous Just Desserts case. The bill stated that any individual convicted of a crime carrying a sentence of ten or more years was a danger to the public. This had the effect of denying such people the right to appeal a deportation order to the Immigration and Refugee Board. The Just Desserts case was widely and sensationally covered in the media (see Henry and Tator 2002; Wortley 2002) and was debated in Parliament. The racialized discourses of politicians and the media – among other White public authorities – focused on the criminal deviance of those foreign 'others' who were bringing their criminal ways into Canada. In the discourses that surrounded the apprehension and trial of the assailants, the racialized chain of signification led from the particularities of the individual murder to the general cultural attributes of its (Black) perpetrators, and finally, to their specific national origins outside Canada. Once it was 'demonstrated' that this crime had been imported, the source of similar crimes could be pinpointed at the 'border' between 'us' and 'them'; in this way crime prevention could be made synonymous with immigration controls.

It is important to emphasize the link between the media and public policy development – a link that was blatantly obvious in the Just Desserts case. The connections the media drew between that specific crime and a particular *type* of crime – and, later, between that type of crime and *immigration* – led to a loud campaign in editorials and opinion columns to reform the immigration system so that it would be easier to weed out and deport immigrant criminals. The moral panic surrounding immigration and deportation led to an agreement among all parties to police immigration more closely (Wortley 2002; Henry and Tator 2002).

In the seven years following the passage of Bill C-44, 325 people were deported from Canada. Reflecting on this number, Barnes (2002, 200) maintains that Jamaicans have taken the biggest hit from this bill; of the people declared a danger to Canadian society and subsequently deported, the overwhelming majority have been from that island.

The 9/11 terrorist attacks in the United States in 2001 opened a new phase in border policing. Some American politicians and media insinuated that Canada's 'weak' immigration policies had allowed the terrorists to enter the United States. These charges, however false, served to heighten fears among White Canadians that dangerous aliens were in their midst. The ensuing desperation to secure the borders resulted in twenty new pieces of legislation, including the Anti-Terrorism Act, the Immigration and Refugee Protection Act, and the Public Safety Act. On top of this, the Criminal Code, the Official Secrets Act, and other acts were amended (Smith, October 2003). The antiterrorism bill, styled C-36, was central to establishing the boundaries separating 'us' and 'them'; it was based largely on racialized assumptions and stereotypes, in that it targeted Arabs and Muslims and other Middle Eastern peoples. In the context of these policies, racial profiling became more overt. Bahdi (2003) maintains that after 9/11 'the central contention was no longer whether racial profiling was in fact taking place or how to best prevent incidents of racial profiling ... Rather, racial profiling debates in the context of the war against terrorism focus on whether Canadian society can morally, legally, or politically condone racial profiling.'

Immigration is a loaded issue in this country. As many polls have demonstrated, many Canadians do not support open immigration; in fact, a racist discourse of fear of immigration is part of the public agenda. In this discourse, racism is caused by both the volume of immigration and the racial identities of immigrants. The argument here is that if immigration is curbed – especially 'Third World' immigration – racism will decrease. But this ignores the fact that racism existed long before the large-scale immigration of people of colour into Canada, as evidenced by the exploitative relationship between White colonizers and Aboriginal peoples throughout Canada's history.

Those who oppose immigration also believe that racism is the inevitable result of different cultures being brought into close proximity; this proximity, the argument goes, cannot but inspire jealousies and cultural conflicts. Yet racism is *not* made inevitable by cultural differences. There is no inescapable tension between groups who are different; racial conflict flares only when one group has power over another. The White majority in Canada enjoys political, economic, and social control over most Canadian institutions. When racial discrimination is entrenched in a society's institutions and value systems, the social and economic exclusion of people of colour is inevitable, and so is racial profiling, which quickly becomes part of this racialization process.

Racism in the Justice System

The law itself is racialized. This is inevitable, because so much of it was written at a time when people of colour and other disadvantaged groups were barred from participating in the justice system and in society as a whole. Only in recent years has racial discrimination been redefined in a way that includes its *effects* as well as its *intent*. In Canada the research evidence is growing that racism exists in the courts; several commissions have outlined the problems faced by Aboriginal people and Blacks in the justice system.

Perhaps the most extensive research conducted on racism in the justice system was included in the Report of the Commission on Systemic Racism in the Ontario Criminal Justice System (Government of Ontario 1995). Its authors found that many people, both within and outside the justice system, believed that differential treatment happens. For example, one-third of Whites believed that judges do not treat Blacks the same as Whites. Most judges and lawyers did not accept that differential treatment of Blacks takes place, but at least one-third of the judges believed it did, and so did nearly 40 per cent of defence lawyers. With regard to prison incarcerations, both Black men and Black women were overrepresented. White accused were more likely to be released by the police and less likely to be detained after a bail hearing. Blacks constituted not quite 3 per cent of Ontario's population, yet they accounted for 15 per cent of the incarcerated population. During the six years from 1986 to 1992, the Black imprisoned population increased by 204 per cent! With regard to drug offences, the commission found that White accused were twice as likely as Black accused to be released by the police. Moreover, Black accused were three times more likely to be refused bail. It also found strong differences with regard to sentencing. Generally speaking, Whites found guilty were less likely to be sentenced to prison, and Whites were sentenced more lightly than Blacks even when they had a criminal record and a more serious record of past criminal activity. Far more Blacks than Whites were sent to prison for drug offences. The commission also found that racist behaviour – both systemic and individual – was rampant in the prisons and that it was directed mainly against Black prisoners.

Researchers have found that minorities are treated differently at every stage in the justice system. Differential treatment is meted out by the police, in the courts, and in the correctional system (Chan and Mirchandani 2002; St Lewis 1996). The problem of racism in the justice system was also acknowledged by the Law Reform Commission of Canada (1992) when it noted that 'racism in the justice system is a consistently expressed and central concern to Canada's minorities.' This racism is visible in the lack of jobs and positions of power and influence for minorities within justice institutions. It is also visible in police harassment, in the lack of access to both legal aid and police protection, and in differential treatment during sentencing. The Law Reform Commission went on to acknowledge that 'the racism of which these groups speak mirrors attitudes and behaviour found in Canadian society as a whole' (ibid., 10).

In recent years the law as reflected in superior court and Supreme Court decisions has begun to change. The courts are beginning to recognize that racism affects the administration of justice. A number of court decisions have had a impact. For example, in *R. v. Parks* it was ruled that Blacks can challenge juries on the cause of racial bias. This right was further strengthened in *R. v. Williams*, which extended this right to Aboriginal people. An Ontario Court of Appeal then allowed the challenge for all racial minorities. In November 2004, in *R. v. Spence*, the same court granted a new trial to a Black appellant whose victim was East Indian. Although the jurors had been asked about racial bias, the Crown had contended that racism was 'greatly diminished' because the victim was also a person of colour. In these decisions the courts accepted that racial bias was difficult to prove and that lesser standards of evidence than normally applied in the courtroom were acceptable. The important issue of judicial bias is rarely addressed by the courts; nevertheless, the Supreme Court of Canada considered that issue in *R.D.S. v. Her Majesty the Queen* (see also Razack 1999; Henry and Tator 2005), in which a Black provincial judge in Nova Scotia who had made statements about the unequal treatment of Blacks was cleared of allegations of judicial bias.

The issue of racial profiling was specifically targeted in September 2004 in *R. v. Calderon and Stalas*, in which the Ontario Court of Appeal ruled that the police could not detain suspects merely because they fit the profile of a drug courier. A month later, in *R. v. Khan*, a Superior Court judge threw out a case in which the police alleged that a young Black motorist had marijuana in his car. Disbelieving the police evidence, the judge ruled that the motorist had been targeted 'for this stop because of racial profiling; because he was a black man with an expensive car ... The evidence is overpowering that the officers' testimony was untrue.'

Race also affects sentencing. This is clear from the exceptionally high incarceration rates for Aboriginals and Blacks in Canada. In fact, Canada's rates for these groups are among the highest in the world. To address this, new sentencing regulations were developed in 1996 that allowed judges greater discretion in alternative sentencing (Tanovich 2004). These guidelines are especially relevant to young single mothers who have been charged with minor offences and for whom a period of incarceration would make their situation worse. Similarly, young Black men charged with drug offences can hardly be expected to find behind bars the rehabilitation and training they need. As the Supreme Court of Canada noted in *R. v. Gladue*: 'Sentencing innovation by itself cannot remove the causes of … offending but judges can play a limited role in "remedying injustice"' (in ibid.). Judicial decisions at all levels of the system are crucial to advancing the cause of equity in the justice system. The past ten years have seen the emergence of more progressive decision making, and it can be hoped that these trends will continue.

Racism in Education

Racial profiling goes on in Canada's schools at all levels. These institutions, after all, are part of the broader assimilationist White culture, which essentializes and exoticizes notions of cultural differences. Such profiling is visible in monocultural curricula and in Eurocentric teaching practices. It is visible in zero tolerance policies, which have a differential impact on Black students, and in those dominant discourses which deny that racism exists while at the same time making claims to colour-blindness and political correctness. And it is visible in how students of colour are marginalized as 'others' and in how their abilities are assessed as a consequence.

Racism in education is about far more than whether teachers and administrators knowingly hold racialized attitudes towards students of colour. Racialized beliefs, assumptions, and norms are reinforced when faculties of education fail to provide teachers with the knowledge, tools, and skills to address racism in classrooms, and they are only strengthened when these teachers join schools where there is no scope for ongoing professional training in anti-racism and educational equity (Calliste and Dei 2000). A great deal of lip service is paid to the idea of ensuring that schools uphold the principles of tolerance, equal opportunity, and individualism. In reality, educators often adhere to traditional approaches to teaching – approaches that continue to embrace Eurocentric curricula and racialized pedagogies.

Racism in classrooms is supported and reinforced when the curriculum largely excludes the contributions of people of colour. Throughout

Canada's history, the voices, stories, and contributions of racialized people have been ignored. Racism manifests itself in non-inclusive approaches to teaching history and science and in the novels and plays that schools choose for study. It is visible wherever education ministries and boards of education have eliminated or significantly reduced their anti-racism and equity units. A number of provinces, including Ontario, have ended the requirement that school boards establish policies for ethno-racial equity; they have also reduced budgets for anti-racism and equity programs. Over the past decades, boards of education operating under significant budget deficits have fired social workers, psychologists, youth workers, and counsellors. Over the same time, the Ontario Ministry of Education has dismantled African Heritage programs and stripped the budgets of ESL programs. Racial bias is also evident in the recent vogue for standardized tests and assessment tools and in the severe shortage of teachers of colour and First Nations teachers. Racism in schools is also linked to new policies on 'zero tolerance.'

Racial minority subcultures are often expressions of resistance against the closed, hierarchical culture of schools. A great deal of recent research points to this phenomenon (see Solomon 1992; Solomon and Palmer 2004; Dei 1996; Kelly 1998; Yon 2000; Codjoe 2001). These studies focus on the everyday experiences and narratives of Black students as they struggle against racialization processes in their schools. This body of research documents the key factors influencing the success of Black students in schools. Its findings also shed light on the impacts that bias and differential treatment have on other ethno-racial minority students. Black students, families, and communities often raise the following issues: persistent discrimination and stereotyping; ethnocentrism and essentialized constructs of cultural identity; the lack of acknowledgment of Black/African perspectives, histories, and experiences; low teacher expectations; and the dearth of Black teachers. Solomon and Palmer (2004, 6) have pointed to the constructions of Black students as 'fearful, deviant, socially dysfunctional, non-conformist and a threat to the safety and smooth functioning of the school as a social system.'

The singling out of Black males and other racial minority males in schools can be linked to the White 'gaze' and to the racialized discourses of other institutions such as the media and the police. As Kelly (1998, 19) observes, when Black youth are seen it is often with a specific gaze that sees the 'troublemaker,' 'the school skipper,' or the 'criminal.'

Students of colour subjected to the constant 'gaze' of White-dominated schools and of other White public authorities – in schools, in malls, on the streets – cannot but react to the constant pressure of being watched (Hérbert 2001). Some students respond by generating 'glare' – that is, by dressing boldly and by expressing their difference physically (for example, with an exaggerated walk). The 'gaze' and 'glare' then feed off each other, further marginalizing individuals who are already marked by the colour of their skin (ibid.).

There is a 'hidden curriculum' in schools, which often manifests itself in the strong emphasis that educators place on sports as a means of keeping Black students in school. The media and the coaches themselves are complicit in this. Black youth, more than any other group, tend to use sports to navigate the myriad barriers identified earlier (James 2005; Spence 1999; Solomon 1992). James (2003) suggests that the construct of the Black athlete may reflect schools' perceptions of how they can best address the academic needs and interests of Black student athletes. He adds that educators need to ask themselves why Black students believe it is 'mainly through sports that they can fulfill their educational needs, aspirations and requirements' (ibid., 34).

Harassment in schools is one of the most painful manifestations of racism. This harassment includes racial slurs, ethnic and racial jokes, and racist graffiti. It can also take the form of bullying, physical threats, and assaults. In Canada, there has not yet been an accurate assessment of the frequency, nature, or distribution of racial harassment, nor has there been any documented analysis of its perpetrators or victims. But researchers, students, parents, and minority communities have made available a body of impressionistic evidence, and a few boards of education have issued reports on this issue. Some educators believe that racial harassment in Canada's schools has been increasing in recent years. More and more teachers and principals are filing reports about racially motivated incidents (Lawson 2003; Ruck and Wortley 2002; Jull 2000).

Solomon (1992) studied a group of Black, mainly male, urban high school students of low socio-economic status and found that they tended to perceive school discipline as being administered arbitrarily by the authorities. Black students contended that they were suspended more often than White students for engaging in similar behaviour. Ruck and Wortley (2002) analysed minority students' perceptions of school discipline, drawing their data from a large, multiracial, culturally pluralistic sample of high school students in Metro Toronto. One of their most striking findings was that students from all four racial/ethnic groups they studied (Black, South Asian, Asian, 'other') were much more likely than White students to read discrimination into the discipline imposed on them (discipline for them included punishment by teachers, suspension by administrators, and the school calling the police). Also, Black students viewed themselves as at a distinct disadvantage, especially with regard to their dealings with the police while at school (see chapter 7). Ruck and Wortley draw a conclusion similar to that of many scholars: 'zero tolerance,' for students, means that the blacker they are the more harshly the school disciplines them and the more likely they are to suffer significant social consequences. Black students are the most likely to notice this, followed by South Asian students, then 'other' students, and finally (at the bottom of the list) White students.

A study by Wortley and Tanner (2003) on Toronto high school students that focused on student's experiences with the police offers some important findings. For example, after controlling for factors such as criminal activity, drug use, gang membership, car use, and leisure activities, police stops were actually higher among students with the lowest levels of criminal behaviour. The authors' findings demonstrated differential treatment in stop and search procedures based on Blackness versus Whiteness. Of Black students who had not engaged in any form of criminal behaviour, 34 per cent reported that they had been *stopped* by police, compared to only 4 per cent of White students in the same category. Similarly, only 5 per cent of non-deviant White students said they had been *searched*, whereas 23 per cent of non-deviant Black students had been searched. The authors concluded that age and social class offer little protection from police stops and searches; furthermore, good behaviour also does not protect blacks from unwanted police attention.

Solomon and Palmer's (2004) analysis of the school records and clinical files of Black students suggests that schools are summoning the police more and more often to reinforce the authority structure. The negative spiral between the authoritarian practices of schools and students' resistance to these practices leads to detention, in-school suspension, short- and long-term suspension, and, ultimately, interventions by the criminal sustice system.

Interviews with incarcerated Black youths offer further important insights into 'the ways arbitrary power and authority operate within the contested terrain of schools.' Their findings highlight just how much fear is generated by this authority: 'Safe school policies of "zero toler-ance" and the ongoing practice of racial profiling appear to converge in moving Black students through the school–prison pipeline' (ibid., 1).

All of the above studies suggest that both schools and law enforce-ment agencies trap Black youths in deep and powerful stereotypes. Yet suggestions that racism exists in the schools are typically challenged by educators, who argue that they are colour-blind as well as 'culture-blind.' The discourse of denial of racism is strong in the educational system; evidence of this is the tension that exists between the everyday racism experienced by students of colour (and educators of colour, for that matter) and the attitudes and practices of educators and adminis-trators, who deny those students' perceptions and experiences. On those rare occasions when someone admits that racism exists, it is interpreted as an isolated and aberrant phenomenon – the 'few bad apples' again – rather than something deeply rooted in the everyday practices, norms, values, and priorities of educational systems (Dei and Calliste 2000).

Racial Profiling by the Media and Other Vehicles of Cultural Production

All media are powerful vehicles for disseminating images and ideas. They help shape identity, be it gender, racial, ethnic, class, or national identity. Media messages also do much to categorize people as 'us' and 'them.' Cultural productions influence how we view the world and play a crucial role in defining society's norms and values. The media and other forms of cultural production inform our beliefs, values, and behaviours.

In a liberal democracy, media institutions are expected to reflect alternative perspectives, to be neutral and objective, and to provide free and equitable access to all groups and classes. They are expected to develop a full range of diverse voices so that the views of all people are represented. But they do not always do this; too often, while espousing democratic values of fairness, equality, and freedom of expression, they reinforce and reproduce racism in a number of ways. For example, they engage in negative stereotyping, they racialize issues such as crime and immigration, they make Eurocentric and eth-nocentric judgments, and they marginalize people of colour in all aspects of media production (van Dijk 1991, 1993; Fiske 1994; Fleras and Kunz 2001; Entman and Rojecki 2000).

Because racial minority communities are not integrated into main-stream society, many White people rely almost entirely on the media for their information about minorities and the issues that concern their communities. Thus the relationship between the White community and these groups is largely filtered through the perceptions, assumptions, values, and beliefs of journalists and other media professionals.

Studies of the print and electronic media (Henry and Tator 2002; Hier and Greenberg 2002; Wortley 2002; Murray 2002; Fleras and Kuntz 2001; Mahtani 2001) demonstrate that in general, the Canadian media present negative views of people of colour – and Black youth and Black men in particular. Racialized discourses in the media involve repertoires of words, images, texts, explanations, and everyday practices; when threaded together, these produce an understanding and a positioning of people of colour. Negative stereotypes are commonly used to reinforce notions that the 'other' is both different and deviant. The media have racialized crime for more than one hundred years, and Canadian newspapers have in the past routinely mentioned the race of offenders. This 'served to identify Asians and Blacks as alien ... and justified to a certain extent their differential treatment by the criminal justice system' (Mosher 1998, 126).

Today, the language of 'otherness' in the media is most commonly associated with Black males (often identified as Jamaican). First Nations people, Muslims and Arabs, and Chinese and Vietnamese immigrants also are racialized and stereotyped in media discourse as well as in other vehicles of cultural production. A consistent message on television (both in the news and in commercial programming) is that people of colour are 'outsiders within,' and this cannot but reinforce the 'we–they' mindset. Research has established that media constructions of race-related stories have a clear impact on public opinion (Entman and Rojecki 2000; Campbell 1995; van Dijk 1991, 1998). bell hooks (1990) suggests that stereotypes of people of colour are developed to 'serve as substitutions for reality.' They are contrived images that are developed and projected onto the 'others.'

One of the most persistent examples of racism in the media relates to the frequency with which people of colour and First Nations people are singled out as 'having problems' that require disproportionate amounts of political attention or public resources. That, or they are portrayed as 'creating problems.' *They* make unacceptable demands that threaten society's political, social, and moral order (Henry and

Tator 2002; Fleras and Kunz 2001; Law 2002; Entman and Rojecki 2000; Cottle 2000; Fiske 2000).

Images of everyday Black life in Canada, the United States, and the United Kingdom are dominated by representations of Black deviance. The racially coded language of 'Black-on-Black crime,' 'Black criminality,' and 'Black crime' has no parallel in discussions of crimes committed by Whites.

Hall and his colleagues (1978) in Britain were among the first to shed light on how news making, race, and crime are interlinked. One of the key factors in the racialization of crime is the overreporting of crimes (especially street crimes) allegedly committed by people of colour – specifically by Black men. As discussed in chapter 1, these researchers established that in 1970s Britain, the media played a crucial role not only in generating fear of crime but also in isolating specific criminal types ('Black urban muggers'). The media were largely responsible for implanting the idea that young Black males were enemies of society rather than the products of depressed socio-economic conditions.

Today, the media commonly construct Blacks as criminally disposed. They do so using racially coded language and images that portray them as dangerous, as less deserving of sympathy than Whites, and as less open to rehabilitation. We noted earlier that many studies in other countries have found a link between the media and the racialization of crime. More recently, Canadian researchers have demonstrated that persistent representations of Black men as criminals lead to fear of and hostility towards Blacks (Benjamin 2002, 2003; Wortley 2002; Henry and Tator 2002).

As the culture of violence expands, and as the phenomenon of crime is increasingly coded as a Black problem, it becomes more and more difficult to distinguish fact from fiction. Newspapers often highlight violent (Black) street crime with sensational headlines and graphic and disturbing images on page 1. Local TV newscasts often lead off with a crime story. The racial coding of crime is found in coverage that associates rap music with gang violence and gang violence with Blackness. Hollywood films are yet another powerful vehicle in reinforcing the interlocking nature of race and violence; these films function as indictments of an entire racial group (Giroux 1995). The media are constantly striving for greater sensationalism by construing real-life crimes as everyday entertainment. More and more frequently, representations of violence are racialized in ways that suggest violence is almost always a Black problem. This is not to suggest that White youths and adult criminals are absent from these cultural discourses. However, White violence and crime (be it youth or adult) is often framed in the language of personal pathology, or it is related to a class-specific nihilism; never is it attributed to the White ethnic group (Giroux 1995). In stark contrast, violence and crime by Blacks is represented as largely stemming from Black/Jamaican culture. This serves to indict the entire Black community for contributing to the social problem of race and crime. As a consequence, that community is held socially accountable for the problem as well as responsible for its solution.

Racialized images and ideas embedded in popular culture and other social institutions fuel moral panic among the White dominant culture (Hall et al. 1978). Moral panic thus becomes the vehicle of the dominant ideology; as such, it marginalizes, inferiorizes, and stigmatizes people of colour. Hall and colleagues (1978, 16) describe this phenomenon:

> When the official reaction to a person, group of persons or series of events is out of all proportion to the actual threat offered, when 'experts,' in the form of police chiefs, the judiciary, politicians and editors perceive the threat in all but identical terms, and appear to talk 'with one voice' of rates, diagnoses, prognoses and solutions, when the media representations universally stress 'sudden and dramatic' increases (in numbers involved or events) and 'novelty,' above and beyond that which a sober, realistic appraisal could sustain, then we believe it is appropriate to speak of the beginnings of a moral panic.

Conclusions

In Canadian society, White elite authorities in diverse institutions have long enjoyed the right to frame discussions about race and crime. In fact, they still do. Images and ideas embedded in political, legal, judicial, educational, and cultural discourses are still contributing to commonsense understandings of what constitutes 'difference,' 'deviance,' and 'danger' to White society. The White gaze acts as a filter through which Blackness is constructed and differentiated from Whiteness.

This analysis has highlighted the fact that racial minorities experience racism both separately (as individuals) and collectively (that is, as communities). Every dominant structure depends on the existence of an 'other' structure for its authority and power. To critically examine how racial profiling actually operates in policing, we must consider the impact of the deeper structures of racism that permeate society.

3 Racial Profiling in Canada, the United States, and the United Kingdom

CHARLES C. SMITH

> As to the portent, the pattern of incidents clearly reflecting policies unspoken, but no less authorized, conveys the message that Black people are now, as they have been throughout the history of this country, expendable. No matter their status, income, or accomplishments, we are at risk of harassment, arrest, injury, or death by those hired to protect the public peace. (Derrick Bell 2000, 88)

Racial profiling is the most recent manifestation of the intensely hostile relationship between police and subordinated racialized communities, especially those of African descent. Racial profiling – especially in the form of 'driving while Black' police stops (DWB) – has its own history, which is squarely situated within this relationship. Indeed, racial profiling is integral to today's so-called 'War on Drugs.' Those who believe anything else have blinded themselves to certain crucial issues in the historical relationship between people of African descent and the White people of Britain and North America. This history has been monstrous. It has included capturing Black Africans and tearing them from their culture, their language, and their homeland; enslaving and forcibly confining them; exploiting their labour; enforcing residential and educational segregation on them; and punishing their transgressions (in the eyes of White people) with violence and death, be these sanctioned by White mobs or by the state itself. And these practices have been justified through the processes of racialization as channelled by religious beliefs, cultural theory, political and economic development, the law, and the social values reflected in all of these. These social values pervade political and institutional structures, the law courts, the educational system, cultural representations, and media depictions (Martinot 2003; Omi and Winant 1986).

This history has laid the foundations for racial profiling, which is especially obvious in how people of African descent are treated and in how these people have been 'constructed' in the United States, the United Kingdom, and Canada. Randall Kennedy (1997) asserts that the relationship between Whites and African Americans in the United States constitutes the most difficult racial divide that country has ever faced. In his book, Kennedy delineates the history of the relationship between these two groups and describes the particular discursive formation in which that relationship operates and how it has been maintained through the law as well as through state-sanctioned and mob violence.

Racialized law enforcement has been an extraordinarily powerful tool for preserving social power, and over the past 150 years police forces have been a central resource for social control (Erez et al. 2003; Pedicelli 1998). Police forces play an important role in maintaining the status quo and ensuring social distance between divergent groups. This is especially true for societies in which race plays a key role in preserving power and privilege. When we examine the histories of people of African descent in Western nations, we find that these forms of social control include intense surveillance by law enforcement authorities resulting in increased rates of interaction between police and people of African descent. These interactions have contributed to higher-than-average rates of arrests, convictions, incarcerations, and acts of violence and have resulted in physical harm and death. As the Institute on Race and Poverty of the University of Minnesota suggests: 'One traditional law enforcement justification for racial disparities in police stops and searches is that it makes sense to stop and search people of colour in greater numbers, because they are more likely to be guilty of drug offences. The reality is that people of colour are arrested for drug offences in connection with vehicle stops at a high rate because they are targeted at a high rate, not because they are more likely than Whites to have drugs in their cars' (2000, 3–4).

Racial profiling in the United States is being chronicled more and more often in media articles, law journals, and government reports. The current spate of racial profiling has led some to wonder whether we are returning to an uglier period in American history – one in which racism was not simply publicly practised but actually sanctioned by state authority. Parallels have been drawn with the impact of slavery on people of African descent both before and after the Civil War, and to the Jim Crow era, when legislators and the courts actively reinforced segregation and the differential treatment of people of African descent (*Plessy v. Ferguson* 1896).

Before these issues can be discussed, it is essential that we define 'racial profiling' and explain how it has become intertwined with criminal profiling. It is widely acknowledged that law enforcement agencies exercise tremendous discretion in deciding whom to investigate. Put simply, police officers make subjective choices. These subjective choices cannot help but be influenced by social values, including biases related to socially constructed boundaries such as race (Holland 2000). Law enforcement agencies and their personnel are part of the broader society in which individuals and institutions interact daily. This interaction is influenced by social values and norms embedded in laws, cultural values, and state and organizational policies that influence individual beliefs and behaviours (Berger and Luckmann 1966; Essed 2000). These individual beliefs and behaviours in turn feed into an accepted understanding of race. For example, Peter Verniero and Paul H. Zoubek, respectively the former attorney general and first assistant attorney general for New Jersey, wrote that there are 'more common instances of *de facto* discrimination by officers who may be influenced by stereotypes and may thus tend to treat minority motorists differently during the course of routine traffic stops, subjecting them more routinely to investigative tactics and techniques that are designed to ferret out illicit drugs or weapons' (1999, 7).

Elizabeth A. Knight and William Kurnik (2002) define a law enforcement 'profile' as 'a set of circumstances, events, or behavior that, when combined with the experience of an officer, may cause heightened suspicion that affects the officer's exercise of discretion in stop and/or arrest decisions' (2002, 3). They add that 'the term "racial profiling" appears to broadly connote discriminatory law enforcement practices.' These practices are based on elective decisions by individual officers and thus differ markedly from responses to calls for help, in that the resulting actions are initiated by officers (ibid.). In other words, racial profiling implies a degree of intent or discriminatory purpose.

All of this provides insight into the blatant racial discrimination experienced by African Americans – experiences that effectively continue their oppression. For example, David A. Harris (2002, 3) discusses the practices of slave patrols and their efforts to ensure that slave labourers would be deterred from escaping and bow to the harsh conditions of plantation life. Adero S. Jernigan (2000, 128) notes the implications of empowering ordinary citizens in the 1600s to 'take up' peoples of African descent who were hanging around and forcing them to submit to unreasonable searches. He goes on to note that 'today, police officers across the country continuously target blacks in a manner consistent with the colonial measures instituted over 300 years ago' (ibid.).

Randall Kennedy (1997, 13–75) describes many episodes of this sort of anti-Black racism. Those who defended slavery alleged that people of African descent had criminal tendencies and a penchant for committing 'horrendous crimes'; this belief was used to justify both slavery and lynching. He goes on to list many instances when people of African descent were not protected by the law – especially from mob violence and lynching. In this way, Kennedy identifies the painful and still unacknowledged impact of racism on people of African descent. Later in his book (1997, 84–135), he discusses how laws were unequally enforced throughout the slavery era and after Reconstruction right up to the current era; here he pays particular attention to the era of segregation and racially biased police misconduct and police violence.

Jernigan describes how 'profiling' during the War on Drugs escalated into 'racial profiling' (2000, 128–9). There is clear evidence that the approach taken by the Drug Enforcement Authority (DEA) in the early 1980s was supported by the federal government and that the DEA Operation Pipeline developed and used training materials that included racial profiles of drug couriers. These materials were employed in the education and training of federal, state, and local law enforcement authorities (Harris 2002, 3-4).

Links between racial profiling and the War on Drugs in Florida have been established. A law enforcement memo titled 'Common Characteristics of Drug Couriers' instructed deputies in that state to watch for 'ethnic groups associated with the drug trade,' and several deputies testified that the memo was widely circulated throughout the department (Morris 2001, 80). Also, in a Maryland lawsuit filed by Robert Wilkins, evidence surfaced during discovery indicating that 'a State Police memo instruct[ed] troopers to look for drug couriers – described as "mostly black males and black females."' Once this memo was revealed, the state police settled with Wilkins (Harris 2001, 115).

Numbers Don't Lie, Do They?

Now that the issue has been defined, it is important to examine the numbers – specifically, interaction rates between police and individuals from subordinated racialized groups, especially African and Latino Americans. Beginning with the recent War on Drugs, and supported by the official and unofficial policies and tactics of the DEA, the practice of racial profiling in the United States was established as a tool for eliminating drug trafficking. However, as was noted earlier, the criminal profiles generated by the DEA were not without strong historical precedents.

Racial profiling mainly involves state and local enforcement authorities stopping motor vehicles on highways and streets. It is common knowledge that moving vehicle violations are difficult to assess. Many motorists who have been pulled over by the police often do not know why they have been stopped and do not believe they have violated any laws. Even so, they are stopped. Many motorists of African and Latino descent have complained that after routine questioning, they are subjected to additional questioning or are required to leave their vehicle to allow the police to conduct a search.

The 'traffic violation' stop is often a pretext for something else, such as a check for drug possession or trafficking. An officer's suspicion has been aroused, and this has triggered a stop-and-search action. In New Jersey, for one example, state troopers pulled over a group of young African Americans travelling on the New Jersey Turnpike to attend a basketball camp. They were subsequently shot by the troopers, who wounded three. In the same state, the governor at the time had her photograph taken while apparently frisking a Black motorist (Lipper 2001, 31). This photo was widely publicized, and reinforced public perceptions that the state and its police were making an orchestrated effort to profile motorists of African descent. Statistical data supporting the concerns raised by these anecdotes appeared shortly afterwards in a number of states:

- In opinion polling, 72 per cent of African Americans between eighteen and thirty-four said they had been stopped by the police because of their race; 37 per cent reported having been stopped more than once, and 15 per cent more than ten times.
- Between January 1995 and June 1996, in Maryland, 732 individuals were detained and searched by the state police. Of these, 75 per cent were African American and 5 per cent were Latino (Morris 2001, 80).
- In Philadelphia, African Americans comprise 79 per cent of those stopped and searched even though they are only 42 per cent of population;
- In Illinois, Latinos comprise 41 per cent of those stopped and

searched even though they are less than 1 per cent of the driving population. Furthermore, one in every 75 African Americans is stopped compared to one in every 163 Whites (Kearney 2001, 62–80).
• In New York City, a review of 175,000 cases indicated that African Americans were stopped six times more often than Whites. Also, even though they were only 25 per cent of the city's population, African Americans accounted for 50 per cent of all individuals stopped (Bobb 2002, 6).

Regarding New Jersey, David A. Harris (2001) points out that Blacks and Whites were equally responsible for traffic violations, yet 73.2 per cent of those stopped and arrested were Black, even though only 13.5 per cent of cars on the road had a Black driver or occupant. Harris examined municipal court records in Ohio (Toledo, Akron, Dayton, Franklin County) and found that 'Blacks are about twice as likely to be ticketed as non-Blacks are. When the fact that 21% of Black households do not own a vehicle is factored in, the ratios rise' (ibid., 117). These disparities in results are statistically significant, so it must be concluded that the racial disparity is not a random result (ibid., 114–17).

These data, and observations of police behaviour, indicate that in the War on Drugs, the police are abusing their powers. Sean Hecker (1997) reviewed data from Orlando, Florida. According to the *Orlando Sentinel News*, the police made 1,084 stops between 1980 and 1992; these led to 507 searches and 55 arrests but only 9 traffic tickets. Of these stops, 70 per cent were of African Americans and Latinos, who incurred an average stop time of 12.1 minutes compared to 5.1 minutes for Whites. Furthermore, of the 507 cars searched, 82 per cent belonged to African Americans and Latinos (ibid., 3–4).

These data point strongly to what Ira Glasser (2001, 22) describes as a matter not of 'rogue' police but of 'rogue' policy. And nowhere is this more obvious than in an examination of what are typically called 'hit rates' for police profiling activities. Harris found that hit rates in the late 1990s showed no distinction between Whites and subordinate racialized groups.

For example, data collected from the Minneapolis and St Paul police indicate that racial profiling is an unsound policing strategy. The problem has mainly to do with circular logic – that is, more stops lead to more arrests, which justify more stops, which lead to more arrests, and so on. John Lamberth's research in Maryland found that the hit rate was the same for African Americans as for Whites (28 per cent) despite the rise in stop-and-searches of African Americans. Similarly, New Jersey data from 1999 indicated an arrest ratio of 10.5 per cent for Whites compared to 13.5 per cent for African and Latino Americans. In New York, stop-and-frisk data from 1998–9 indicated a hit rate of 12.6 per cent for Whites versus 11.3 per cent for Latinos and 10.5 per cent for African Americans (Institute on Race and Poverty 2000, 2–3). The New York Police Department had to stop 9.5 African Americans to generate one arrest, whereas they had to stop 7.9 Whites for the same result (Bobb 2002, 6–8).

There is overwhelming evidence of discriminatory policing, yet the police and their supporters strongly deny that it exists. Instead of accepting the evidence of racial profiling and developing strategies to address it, these groups have attacked the statistics. According to them, the data do not include all stops or violator rates, do not account for different levels of police discretion, and have not been adjusted to reflect the differential deployment of police as a function of crime rates (Harris 2001, 112–20). They discuss their 'success' in terms of 'batting averages,' or they contend that they use race in conjunction with other factors (Glasser 1999, 5; Hecker 1997).

What is frightening is that in the face of this backlash and denial, official state reports and analyses indicate results similar to those noted above. For example, Verniero and Zoubek (1999, 6–33) made these observations in their report for the State of New Jersey:

- There is wilful misconduct by some officers and – even more common – de facto discrimination by officers influenced by stereotypes.
- The data on traffic stops by race indicate that nearly 40 per cent of stops involved African, Latino, or Asian Americans (27 per cent African Americans, 6.9 per cent Latinos, 3.9 per cent Asian Americans).
- According to an internal audit, 52.6 per cent of searches were of African Americans.
- Motorists from subordinate racialized groups were disproportionately subject to consent searches. African-American motorists were ticketed disproportionately. For example, 18 per cent of tickets written by the Radar Unit, 23.8 per cent of those written by the Tactical Patrol Unit, and 34.2 per cent of those written by the Patrol Unit on Exits 1 and 7A of the New Jersey Turnpike, were written against African Americans.

Similar data are encountered in other federal and state reports, including these: *The New York City Police Department's 'Stop and Frisk' Practices* (1999), *Vehicle Stop Study Mid-Year Report* (2000), *Evaluating North Carolina State Highway Patrol Data: Citations, Warnings, and Searches in 1998, Interim Report of Traffic Stop Statistics: January 2000 to June 2000* (2000), and *1st Annual Report Denver Police Department Contact Card Data Analysis: June 1, 2001 through May 31, 2002* (2002). In addition, there has been considerable media coverage of the DWB issue. Articles have appeared in the local and national press. Examples: Dan Olsen, 'Justice in Black and White: The Justice Gap,' *MPR News*, 13 April 2000; Amy Randal, 'Racial Profiling Allegations Bring Calls for Statewide Data Collection,' 15 June 2000; Byron Bain, 'Walking While Black,' *The Village Voice*, 26 April–2 May 2000; and John Cloud, 'What's Race Got to Do with It?' *Time Canada*, 31 July 2001.

We Are What We Eat

Having reviewed the statistical data and the systemic practices that bring about these numbers, it is time to look at the jurisprudence that sanctions law enforcement's use of racial profiling. Legal challenges relating to the differential impact of policing and the criminal justice system on subordinate racialized groups – especially people of African descent – have not addressed the concerns of these communities. Beginning with *Terry v. Ohio* (1968), followed by *Robinson v. U.S.* (1973) and culminating in *Whren v. U.S.* (1996) and *Atwater v. Lago Vista* (1996), the United States Supreme Court has upheld the right of police to take extraordinary actions, even if they may violate the letter and spirit of the 4th and 14th Amendments.

In particular, the Supreme Court has continued to support policing practices such as racial profiling even in the face of social science evidence presented to it over the years (for example, in *Terry* and *Whren*). The Court seems to have ignored the NAACP Legal Defense Fund presentation of data on Blacks and stops; instead it has relied on the 'police as expert' narrative, which was central to the post-*Terry*/pre-*Whren* era. This is evident in other cases as well. In its approach to 14th Amendment cases, the Supreme Court has consistently taken a 'race-free' approach to 4th Amendment jurisprudence and ignored the social science data, including data on the use of deadly force (Thompson 1999, 962–91; Colby 2001).

These cases demonstrate how hard it is to overcome the evidentiary threshold associated with proving race-based discrimination in the

United States, especially in the context of the 4th and 14th Amendments. Although there are abundant 4th Amendment cases requiring reasonable suspicion to justify an investigatory police stop, the Supreme Court has imposed 'constrictions [on the use] of Fourth Amendment protections over the last several decades' (Johnson 2000, 686–7). Furthermore, efforts to press for an examination of racial profiling practices under the equal-protection clause have been hindered by the heavy burden of proof necessary under that clause.

The U.S. Supreme Court's failure to acknowledge the disproportionate impact of policing practices on subordinated racialized groups has undoubtedly contributed to the increased use by law enforcement authorities of criminal profiling, which has an obvious racial component. Whren has had dire consequences for African Americans and Latinos. It has given law enforcement authorities the go-ahead to keep relying on racial profiling; the impact of this is visible in the data collected in many states, including Florida, Maryland, Illinois, and Colorado.

Based on the pervasiveness of racial profiling and the extraordinary number of individuals stopped, it is hard to dismiss concerns that racial profiling has amounted to a state-orchestrated attack against individuals from subordinated racialized groups, especially people of African descent. Given the 'success' of the practice in apprehending criminal suspects and the conviction rates of these suspects, one can only wonder why police keep using racial profiling, especially when the evidence shows that it not a productive use of police resources and when its impact on police–minority relations has been disastrous.

The United Kingdom's Experience

> The history of police race relations in Britain has a strong strand of conflict running through it, with pressure for change arising from public inquiries. Change has not been driven spontaneously by the police but required by the findings of various inquiries into insensitive and inappropriate police work. This context begs researchers to take seriously and understand processes of conflict. (Holdaway 2003, 64)

The relationship between the police and people of African descent in the United Kingdom differs in some particulars from the American experience, but the nature of that relationship is fundamentally the same. In his introduction to *Black Youth, Racism, and the State: The Politics of Ideology and Policy,* John Solomos (1988, 1) stated:

The issue of the position of young blacks within British society, and their role in the future of 'race relations,' has been a hotly debated question for nearly two decades. Moreover, in the aftermath of the violent protests that have taken place since the 1980s, numerous state agencies, political organizations, voluntary bodies, academic researchers and media commentators have addressed themselves to the 'crisis of black youth' ... It [therefore] came as no surprise when Lord Scarman's report on the Brixton riot of 10-12 April 1981 concluded that: 'The riots were essentially an outburst of anger and resentment by young black people against the police.'

Similar comments about African Americans in the United States would be just as apt.

The experiences of British people of African descent in their relationships with the police suggest a worrying commonality with African Americans with respect to racial profiling (ibid. 1988, 91, 101–2). This is related to the unique discursive formation between the police and people of African descent – a formation that seems to have defied national borders and vastly different historical developments to arrive at the same axis: police forces treat people of African descent quite differently than they do Whites. They even treat them differently from members of other subordinated racialized communities. And this differential treatment is the very basis of the hostile relations between these two groups (Holdaway 2003).

To understand racial profiling in Britain, we must consider first the impact that immigration from the Caribbean and African countries has had on Britain's national character and identity (Ware 2001, 184–213). After the Second World War, changes to the composition of British communities came about as a result of immigration from recently established Commonwealth nations in the Caribbean, Africa, Asia, and South Asia. This change in Britain's racial composition had an almost immediate impact on policing. Racist attacks on individuals from subordinated racialized groups throughout the 1950s and 1960s and the failure of the police to protect these new British residents adequately led to increasing polarization between the police and these groups. According to Paul Gilroy (1991, 79–85), the British police and political leaders in the 1940s and 1950s actively constructed images of crime as being perpetrated by individuals of African descent; meanwhile, their failure to protect people of African descent from racist attacks became the springboard for the 1958 riots in Nottingham and London.

The linking of crime with people of African descent continued in the aftermath of the riots. Solomos notes that with rising immigration, 'black settlements rapidly became identified as localities with crime-related behaviour and other "social problems."' Solomos suggests that the 1960s saw a growing politicization of this question, and continuous attempts by the police and by governments to deal with the danger of conflict between the police and black communities. During these years, individuals of African descent increasingly complained of racial discrimination at the hands of the police. This led to the release in 1967 of a Home Office circular to police chiefs titled 'The Police and Coloured Communities,' which made several recommendations for improving relations between the two. For example, it called for improved officer training and for the launching of community liaison initiatives. A series of reports and articles on relations between police and subordinated racialized communities were released in the wake of this circular. All of this helped politicize the issue of 'race and policing' and led to communities demanding investigations into cases of alleged police harassment (Solomos 1988, 92–4).

Conflict and advocacy pervaded the 1970s. With the introduction of the 'Sus laws,' which extended to the police the power to stop people without reason, allegations surfaced that the police were targeting people of African descent for unreasonable stops and searches. In 1972 the Select Committee on Race Relations and Immigration described relations between police and youth of African descent as 'difficult and explosive.' A representative from the community-based West Indian Conference told the select committee in writing: 'To state that a sizeable proportion of the West Indian Community no longer trust the police is to confer a euphemism upon a situation which, for many, has reached a level equal to fear [and] if urgent action is not taken to give effect to the grave issue at hand, violence on a large scale cannot be ruled out. The solution rests largely in the hands of the police' (in Gilroy 1991, 88)

Shortly after the select committee released its report, the police and youth of African descent clashed violently in Brockwell Park (South London, 1973), Chapeltown (Leeds, 1973, 1974, 1975), the Notting Hill Carnival (1976, 1977, 1978), Ladywood (Birmingham, 1977), and Lewisham (London, 1977). These clashes took place just as the police were beginning to recognize the permanence of these new communities and to consider approaches to policing them. In this regard, Holdaway (2000) writes: 'Until the early 1980s, the police took the widely accepted view that immigrants would gradually assimilate into our apparently homogenous culture. The initial task for police was to understand the different immigrant cultures and for people from those cultures to understand the traditions of English policing.' Holdaway continues: 'This approach had two main effects. It located police race relations within specialist departments, not within routine policing. The problems of policing "those people" became the concern of specialist officers who understood immigrants and their culture. The work of the rank and file was largely unaffected by police community relations policies' (ibid., 103–9). As a consequence, 'race relations were of little relevance to a local police commander and his officers' (ibid., 52–4).

Despite this approach – or perhaps because of it – conflicts between police and subordinated racialized communities were inevitable, especially since this approach did nothing to address the 'negative ideas about black people as criminals and drug users' (ibid., 5) that the police had nurtured. The inadequacy of this approach contributed greatly to the Brixton riots of 1981. A police stop-and-search operation mainly targeting people of African descent inflamed the community; the result was three days of looting, arson, property damage, and violent exchanges between the police and the predominantly 'black' community.

Other riots flared across Britain throughout the 1980s, pitting police against young people of African descent. The locations included Bristol, Toxteth, Manchester (Moss Side Police Station), London, Liverpool, Birmingham, Wolverhampton, Leicester, Derby, Nottingham, Leeds, and Huddersfield. The Metropolitan Police released a report that provided a racial breakdown of those engaged in street robberies; it indicated a disproportionate involvement of youth of African descent (Solomos 1988, 102, 181, 115–16). Also during this period, individuals from subordinated racialized groups died while in police custody or in prison. The Independent Race and Refugee News Network (2002) compiled a list of these deaths, and suggested that they had not been explained, nor had those of blacks in psychiatric custody between 1969 and 2002. The network cited around ninety such deaths in all. The group wanted to know how these people died, and whether there had been 'maltreatment, dereliction of duty or brutality.'

In response to the rioting, the Police and Criminal Evidence Act (PACE) was adopted in 1984 to provide national authority for stopping and searching suspects for stolen or contraband items. PACE required reasonable grounds for suspecting that a search would uncover 'stolen or prohibited articles'; it also required the police to record all stops (pedestrian and vehicle) that concluded with searches. PACE offered police the power to conduct full searches of individuals as well as any items they were carrying and their vehicles. On top of this, in 1993 Her Majesty's Inspectorate of Constabulary (HMIC) made it compulsory for all police forces to record the ethnicity of persons searched. The Home Office began monitoring the ethnicity of these individuals in 1996.

Even though the Scarman Report of 1981 noted the discriminatory impact of police stops and searches of youth of African descent, the practice continued. According to Bowling (2003, 24), 'it was doubtful that searches were always based on reasonable suspicion; [and] so-called voluntary searches were rarely based on informed consent and often not officially recorded.' A 1997 review of the police's race relations practices conducted by Her Majesty's Chief Inspector of Constabulary declared that 'racial discrimination, both direct and indirect, and harassment are endemic within our society and the police service is no exception ... There was continuing evidence during the inspection of inappropriate language and behaviour by police officers, but even more worrying was the lack of intervention by seargents and inspectors' (ibid., 24).

This research has underscored the concerns of subordinated racial-ized communities and their lack of trust and confidence in the police. It was in this context that the Stephen Lawrence Inquiry was held, chaired by Sir William MacPherson of Cluny. This inquiry was prompted by the failure of the police to properly investigate the racially motivated murder of a youth of African descent. The Lawrence Inquiry contrasted with the Scarman Report, which studiously avoided addressing the possibility of institutional discrimination. It concluded that institutional racism was a central issue in police rela-tions with subordinated racialized groups, especially those of African descent. MacPherson defined institutional racism as 'the collective fail-ure of an organization to provide an appropriate and professional ser-vice to people because of their colour, culture, or ethnic origin. It can be seen or detected in processes, attitudes and behaviour which amount to discrimination through unwitting prejudice, ignorance, thoughtless-ness and racist stereotyping which disadvantage minority ethnic peo-ple' (McPherson 1999, 29; Bowling 2003).

This definition, and the adoption of recommendations from the Lawrence Inquiry, set the stage for significant amendments to the U.K. Race Relations Act and for the introduction of requirements that *all* public authorities – including the police – develop and implement comprehensive plans for improving race relations.[1] In particular, the police would be expected to establish policies and actions to address the discriminatory impact of stops and searches.

The Numbers across the Atlantic

As previously noted, current police stop-and-search powers as well as requirements for ethnic data collection were introduced in the mid-1980s and 1990s. Since then a raft of information has been gathered related to the practices of police officers in fulfilling their duties in this regard. Published one day before the tenth anniversary of Stephen Lawrence's murder and three years after the inquiry into his death had been concluded, a recent newspaper article based on a report by Dr Benjamin Bowling asserted that 'Afro-Caribbean people are 27 times more likely than White people to be stopped and searched under a special police power designed to tackle ravers and football hooligans' (Dodd 2003).

According to the Home Office, stop-and-search statistics demonstrate clear disparities. People of African descent are stopped more frequently, cautioned less than other groups, and held in custody more often than other groups. In terms of the magnitude of continued stops and searches, a recent report of the Metropolitan Police Authority (MPA) provides a racialized breakdown, borough by borough, for the years 1997 to 2002 (2003). Some of these boroughs are more intrusive than others when it comes to stopping and searching people of African descent. For example, the MPA report indicates that during this period, searches of people of African descent rose dramatically, from 75,583 in 1996–7 to 89,916 in 2002–3; within the same time frame, there was a significant reduction in searches of Whites, from 187,105 to 130,635. Fur-

---

1 Bowling also notes the support to this definition provided by John Newing, then head of the Association of Chief Police Officers and Chief Constable of Derbyshire, who appeared before the Lawrence Inquiry and stated in his submission that 'institutional racism [is] the racism which is inherent in wider society which shapes our attitudes and behaviour. Those attitudes and behaviour are then reinforced or reshaped by the culture of the organization a person works for. In the police service there is a distinct tendency for officers to stereotype people. That creates problems in a number of areas, but particularly in the way officers deal with black people. I know because as a young police officer I was guilty of such behaviour.'

thermore, individuals from subordinated racialized communities – especially people of African descent – were subject to an increasing number of searches, even though total searches decreased during this period from 303,546 to 262,903 (Metropolitan Police Authority 2003, Appendix E).

An examination of police stops and searches in the West Midlands indicates that a total of 79,000 stops/searches took place from 1998–9 to 2001–2 – around 20,000 stops per year. During 2000–1, 64 per cent of those stopped were White, 16 per cent were people of African descent, and 19 per cent were Asian. These latter two figures are strongly disproportionate to the presence of these groups in the West Midlands. Under Section 60 of the Criminal Justice and Public Order Act, 1994 (CJPOA), stops/searches do not require an objective basis. West Midlands data indicate that over the two most recent years the study considered, individuals from subordinated racialized communities were stopped more often in absolute numbers. For example, in 2001–2, 2,209 Whites were stopped compared to 1,921 people of African descent and 1,380 Asians. Stops under the Prevention of Terrorism Act 1989, which was 'designed specifically to combat terrorism from the Provisional Irish Republican Army,' indicate that in 1996–7, 11 per cent of the 43,700 stops in England and Wales were of individuals from subordinated racialized groups. In 1997–8, 7 per cent of those stopped were people of African descent (Bowling 2003, 6).

The 2001–2 West Midlands statistics comparing resident populations tell us that 5 Whites, 41 individuals of African descent, and 17 Asians were stopped/searched per 1,000 of each of their cohorts. This indicates that people of African descent were eight times more likely, and Asians three times more likely, to be stopped/searched than their White counterparts. This is consistent with the national average of racial disproportionality across England and Wales: 13 Whites were stopped per 1,000 of the population, whereas people of African descent were stopped 106 times per 1,000 and Asians 35 per 1,000. Furthermore, stops/searches under CJPOA indicate that per 1,000 population, 1 White is stopped/searched; 26 individuals of African descent and 7 Asians are similarly treated. In England and Wales this compares respectively as 0.5 per 1,000 for Whites, 5.5 per 1,000 for people of African descent, and 3.6 per 1,000 for Asians; in other words, people of African descent are '28 times more likely to be searched and Asian people 18 times more likely to be searched in comparison with their White counterparts' (Bowling 2003, 9–10).

According to the recent British Crime Survey (BCS), in terms of multiple stops, 77 per cent of Whites were stopped only once compared to 53 per cent of individuals of African descent and roughly 64 per cent of individuals of South Asian descent. In addition, 14 per cent of individuals of African descent reported being stopped five or more times compared to 4 per cent of Whites. Also, only 9 per cent of stops of Whites resulted in a search, compared to 34 per cent for individuals of African descent and 14 per cent for Asians. Furthermore, people of African descent were subject to:

- more multiple vehicle stops – 14 per cent were stopped five or more times compared to 4 per cent of Whites, 6 per cent of Indians, and 2.7 per cent of Pakistani/Bangladeshis;
- more multiple pedestrian/foot stops – 18 per cent were stopped five or more times compared to 12 per cent of Whites, 10 per cent of Indians, and no Pakistani/Bangladeshis; *and*
- increased traffic stops/searches – 9 per cent of White people were searched compared to 34 per cent of people of African descent and 14 per cent of Asians (Clancy et al. 2001, 59–71).

According to 1991 census data, although people of African descent were only 5 per cent of the population of Greenwich, they comprised 16 per cent of those stopped and 14 per cent of those searched. In Hounslow, they comprised 3 per cent of the population but 16 per cent of those stopped and 14 per cent of those searched. In Central Leicester, they comprised 1 per cent of the population but 11 per cent of those stopped and 13 per cent of those searched. Ipswich and Chapeltown reported similar results. The police in these communities show a penchant for stop-and-search activity and 'focus on areas with a disproportionately high number of minority ethnic residents' (Miller 2000, 13–36).

The British data on racial profiling offer significant evidence that policing has a disproportionate impact on subordinated racialized groups. This, despite substantial under-recording of stops and some doubt as to the accuracy of police statistics (Miller, Bland, and Quinton 2000, viii and x). On a related point, one of the main reasons for police stops is to stem illegal drug sales and use, yet the self-reporting of such offences to Britain's Home Office indicates that throughout the 1990s, drug use was highest among Whites. Having reviewed these data, Bowling declares: 'The findings from these surveys are remarkable in their consistency – they all point to the conclusion that offending rates are no higher among ethnic minority communities than among the White majority community. If these statistics were accepted as accurate, and applied to the West Midlands, then the extent of disproportionality in the use of stop/search will be of similar magnitude to those based on resident population' (Bowling 2003, 14).

This is an astonishing finding, especially given the controversy surrounding police assertions that people of African descent are heavy users of drugs and the impact of this perception on police interactions with this community during the 1970s and 1980s. Unfortunately, these findings are mirrored by other 'hit' rates in terms of the policing of people of African descent. For example, Holdaway (2003, 51–3) maintains that 'the use of negative ideas about black youths, as drug users and offenders, for example, played a key role in the police action that led to the near riots on the streets of Brixton, London, in 1981.' In a society estimated to be 94.1 per cent White, 1.8 per cent people of African descent, 2.9 per cent South Asian, and 1.2 per cent Chinese, the racialized composition of hit rates is mind-boggling. These figures make it abundantly clear that racial profiling is a major activity of law enforcement in Britain, notwithstanding the government's avowed intention to stop the practice, the requirement to collect data on this practice, and the requirement for police forces to adopt positive actions in the context of recent amendments to the Race Relations Act.

The Canadian Experience

First, what we are dealing with, at root, and fundamentally, is anti-Black racism. While it is obviously true that every visible minority community experiences the indignities and wounds of systemic discrimination throughout Southern Ontario, it is the Black community which is the focus. It is Blacks who are shot, it is Black youth that is unemployed in excessive numbers, it is Black students who are being inappropriately streamed in schools, it is Black kids who are disproportionately dropping-out, it is housing communities with large concentrations of Black residents where the sense of vulnerability and disadvantage is most acute, it is Black employees, professional and non-professional, on whom the doors of upward equity slam shut. Just as the soothing balm of 'multiculturalism' cannot mask racism, so racism cannot mask its primary target. (Lewis 1992, 2)

When racial profiling is discussed in Canada, the focus is mainly on recent experience, which tends to support the notion (just as in Britain) that this profiling is a recent phenomenon and largely a consequence of changes in immigration patterns. This is a short-sighted perspective that ignores the weight of experience of African Canadians, especially with regard to their relationship with law enforcement authorities (Walker 1997; Mosher 1998).

People of African descent have a long history in Canada, one which has been marked by racist laws that have severely impeded African Canadians' advancement. In early Canada, the enslavement of Blacks was legal, and even after slavery was abolished here, the law forbade Blacks to own land. This included those Blacks who had come to Canada with the British Loyalists during and after the American Revolution. Subsequently, laws were passed so that schools and residential areas were segregated. Constance Backhouse (1999) has documented how restrictive land covenants and other practices prevented people of African descent from finding work, accessing land and housing, joining the military, entering orphanages and poorhouses, attending churches, taking public transportation, using services such as restaurants, hotels, and theatres, and being buried in certain cemeteries.

For example, Backhouse describes how in 1930 the Ku Klux Klan entered the town of Oakville, Ontario, in full robes and hoods to forcibly end the marriage between an African-Canadian man and a White woman. These racist actions were supported by law enforcement authorities, and the charges laid in the case did not specifically address the obvious racism in the Klan's actions. She later discusses the experiences of Viola Desmond, who in 1946 was arrested, charged, and prosecuted for attempting to sit in the White section of a movie theatre in Nova Scotia (ibid., 173–229).

Like Backhouse, Clayton James Mosher (1998) cites experiences related to access to housing, employment, and services. In each instance, he notes the particular impact of the racist actions of White Canadians. For example, he shows how restricting access to housing led to the formation of segregated communities. Here, he cites a covenant in Hamilton, Ontario, that prevented the sale of land to people of African descent (as well as to others). Similar regimes were in place in parts of southwestern Ontario. Mosher also examines access to services such as hotels, theatres, restaurants, and taverns, and concludes that 'denial of services to Blacks was pervasive in Canadian society, and Canadian judicial officials frequently upheld the right of businesses to discriminate' (ibid., 96–7).

In his account of the racialization of criminal justice, Mosher (1998, 162–81) makes the following observations:

- In six cities in Ontario, including Windsor, Hamilton, London, and Toronto, 12 per cent of all public order charges were against African Canadians, 11 per cent against Aboriginal people, and 2 per cent against Chinese. This was vastly disproportionate to their actual numbers in these cities. Of those charged, African Canadians and Aboriginal people were the most likely to be imprisoned.
- In their efforts to control public order offences, the police in these Ontario cities tended to focus on African Canadians. This led to the use of 'disorderly-house and other public-morals laws ... to control Black populations.'
- African Canadians were required to appear in court more often than other groups to defend themselves against charges of property crime, and they received longer sentences when convicted.
- African Canadians found in areas where property offences had occurred 'were often identified as suspects, and the courts often found them guilty on the basis of such limited evidence.'
- The mean sentence length for African Canadians for property offences was 10.51 months, compared to 8.33 for Aboriginal people and 6.26 for Whites.

Mosher's analysis focuses on the seventy years between 1892 and 1961. His research provides insight into the media's influence on public values and judicial rulings; it also highlights the propensity of police to apprehend suspects based on prevailing racial biases. In 1995, the Commission on Systemic Racism in the Ontario Criminal Justice System addressed similar issues and reached strikingly similar conclusions. The African Canadian Legal Clinic recently released a report (Smith and Lawson 2002) that identified the cumulative impact of anti-Black racism on the criminal justice system and on Canadian society as a whole. Both these reports built on the many community concerns expressed earlier in this chapter. The latter report also discussed the apparent reluctance of governments to hold the police accountable for their actions.

These accounts make it clear that racism has always infected Canada's criminal justice system, that it is embedded in the law itself, and that this has had a profound impact on African Canadians. Anti-Black racism in law enforcement did not just appear in Canada and its urban centres following changes in immigration policies.

Recent research has also looked at racism in law enforcement. Several of these studies have taken a statistical approach to examining the impact of policing on subordinated racialized groups, especially African Canadians. Whatever their scope, these studies reach the same conclusions: African Canadians are treated very differently by the police and other key players in the criminal justice system, and this has damaged the lives of Black individuals and their communities. These same studies contextualize the practice of racial profiling and offer a full account of its social backdrop.

One of the first of these studies was conducted by Phillip Stenning (1994), who described the differential treatment of African-Canadian inmates in three Toronto detention centres. His research revealed the following:

- African Canadians were significantly overrepresented in the 'major' offence category: they accounted for 58.8 per cent, compared to 25.0 per cent for Whites and 28.9 per cent for 'others.' This category included robbery (Whites, 5.0 per cent, African Canadians, 29.4 per cent, 'others,' 2.6 per cent) and drug offences (Whites, 10.0 per cent, African Canadians, 19.6 per cent, 'others,' 15.8 per cent).
- In responding to 'minor offences,' police drew their weapons when arresting African Canadians more often than with other groups (25 per cent of the time, compared to 6.7 per cent for Whites and 6.7 per cent for 'others').
- Rates of police use of force – at the time of arrest as well as after arrest – were significantly higher for African Canadians (33.3 and 31.4 per cent respectively, compared to 25.0 and 25.0 per cent for Whites and 30.8 and 23.1 per cent for 'others') (ibid., II.9–II.24).

These data tell us some things about the unequal treatment of African Canadians, Whites, and 'others' at the hands of the police. In noting these differences, it must be acknowledged that Whites and 'others' were sometimes treated less favourably than African Canadians. Other studies besides Stenning's support the assertion that African Canadians face differential treatment. For example, in 1993 the Canadian Civil Liberties Association conducted a survey of 150 youth; it found that 71 per cent of individuals from subordinated racialized groups had had negative experiences of the police, compared to 50 per cent of Whites. Several of these youth alleged that they had been subjected to racial slurs by police officers during questioning (Mosher

1998, 18). These statistics are supported by Scot Wortley's research (1997), which found that:

- 28.1 per cent of African Canadians reported having been stopped by police, compared to 18.2 per cent of Whites and 14.6 per cent of Chinese Canadians;
- 16.8 per cent of African Canadians reported having been stopped twice by police, compared to 8.0 per cent of Whites and 4.7 per cent of Chinese Canadians;
- 11.7 per cent of African Canadians reported having been stopped by police 'unfairly' in the past two years, compared to 2.1 per cent of Whites and 2.2 per cent of Chinese Canadians;
- 42.7 per cent of African-Canadian males reported having been stopped by the police in the past two years, compared to 22.1 per cent of Whites and Asians; *and*
- 28.7 per cent of African-Canadian males reported having been stopped twice in the past two years, compared to 9.9 per cent of Whites and Asians (ibid., 18–19).

Anecdotal accounts and statistical data pointing to the use of racial profiling have been supported by the Commission on Systemic Racism in the Ontario Criminal Justice System (1995). This commission reported the following findings:

- The police stop African Canadians (especially African-Canadian males) twice as often as Whites.
- Whites are less likely to be detained before trial than African Canadians (23 per cent against 30 per cent), especially for drug charges (10 per cent against 31 per cent).
- Between 1986–7 and 1992–3, incarcerations of African Canadians for drug trafficking rose by 1,164 per cent, from 25 per cent of 524 admissions to 60 per cent of 2,616 admissions. This compares to a 151 per cent increase for Whites during the same period.
- With regard to drug charges, White accused were released more often than African Canadians. Also, African Canadians were denied bail more often, and the conviction rate was higher for African Canadian men: 69 per cent, compared to 57 per cent for White men.
- In the six years leading up to 1993, the African-Canadian population of Ontario increased by 36 per cent; over the same period, the number of African-Canadian prisoners admitted to Ontario correctional

facilities increased by 204 per cent! The number of White prisoners admitted increased by only 23 per cent.

The commission also noted that 'no evidence shows that African Canadian people are more likely to use drugs than others or that they are over-represented among those who profit from drug use. Events of the last few years do show, however, that intensive policing of low-income areas in which African Canadian people live produces arrests of large and disproportionate numbers of African Canadian male street dealers. Once the police have done this work, the practices and decisions of the crown prosecutors, justices of the peace and judges operate as a conveyor belt to prison' (ibid., 83).

The commission suggested that the American practice of drug profiling was introduced to Canada in 1994, and that the RCMP had trained some ten thousand law enforcement personnel in its use (Tanovich 2002, 152). Despite the commission's findings, the training continued.

And the trail of evidence does not stop there. In another report, African Canadians described other examples of 'policing Black'; young males in particular reported being exposed to excessive policing. This study was conducted by the Ontario Coalition Against Poverty (OCAP) in 2000; many of the 167 interviewees were African Canadians from low-income populations who used social agencies. Two-thirds of those surveyed reported having been assaulted or threatened with assault by the police. The actual assaults included being beaten, slapped, punched, and Maced. Threats included threats of death (37 per cent). Other intimidation tactics used included harassment (74 per cent), threatening arrest (59 per cent), searches without good cause (54 per cent), arrest on false or improper charges that were eventually thrown out of court (35 per cent), and taking photographs of individuals on the street without their consent (25 per cent).

Separate studies, both based on interviews by Carl James (1998) and Robynne Neugebauer (2000), offer remarkably similar findings. African-Canadian youth told these researchers that they were stopped by police, mainly because of their skin colour. These findings are supported by Wortley and Tanner (2003), who surveyed 3,400 Toronto high school students. Among their findings:

• Over 50 per cent of African Canadians surveyed claimed to have been stopped and questioned by the police on two or more occasions in the past two years, compared to 23 per cent of Whites, 11 per cent of Asians, and 8 per cent of South Asians.

- Over 40 per cent of African Canadians claimed to have been searched by the police in the past two years, compared to 17 per cent of Whites and 11 per cent of Asians.
- Of African Canadians who had not been involved in criminal activity, 34 per cent claimed they had been stopped by the police on two or more occasions in the past two years, compared to 4 per cent of Whites.
- Of African Canadians not involved in 'deviant' activity, 23 per cent claimed to have been searched by police, compared to 5 per cent of Whites (ibid., 7–9).

In assessing the impact of these statistics, David A. Tanovich (2002, 162) suggests:

Racial profiling has, thus, created a disproportionately large class of racialized offenders. It has also criminalized many predominantly black neighbourhoods in Toronto that are commonly referred to by the police as 'high crime areas.' This criminalization has contributed to the perpetuation of the belief that there is a link between race and crime. For example, a 1995 Angus Reid Gallup poll indicated that 45 per cent of those surveyed believe that there is such a link. The widespread belief that the face of crime is black has stigmatized the black community, and has had a tremendously negative impact on their dignity and self-worth.

Racial Profiling in Quebec

Racial profiling by police and other institutions is pervasive in Montreal, which has the province's largest population of people of African descent. Montreal's communities include the African Canadians of 'Little Burgundy' as well as more recent immigrants from Haiti. There is also a significant group of immigrants from the English-speaking Caribbean. The city is also home to large numbers of other migrants; its population, like Toronto's, is becoming increasingly diverse.

African Canadians in Montreal have long complained about racial profiling by police. The flashpoint in hostilities between the two was the shooting of Anthony Griffin, a nineteen-year-old African Canadian, in 1987. Griffin had been picked up by the police because he had an outstanding warrant against him. He was placed in the back seat of a police cruiser, and as it reached the police station, he bolted and ran. The police pursued him, yelling at him to stop, and when he did not, they shot him in the head. The African-Canadian community was outraged, especially after they learned that during shooting practice, the police had been placing pictures of people of African descent over their targets. Charges of police racism raged through the city. Egbert Gaye, the editor of the West End African-Canadian newspaper *Community Contact*, suggests that Griffin's death brought to light something that had long been known but never been spoken: 'Fifteen years ago, it seemed like open warfare between people of African descent and the police. And only one side was armed. The community felt under siege at the time' (Lejtenyi 2002).

Relations between the police and Montreal's African-Canadian communities have improved since then, but as Dan Philip, president of the Black Coalition of Quebec, says: 'That's in large part because they couldn't have gotten worse' (ibid.). Like police everywhere, the Montreal police deny they use racial profiling and insist they are not targeting specific groups but rather the criminal element in every community. But African Canadians in Montreal do believe that their community is being targeted – especially its young people. Anecdotal accounts of this are legion:

- Five African-Canadian women, including two in their seventies, say they were victims of police brutality (Rocha 2005).
- A twenty-four-year-old man named James Hamilton says he has been handcuffed six times by the police over the years; he was thirteen the first time. The most recent occasion was in 2003 – he and two other drivers ran a yellow light, but his was the only car pulled over by the police. He contends it was because he was the only African-Canadian driver among the three and was driving a new Audi. When Hamilton was detained by police, he called his family. When his mother and seventy-four-year-old grandmother arrived, they too were detained (ibid.).
- A fifteen-year-old girl says the police did not believe her when she said she was waiting for a specific bus, so they made her board the next bus that arrived (ibid.).
- One young man alleged that the police invaded his apartment for no reason, shot him with a rubber bullet, and threw him against their police car. The officers maintained they believed he was holding his

family hostage in the apartment, despite his mother's claims to the contrary (Canadian Race Relations Foundation, cited in the United Nations Economic and Social Council, UN Commission on Human Rights, 60th session, March 11, 2004).

- In Beaconfield, a suburb of Montreal, a young woman was distributing Christmas baskets to needy families when she was stopped by the police. She was wearing a hat and a down jacket and was apparently mistaken for a man. When she asked why she was being detained, the officer said it was 'just a routine check' because robbery suspects had been seen in the area (Branswell 2005).
- James Fraser has also had experience with 'routine checks.' He owns a barbershop in Little Burgundy and has neither a criminal record nor any outstanding tickets. Yet he is so accustomed to being stopped by the police that he leaves his licence, registration, and insurance in the ashtray for easy access when he is stopped. He does not drive a new or expensive car and believes he is stopped because he is of African descent (ibid.).

The racial profiling of African-Canadian youth has become endemic in Montreal. These youth have been charged for merely 'sitting down at the wrong place,' and they are routinely subjected to racist comments by officers such as 'go back to your country.' The police also closely watch street gangs, some of whom contain members of African descent.

Over the past few years, the Montreal police have made an effort to address the many complaints about racial profiling. Recent events have led them to finally admit to the public that racial profiling is widespread. A major initiative was launched by the police chief at the time, Michel Sarrazin, who sent a memo to all officers stating that racial profiling was against policy and that he would not tolerate it. Jacques Lelievre, an assistant police director, admitted that the practice occurred and confirmed that a number of new measures were being undertaken to put a stop to it. He also said that Quebec was ahead of other provinces in trying to end racial profiling. He described the problem: 'Officers see street gangs ... They see some black people doing wrong. They get used to that and myths develop. So when they see a black guy in a Lexus, they assume he's in a gang. We're trying to break that ... We're building contacts with communities ... This is how you create a climate of trust' (Rocha 2005).

The Montreal police have launched a number of initiatives to combat racial profiling. These range from community activities such as playing basketball with youth of African descent to monitoring officers who seem to be more aggressive and intolerant. New graduates of Quebec's police academy will have taken courses on racial profiling, and those of the province's community colleges (CEGEPs) which offer police technology programs will offer similar courses. These initiatives reflect the recommendations made by a community/police/government commission into the matter.

The police say they are making greater efforts to contain racial profiling; meanwhile, community leaders like Fo Niemi, head of the Centre for Research Action on Race Relations, and Dan Phillip, president of the Black Coalition of Quebec, as well as the many victims of racial profiling, have generally adopted a wait-and-see attitude to these planned changes. An editorial in *The Gazette* (3 February 2005) summed up the situation: 'What is really at issue now is how common this kind of pre-judgment – "driving while black" ... really is in our police force, and what the department is doing to wipe it out.' The editorial went on to criticize the police for not spreading their corrective strategies far enough, and ended by suggesting: 'It would be healthy for the force to spell out what's being done to educate our men and women in blue on this issue. It would be heartening to hear that visible-minority hiring is being emphasized. It would be encouraging to see efforts, at all levels of the police hierarchy, to communicate better with visible-minority communities and individuals.'

Racial Profiling of Aboriginal People

Numerous research reports have documented the racialization of Aboriginal people during all stages of the criminal justice system. One good example is the Report of the Royal Commission on Aboriginal Peoples (1996).

One of the first public inquiries to identify racism in the criminal justice system was the Royal Commission on the Donald Marshall Jr Prosecution. Marshall was a seventeen-year-old Mi'kmaq who in 1971 was wrongfully convicted of a murder in Sydney, Nova Scotia. He spent eleven years in provincial and federal prisons. In 1986 a commission was appointed to investigate how this happened, but it was not until 1991 that he was finally absolved of any wrongdoing. The commission found that systemic racism existed in the criminal justice system and that it had contributed to his wrongful imprisonment. It also pointed to the important role the Sidney Police had played in Marshall's arrest and wrongful conviction. Also to be blamed were prosecutors, the courts, and the political system itself (Samuelson and Monture-Angus 2002). The commission made many recommendations, among them that a tribal police force be established. Bernd Christmas (2001), an Aboriginal lawyer, argued that a force like this would ensure a proactive approach to policing and would involve the Mi'kmaq community positively rather than as adversaries. It would be able to engage Aboriginal people as equals rather than as outsiders. The recommendation was implemented, but only for a brief period.

The most glaring evidence of racism in the criminal justice system is found in inquiries and research studies which consistently show that Aboriginal people are heavily overrepresented in correctional facilities across Canada. According to Corrections Canada's own statistics, Aboriginal adults are incarcerated over six times more often than anyone else. A one-day 'snapshot' of all offenders in this country's correctional facilities by the Canadian Centre for Justice Statistics conducted in 1996 (see Hylton 2002, 140) showed that although Aboriginal people are 2 per cent of the adult population of Canada, they account for 17 per cent of federal inmates. In Saskatchewan, Aboriginal people were being incarcerated at almost ten times the overall provincial rate; they were 76 per cent of that province's inmate population. In Manitoba, 61 per cent of inmates were Aboriginals; in Alberta, it was over 35 per cent. Another shocking statistic: in Saskatchewan, 70 per cent of sixteen-year-old Treaty Indian males can expect to be incarcerated at least once by the time they reach twenty. Hylton notes: 'There is no indication that the extent of the overrepresentation of Aboriginal people is diminishing over time' (2002, 140–1). Samuelson and Monture-Angus (2002, 165) contend that these patterns of overincarceration of Aboriginal youth have become 'the contemporary equivalent of what the Indian residential school was for their parents.'

In recent years, several Aboriginal men have been found frozen to death in Saskatoon following police interventions. In November 1990 the body of an Aboriginal teenager named Neil Stonechild was found frozen in a field just outside the city. The injuries and marks on his body were probably caused by handcuffs. A friend reported that he last saw Stonechild bleeding in the back of a police car, screaming that the police were going to kill him. An inquiry was called in 2003, in the course of which Justice David Wright determined that two officers had had Mr Stonechild in their custody before he died and that they had tried to conceal this fact while testifying at the inquiry. Wright concluded that the police had prematurely closed their investigation into Stonechild's death, probably because the detective leading it was aware that members of the force could have been involved. Wright wrote: 'As I reviewed the evidence in this inquiry, I was reminded again and again of the chasm that separates Aboriginal people and non-Aboriginal people in this city and province ... The deficiencies in the investigation go beyond incompetence and neglect. They were inexcusable' (Canadian Press 2004).[2]

In January 2000, the body of Lloyd Dusthorn was found frozen to death outside his locked apartment after he had been seen in police custody. That same month, the frozen body of Rodney Naistus was found on the outskirts of Saskatoon near the Queen Elizabeth II Power Station. Five days later, Lawrence Wegner, a social work student, was last seen alive banging on the doors of relatives' homes in Saskatoon. Later testimony would indicate that he ran away when the police were called. His frozen body was later found near the power plant. After Wegner's body was found, another man, Darrell Night, came forward. Night reported that he had been dropped off by the police south of the city on a bitterly cold night but had managed to get to a nearby power station for help. These deadly excursions became known among Aboriginal people as 'starlight tours.' Two Saskatoon police officers were found guilty of unlawful confinement in the *Night* case and were sentenced to eight months in jail (ibid.).

Saskatchewan's Commission on First Nations and Métis Peoples and Justice Reform was established in 2001 to investigate Saskatchewan's justice system, and released its findings in June 2004. It found racism against Aboriginal people in the police services. The commissioner, Wilton Littlechild, said that when interviewed, police officers expressed frustration at the number of false accusations. Even so, on the basis of the evidence presented, he believed such racism to be widespread. Among the commission's 122 recommendations were that an agency be established to handle complaints against police and that police stations have Aboriginal liaison officers. Also recom-

---

2 See also Joyce Green, 'From Stonechild to Social Cohesion: Anti-Racist Challenges for Saskatchewan,' paper presented at the Canadian Political Science Association, University of Western Ontario, 24 June 2005. For an in-depth analysis of this case, see *Starlight Tour: The Last Lonely Night of Neil Stonechild* (Toronto: Random House, 2005).

mended was that an independent body be established to handle allegations of police abuse and excessive force.

In Winnipeg, Manitoba, in 2005, Aboriginal leaders demanded answers after the police shot and killed two young Aboriginal men within a few weeks of each other. In January in Norway House, an RCMP officer shot and killed Dennis St Paul after trying to arrest him for parole violations. The following month, Matthew Dumas, eighteen, was fatally injured when the police fired two shots during what they referred to as a 'scuffle.' The police stated that Dumas was a robbery suspect armed with an unspecified weapon. Many Aboriginal leaders claim that the relationship between the community and police continues to be difficult. An anti-racism group in Winnipeg, United Against Racism (UAR), which is led by the Aboriginal group Ka Ni Kanichink, says it is constantly receiving calls to report police malfeasance, including beatings of Aboriginal people.

In Vancouver, a public inquiry was called by the Union of B.C. Indian Chiefs as well as the B.C. Police Complaints Commissioner in the matter of Frank Paul, who froze to death in 1998 after police dumped him in an alley. In 2000, the Vancouver Police Department suspended one of the officers involved in Paul's death for two days; another officer received a one-day suspension. When rumours began to circulate that police were dumping 'drunks and troublemakers' in remote areas, police chief Jamie Graham defended the provision in the Criminal Code that allows police to remove citizens to other parts of the city for breaching the peace: 'It's a good law. It's a good tool for police officers to quell those disturbances that require people to be removed from certain areas' (Carmichael 2004).

Benedijt Fischer, a criminologist at the University of Toronto's centre of criminology, has noted that although it is not rampant, officers all over Canada abuse the breaching provision and use it to hand down punishments of their own design: 'It's brushed under the carpet. It's difficult to get at evidence beyond the infamous blue line, it's difficult even to investigate' (ibid.).

Making a similar point, John Richardson, the executive director of Pivot Legal Society, say his clients in Vancouver's Downtown Eastside contend that police take them for a drive if they talk back: 'What you have is a very discretionary remedy available to police to punish people for whatever they decide constitutes a breach of the peace' (ibid.).

On 6 September 1995, Dudley George, a Chippewa from Stoney Point, Ontario, became the first Aboriginal person in this century to be killed in a land rights dispute. He was one of around thirty unarmed protesters, including elders, women, and children, who had peacefully occupied Ipperwash Provincial Park to protest the destruction of their burial ground and a fifty-year delay in returning tribal lands. The newly elected provincial government of Mike Harris immediately ordered the Ontario Provincial Police (OPP) to 'take steps to remove the Indians in the park.' The following night the police opened fire on the protesters, and Dudley George was left dying as almost two hundred OPP officers fled the site. It took eight years of unrelenting pressure from Mr George's family, the demands of a broad-based coalition of groups for a full investigation, and the election of a Liberal government in Ontario to convene a public inquiry (Edwards 2001).

One day before Dudley George was shot, police surveillance tapes recorded a conversation between two OPP officers posing as a media crew at the standoff. The tapes, which were obtained by CBC News through a Freedom of Information request, revealed the following exchange between police officers:

> 'Is there still a lot of press down there?'
> 'No, there's no one down there. Just a big fat fuck Indian.'
> 'The camera's rolling, eh?'
> 'Yeah.'
> 'We had this plan, you know. We thought if we could get five or six cases of Labatt's 50, we could bait them.'
> 'Yeah.'
> 'Then we'd have this big net and a pit.'
> 'Creative thinking.'
> 'Works in the [U.S.] South with watermelon.' (CBC News 2004)

As this book was going to press, the inquiry was still under way.

Finally, the 2003 Ontario Human Rights Commission inquiry report, *Paying the Price: The Human Cost of Racial Profiling*, documents how Aboriginal people experience racial profiling. Many narratives have expressed the everyday experiences of fear, humiliation, and differential treatment that Aboriginal people – especially Aboriginal youth – suffer at the hands of the police. These accounts have described how useless it is to complain to the police or any other body. The commission looked at the effects of profiling and attempted to measure the impact of this practice on individuals, families, communities, and society.

Almost every inquiry and commission has focused its recommendations on the police. Policing is the primary point of contact between the Aboriginal community and the criminal justice system. As stated in the Report of the Saskatchewan Indian Justice Review Committee (1992, 20): 'Policing is a crucial focal point for any alienation, cultural insensitivity or systemic racism which Aboriginal people might encounter in their dealings with the criminal justice system' (Samuelson and Monture-Angus 2002, 165–6).

Public Perceptions and the Media

It can be argued that the effects of racial profiling have been magnified as a result of the media consistently presenting images of African Canadians as troublesome, criminal, and dangerous. The lesson embedded in such images is that Blacks deserve the attention paid to them by the police. In her thesis 'The Black/Jamaican Criminal: The Making of Ideology', Akua Benjamin (2003) examined media perspectives on policing in the African-Canadian community. To this end, she reviewed 266 articles in the *Toronto Sun* on 'Black/Jamaicans' involved in criminal activities. She found that the language and discourse of these articles reproduced stereotypes and racist ideologies about African Canadians and crime. Her conclusion: being 'othered' in this way has negative consequences for African Canadians in terms of social exclusion, marginalization, and banishment through deportation (ibid., 1–8).

Benjamin refers to many media articles that have stereotyped African Canadians. She then focuses on the connections between these stereotypes and the criminalization of African Canadians. In her summary she states: 'In the *Sun's* news reports on Jamaicans and crime, language and discourse readily recognizable and conveying of a racial profile was used to identify the suspect or perpetrator of the crime' (ibid., 250). In drawing this conclusion, she points to the findings of several other studies. For example, in citing Wortley's 'Misrepresentation or Reality: The Depiction of Race and Crime in Toronto Print Media' (2002), she notes that he reviewed more than nine thousand stories in Toronto-area newspapers over a four-month period in 1997–8. Wortley found that '90% of the stories involving Black people deal with crime, sports or entertainment. Black people are especially likely to be affiliated with crimes of street violence and drug trafficking [and] that Black crimes were often attributed to problems within the Black community or to aspects of Caribbean culture' (Benjamin 2003, 33).

Benjamin notes similar findings in the research conducted by Wortley (2002), McCarthy and Hagan (1995), and Visano (2002), all of whom studied the Just Desserts incident. She quotes Wortley: 'The mass media provide a symbolic platform on which crimes and criminals are paraded before the public and collectively condemned. These media portrayals can be understood as simple morality plays that reaffirm ideas about right and wrong and consolidate the collective conscience' (in ibid., 34). These concerns had already been explored by Frances Henry and Carol Tator (2002) in their own investigation of racism in the media, in which they noted that African Canadians are problematized as requiring a disproportionate amount of political attention and public resources. Henry, Hastings, and Freer (1996) examined articles in the *Toronto Star* printed on 27 April, 5 and 9 May and 1 and 12 June 1996, and found considerable evidence that Jamaicans had been stereotyped as a criminal element.

Henry and Tator (2002) reviewed 2,840 news articles on crime from the *Toronto Star*, the *Globe and Mail*, and the *Toronto Sun* over two months in each of the years 1994, 1996, and 1997, They found the following:

- Thirty-nine per cent of the articles in the *Star* and the *Sun* about Jamaicans related to issues such as crime, justice, immigration, and deportation.
- In stories about individuals from subordinated racialized groups – African Canadians in particular – racial identifiers were used twice as often as they were for Whites.
- Forty-six per cent of all crime articles in the *Globe*, 38 per cent of those in the *Star*, and 25 per cent of those in the *Sun* 'used a racial or ethnic descriptor [that] involved Blacks or people of Caribbean origin.'
- Approximately 33 per cent of all photos in crime stories depicted individuals from subordinated racialized groups; African Canadians accounted for 44 per cent of these images despite being only 7 per cent of the Toronto-area population (ibid., 167–8).
- Tator and Henry also applied discourse analysis (including critical linguistic analysis) to the media reporting around the Just Desserts incident. Having analysed 210 articles, they asserted that the media have developed three discourses relating to law and order: the discourse of gun control (fifty-one articles), the discourse of the young offender (eighteen articles), and the discourse of immigration/ deportation (thirty-four articles) (ibid., 168–80).

All of these findings make it clear that the media's approach to covering African Canadians is itself a form of racial profiling. Furthermore, this reporting supports and contributes to police values and beliefs and in that way helps perpetuate *their* form of racial profiling.

Thank God the Judge Was Awake Some of the Time

The police and the media seem to have developed a common perception of African Canadians. Something very different apparently is taking place in courtrooms. Case law, public inquiries, and tribunal rulings have consistently applied a critical lens to police practices of racial profiling; they have named these practices directly and have indicated quite openly the impact these practices have, especially on African Canadians.

In *R. v. Ladouceur* (1990), the Supreme Court of Canada considered whether routine traffic stops violate the Charter of Rights and Freedoms, in particular Sections 7, 8, and 9. Although the majority ruled that these sections had not been violated, the Court expressed concern about the potential abuse of police power and commented on the need for officers to have a legal basis for stopping vehicles – for example, to check a driver's sobriety or the condition of the vehicle. The dissent (ibid., 1267) in this case expressed concern that allowing roving, random stops would give any officer the power to stop any vehicle, at any time and place, even if the reason was based on subjective factors such as the race of the vehicle's occupants:

> Indeed, … racial considerations may be a factor too. My colleagues state that in such circumstances, a Charter violation may be made out. If, however, no reason need be given nor is necessary, how will we ever know? The officer need only say, 'I stopped the vehicle because I have the right to stop it for no reason. I am seeking unlicensed drivers.' If there are bound to be instances where admittedly Charter violations which cannot be justified will occur, can we overlook these and approve a practice even if in its general application Charter breaches can be justified? … How many innocent people will be stopped to catch one unlicensed driver?

In *R. v. Simpson* (1993), in reviewing whether a vehicle stop constitutes a detention within the meaning of Section 9 of the Charter, it was determined that if a stop or detention is unrelated to road safety concerns or to the operation of a vehicle, a police officer has no general detention power. In reaching this conclusion, the Court wrote (ibid., 492–5) that it is

> essential to keep in mind the context of the particular police-citizen confrontation. Constable Wilken [the officer in this case] was investigating the appellant and the driver of the car ... It was an adversarial and confrontational process intended to bring the force of the criminal justice process into operation against the appellant. The validity of the stop and the detention must be addressed with that purpose in mind.

Yet different criteria may apply in non-adversarial environments where a crime prevention objective may not be at play. For example, the Court expressed concern that 'subjectively based assessments can too easily mask discriminatory conduct based on such irrelevant factors as the detainee's sex, colour, age, ethnic origin or sexual orientation.' The Court further argued that an officer must have an articulable cause to detain a person in order to determine his or her involvement in criminal activity. It described an articulable cause as 'a constellation of objectively discernable facts which give the detaining officer reasonable cause to suspect that the detainee is criminally implicated in the activity under investigation' (ibid., 500–4).

R. v. Richards (1999) is the case most often cited with respect to racial profiling. In it, racial profiling is defined clearly as

> criminal profiling based on race. Racial or colour profiling refers to that phenomenon whereby certain criminal activity is attributed to an identified group in society on the basis of race or colour resulting in the targeting of individual members of that group. In this context, race is illegitimately used as a proxy for the criminality or general criminal propensity of an entire racial group. (ibid., 295)

In R. v. Golden (2001), the Supreme Court suggested that minority groups in Canada are overpoliced and that Charter standards must be developed to 'reduce the danger of racist stereotyping by individual police officers' (Tanovich 2002, 52). Shortly after this case, the Ontario Superior Court of Justice in R. v. Peck (2001) addressed profiling in a case that involved two African-Canadian youths and two young women. They were stopped and searched in an alleyway by an undercover officer, who indicated race and other factors (such as the street location, which was suspected of being a place for drug transactions) as the basis for suspicion. In finding that the race of the accused was a significant factor in the officer's decision to stop them for questioning, the court determined that there was neither a basis for investigative detention nor reasonable grounds to suspect criminal activity. They found that race – especially the race of a young male – either alone or in the context of facts, does not provide reasonable grounds for suspecting criminal activity. The court concluded that 'stereotypical assumptions linking young black men and the illegal use of narcotics do not provide a lawful basis to detain or arrest them' (ibid., paras. 16–18).

R. v. Brown (1998) was determined by the Ontario Court of Appeal on 16 April 2003. Here, an African American argued that he had been the subject of a racially discriminatory stop, as a consequence of which he was charged with impaired driving. On appeal of the conviction, the defence submitted evidence of racial profiling and raised Section 9 of the Charter. It argued that the trial judge had repeatedly assisted the Crown witness (a police officer), and that he had denounced the defence counsel's allegations of racial profiling as 'nasty' and 'completely unwarranted'; the same judge suggested that the defendant should apologize to the officer. The appeal court determined that the trial judge's conduct gave rise to a reasonable apprehension of bias; it overturned the conviction and ordered a new trial.

A recent publication of the Ontario Human Rights Commission (OHRC) and a ruling by the Nova Scotia Human Rights Tribunal suggest the reality and impact of racial profiling. After the *Toronto Star* racial profiling series, the OHRC conducted a public inquiry into the matter. The purpose of this inquiry was to raise public awareness of this contentious issue and to respond to community concerns about racial profiling and its effects on individuals, families, and society as a whole. The inquiry delved into various topics, including housing, services, education, and private security. It heard more than eight hundred submissions; around half of these these concerned racial profiling, especially as practised by the police. The OHRC included several witness accounts in its published findings.

In December 2003, the Nova Scotia Human Rights Tribunal buttressed the work of the OHRC with its ruling in the case of Kirk Johnson, a well-known boxer, who had filed a complaint against the Halifax Regional Police alleging that he had been racially profiled on 12 April 1998 while a passenger in a vehicle travelling on Highway 111 near Dartmouth. The board of inquiry accepted his version of the incident and recommended that the Halifax police hire two consultants to develop and implement anti-racism and diversity training and that these consultants prepare a report on this matter. The ruling also called on the police to review their policies on stops and searches and to pre- pare proposals, for the commission's review, on how information on the role of race in traffic stops could be gathered (Girard 2002, 40–1).

What's All the Fuss?

All of these perspectives, based on anecdotal and statistical research, preceded or ran parallel with the *Toronto Star* series. So it should not be surprising that the *Star*'s research replicated and extended the evi- dence already in the public domain. What *is* significant about the *Star*'s series is the massive amounts of data it examined and the period of time that came under scrutiny. The data reviewed included informa- tion on 480,000 incidents in which an individual was charged with a crime or ticketed for a traffic offence. These data represented the total population of criminal charges (around 800,000) for the years follow- ing the release of the Report of the Ontario Commission on Systemic Racism in the Criminal Justice System (1996–2002). When matched against the findings reported by the commission, these data enabled an examination of more than a decade's worth of experience (1989–2002). The findings of all this work supported the premise that African Cana- dians are 'singled out' by the police. For example, the *Star* reported the following:

- Although only 8.1 per cent of Toronto's population, African Canadi- ans accounted for 34 per cent of drivers charged with out-of-sight violations.
- African Canadians were overrepresented by 4.2 times for out-of- sight driving offences, by 3.8 times for cocaine possession, and by 2.1 times for simple drug possession.
- Though Whites comprised 63.8 per cent of those charged with sim- ple drug possession (more than ten thousand cases), Whites were released at the scene 76.5 per cent of the time, compared to 61.8 per cent for African Canadians.
- After being taken into custody, African Canadians were held for court appearance 15.5 per cent of the time, compared to 7.3 per cent for Whites;
- For cocaine possession (more than two thousand cases), 41.5 per cent

of African Canadians were released at the scene, compared to 63 per cent of Whites.

- African Canadians comprised 27 per cent of all violent charges, even though they were only 8.1 per cent of the population.
- In 51 Division, 40 per cent of African Canadians charged with one count of cocaine possession were held for bail hearings, compared to 20 per cent of Whites.
- African Canadians were overrepresented at police divisions with low African-Canadian populations. For example, they were four times overrepresented in out-of-sight traffic offences at 42 Division and seven times overrepresented at 52 Division, even though these divisions do not have significant number of African-Canadian residents. These data supported the African-Canadian community's anecdotes that they were being singled out by police (Rankin et al. 2002).

The *Star*'s data support the contention that African Canadians are overrepresented in police records and that racial profiling is an alarming reality. They also reveal that African Canadians may be treated more harshly by the police after arrest than Whites and may be more likely to be detained and taken in for processing than Whites. At police stations, African Canadians are more likely to be held in custody for a bail hearing than Whites.

Although racial profiling by the police is a crucially important issue in itself, the continued prevalence of this practice must be placed in an overall social and historical context. People of African descent in Canada have always been marginalized and oppressed. Racial profiling reinforces this oppression and magnifies its impact on African Canadians in every facet of public and private life.

4 The Culture of Policing

Until advocates of police change recognize the importance of culture, they
will continue to be surprised as they have been for 100 years at the profound limitations of reform efforts to yield real and enduring changes.
(Crank 1997, 6)

Policing culture is central to an understanding of how this crucial
agency of social control relates to the changing needs of an ethno-
racially pluralistic society. There is now a very substantial literature on
the 'culture of policing' (Manning 1977; Reuss-Ianni 1983; Skolnick
1996; Crank 1997; Chan 1997). The increased interest in policing organizations is probably related to the growing heterogeneity of modern
and postmodern society as a consequence of globalization and transna-
tionalism. Postmodern societies are increasingly characterized by difference and diversity based on ethnic, cultural, and racial origins. In
this chapter we attempt to demonstrate that despite recent reforms in
police recruitment and management, little if anything has altered the
basic culture of policing.

Notwithstanding Canada's reputation as a 'peaceful' state, the
debate over policing practices has escalated to the point where policing
issues have become a high priority on the political agenda and on that
of the public. The organization of policing and its general role in society has long been at issue; but so, nowadays, is the 'culture of policing.'
This last issue is central to our understanding of how the police operate. It is sometimes assumed that police culture is responsible for some
of the deficiencies in today's law enforcement agencies. But what pre-
cisely is the 'culture of policing'? The literature on this subject reveals

broad similarities in police culture in societies as diverse as the United States, Britain, Australia, and the Caribbean. In this chapter we examine closely some aspects of the organizational culture of the police. We will be assuming that an understanding of police culture will help us understand in turn why police–minority relations are so fragile and so often hostile; and how the culture of both policing and the dominant White society help produce and sustain an ethos in which racism continues to flourish.

Aspects of Police Culture

An important point that needs immediate clarification here is that 'police culture' is actually a *subculture*, in that police officers are first and foremost members of the society in which they live. Their cultural beliefs, perceptions, values, and norms are therefore influenced as much by the standards of the White dominant culture as by the values unique to their occupation. Thus, to better understand racism in police culture, we must look beyond the characteristics of the police themselves. In order to critically analyse police culture, we must take into account the economic, social, political, and geographic factors that contribute to the racialization of contemporary society (Crank 1997).

For example if racism is always present and systemic in a society, we can assume that by the time a woman or man is recruited and selected for the police force, that person has probably already absorbed society's racialized assumptions, stereotypes, and commonsense understandings about particular minority groups (such as Blacks, Aboriginals, Muslims, Southeast Asians, and gays and lesbians). As noted in chapter 2, there is strong evidence that the images, beliefs, and everyday discourses produced and reproduced by educators, journalists, broadcasters, filmmakers, politicians, judges, and other White elites exert enormous power and influence on personal belief systems and collective ideologies (Henry and Tator, 2002, 2005; Dei et al. 2004).

Also, police organizational culture is not monolithic. Rather, it is complex and multilayered and is strongly influenced by the multiple roles played by law enforcement officers and by the changing demands made on the police.

This chapter outlines some of the key elements of police culture and discusses how these relate to the issue of racism in policing. The literature on policing culture suggests that the same patterns arise over and over again. Also, we will be focusing on studies of large, urban police organizations; smaller, more rural ones are often influenced more heavily by local conditions and do not always evidence some of the key dynamics of the larger agencies. Finally, most of the research in this field has been conducted in the United States, and to some extent in Britain and Australia. Few Canadian studies have focused specifically on police culture.

The Subculture of Policing: Social Science Approaches

'Culture' refers to the sum total of an organization's key values, beliefs, and norms. It includes its general belief and value system as well as the behaviours it defines as appropriate. Various perspectives can be applied to shed light on multidimensional organizations such as police services. The most salient of these have been developed by sociologists, psychologists, anthropologists, and other social scientists. To start with, we must distinguish between two levels of police culture: the management culture of the organization, and the everyday culture of the 'beat cop.' Obviously, the former strongly affects the latter. At the same time, though, the management culture is affected by the peculiarities of the local environment, which *include* the behaviour of the beat cops being supervised. The two parts of the organization interact constantly, and each must be sensitive to the other if the organization is to function smoothly. However, as Chan (1997) has noted, there is often a profound schism between police management and the everyday life of the officers on the street.

The police are responsible to many other organizations besides their own. First of all, police services are creatures of governments, which enact the laws that mandate their activities as organizations of social control. In the Canadian case, the federal police, the RCMP, fall under the aegis of the justice ministry. At the provincial level – in Ontario, for example — the Ontario Provincial Police are the responsibility of the Minister of Security and Public Safety. In turn, municipal police organizations are funded and legislated by the municipal governments and are overseen by police boards, which include private citizens as well as representatives from provincial and municipal levels of government.

Next, most large police services have associations or unions, which do much to determine the direction of police activities. These organizations have significant clout, as they are often able to mobilize their members to support or reject certain policies and actions; some even use their power to influence their members to support particular politicians (see chapter 6). In Ontario's last provincial election, the president of the Toronto Police Association, Craig Bromell, announced to voters that the union would be supporting the Conservatives and that if the Liberals won, his members would be prepared to march on the legislature in order to express their displeasure. Bromell also declared that the police would simply ignore any proposed new rules restricting their political involvement. The police association then retained a lawyer to challenge the proposed new policies.

Next, the media and the police are strongly linked. The print and electronic media are constant watchdogs (lapdogs, some would argue) of police activity. Many newspapers and radio and television stations have one or more reporters on the police beat, and police activities often dominate media reportage. The print and electronic media tend to focus on criminal activities – especially those involving people of colour. They slavishly follow daily police investigations, the apprehension of alleged criminals, and their trials (see Wortley 2002; Henry and Tator 2002, Benjamin 2003). ·

Yet another key element in police culture is the relationship between police and the multitude of publics they serve. Each of these constituencies is likely to view and evaluate police conduct in the context of its own social location. The police – especially in big cities – thus have many overseers, to whom they are accountable to varying degrees. Clearly, then, a police service is an extraordinarily complex organization, one that faces a multifaceted internal and external structure and that must adapt to a very often conflicting set of values, norms, and world views.

Police services must respond constantly to the changing social, cultural, political, and especially demographic circumstances in which they operate. Yet the literature on police culture indicates strongly that resistance to change is one of its most prominent features (Chan 1998; Crank 1997; Harrison 1998; Skolnick 1996). Embedded in policing as an occupation are factors that systematically discourage innovation and that perpetuate the status quo (Manning 1993).

The Perpetuation of Police Culture

Police culture tends strongly to perpetuate itself in large part because of how officers are recruited and selected. Most police organizations have developed rigid methods for recruiting new officers. These methods ensure that new entrants will sustain the organization's existing culture – that their values and norms are already consistent with those of the organization. In this way the selection process is the first step in the process of cultural assimilation, since individuals who can demonstrate they have characteristics similar to present-day officers have a greater chance of being hired (Harrison 1998).

After passing through a rigorous selection procedure, recruits are sent to a police academy for training. Besides teaching them basic policing skills, the academy transmits organizational values. For example, most courses at these academies tend to reinforce the notion that police work is dangerous and – it follows – that firearms training is a crucial component (Drummond 1976, 14, in Harrison 1998). Courses in report writing and interrogation methods tend to emphasize the need to be suspicious of people. Guidelines are provided on how to deal with aggressive defence attorneys when testifying in court.

Criminal profiling is now a regular practice in policing, as well as a component of training. For example, recruits are trained to identify the characteristics of a killer. Harris (2002) argues that when these characteristics include race or ethnicity as a factor in predicting crime, criminal profiling can become racial profiling. In sum, the training that police receive encourages stereotypical thinking about particular racial and cultural groups and leads to the belief that 'skin color is a valid indicator of a greater propensity to commit crime' (ibid., 11). These perceptions are shared through anecdotes and warnings in the course of officer training. Through this socialization process, racial biases become fixed ideas and images, which are later incorporated into departmental norms. All of this reinforces pre-existing fissures based on race; it also reinforces notions as to which groups ought to be regarded as inherently suspicious and thus requiring greater police scrutiny. In this way, groups are divided into 'the good and the bad,' 'the citizen and the criminal' (ibid., 13). It may well be that no ethics course or cultural sensitivity training can erase the 'commonsense' understandings that are deeply embedded in the belief systems of police organizations. Crank (1997, 207) suggests that 'cultural racism in a police organization is a self-fulfilling phenomenon that can neither be vanquished, perhaps not even contained.'

After a recruit graduates from the academy, socialization into police culture continues. The officer is assigned to street duty under the tutelage of a police training officer or mentor. These training officers are likely to be older and experienced members of the force; their job is to provide training that not only focuses on behaviour but also – more importantly for our purposes here – transmits the organization's values, standards, norms, and patterns of thought. Yet given the complexity of the organization as a whole, its norms and values are inculcated and reproduced through the ranks in many others ways besides this.

For example, as part their routine activities, police develop commonsense profiles of the probable behaviour of individuals with specific cultural, ethnic, or racial characteristics. Skin colour, accent, and style of dress become markers of social 'difference' and a quick means of identifying suspicious individuals. Over time these processes of profiling by skin colour and/or accent become widely accepted and are seen as the obvious and most effective way of policing the street (Harris 2002; Crank 1997).

Dominant Attributes of Police Culture

Social Isolation

Beginning with the pioneering work of Skolnick (1966, 1996), sociologists have identified social isolation as one of the main features of police culture. Police view themselves as outsiders. They trust neither the publics they serve nor the managers who oversee them (Crank 1997). Because they so often face real or perceived danger, they isolate themselves from former friends, the community, and sometimes even family members as a means to protect themselves. Police are commonly perceived as authority figures, and to a certain extent this also limits their social interactions. Police socialize mainly with other police and their spouses; it follows that their social networks are limited.

Another factor that encourages isolation and suspiciousness among the police is that they are required to enforce laws. To protect themselves from stress, from social rejection, from real and imagined dangers, and from the loss of personal and professional freedom, they may choose to isolate themselves socially (Skolnick 1966; Crank 1997; Harrison 1998). As a consequence of this, they often develop a polarized view of the world in which they function. Their resulting 'we–they' perspective encourages them to believe that the public cannot possibly understand the special demands made on police. The attitudes that characterize 'us,' according to Reuss-Ianni in another seminal work (1983), are:

1. 'Protect your ass.' This relates to the need to distrust everyone, including citizens who are attempting to complain about police, and even including their own supervisors, who are in a position to discipline those under their command.

2. 'Don't trust the new guy until you have him checked out.' New recruits as well as officers transferred from other stations must prove themselves before they can be trusted.
3. 'Don't trust bosses to look out for your interests.' This suggests that when faced with a decision, supervisors will look after their own interests rather than those of the officers under their command. This can lead to a distancing between officers and management. (Cited in Harrison 1998)

Solidarity

Solidarity follows social isolation as another key element of policing culture. Bonding between members is an important aspect of any organizational culture, but such solidarity is especially strong among police (Chan 1997; Crank 1998). Police officers often feel highly vulnerable because of the unpredictable and volatile nature of their work, the hostility of citizens, the demands of making arrests, and the need to apply force. Their fellow officers may be the only protection they have, and this intensifies the camaraderie among officers. This is motivated only in part by friendship or colleagueship; more than either, it involves a proven certainty that officers will watch each other's backs (Skolnick 1996). Newcomers or recruits to the organization must prove their mettle in situations that involve danger before they are fully accepted by their peers. Again, the strong sense of cooperation and support that develops among officers is related to the dangers they perceive themselves as facing on the street.

Solidarity also involves the commitment to secrecy when the organization is investigated by outside agencies. In fact, there appears to be a 'code of silence' within police organizations that not only shields members from outside investigation but also involves keeping silent about the deviant behaviour of fellow officers. Police culture provides many avenues of access to deviant or illegal behaviour. One reason is the discretion officers enjoy in making decisions in any situation. This discretion allows them access to events, situations, and people who are conduits to illegal activities, and some officers succumb. If there is so much deviancy in police culture, as has been alleged, perhaps this is why (Crank 1998).

The intense nature of police culture prevents officers from informing on one another; it is common for officers to 'turn a blind eye' to any form of error or misconduct committed by a fellow officer. This pervasive secrecy allows police to do their work and 'cover their ass' without constant intervention from managers. Police are constantly attempting to stay invisible and avoid trouble (Chevigny 1995).

In comparing police organizations with other occupational groups – especially with other groups that wear identifying uniforms – Skolnick (1996, 96) comments: 'It is doubtful that [other] workers have so close-knit an occupation or so similar an outlook on the world, as do the police. Set apart from the conventional world, the police officer experiences an exceptionally strong tendency to find a social identity within the social milieu.' Police culture is reinforced by rites and rituals, traditions and dress codes; all of these serve as markers of difference that separate police from the various publics they serve. The dangers of the work environment intensify the loyalty and solidarity the police extend to one another; at the same time, these dangers contribute to a stressful work environment.

Crank (1997) draws an important distinction between the cultural value of solidarity and the notion that police see themselves as outsiders. The cultural themes of solidarity and 'outsidership' raise different questions about police culture as it is linked to racial profiling. As discussed earlier, the cultural value placed on solidarity underscores the ties that bind police together and emphasizes similarities among them. The concept of officers as outsiders points to the commonly shared belief among police that as an occupational group, they are distinct from society. As outsiders, they often develop a 'we–them' attitude. This is most visible in the relationship between White officers and racialized minority communities.[1]

In Canada, York (1994) identified many of these same elements in police culture, which is sometimes referred to as 'canteen culture.' These features include isolation, conservatism, machismo, a sense of mission, a siege mentality, and what is referred to as the 'thin blue line' mindset. Police organizations resemble other closed institutions in their cultural patterns and orientations. Such institutions arise in 'pre-modern' social settings such as armies, religious orders, asylums, jails, and hospitals. What Skolnick (1966) called the 'working personality of a police officer' includes the following important identifiers of police culture: a sense of mission about police work, an orientation towards

---

1 Crank (1997) suggests that solidarity is powerfully manifested in particular cultural rites. The most dramatic of these rites are funeral ceremonies, in which displays of police unity act as symbols of strength and solidarity.

action, a cynical or pessimistic outlook towards the social environment, political conservatism, racial prejudice, and an attitude of sustained suspicion (Chan 1997).

Other elements of police culture include the following: the exercise of authority and discretion; efficiency; pragmatism, cynicism, and pessimism (developed over years of observing criminal behaviour and apprehending felons); and conservatism in the sense of clinging to established ways of doing the job instead of trying new methods. The bottom line for many is this: 'Police officers are concerned to get from here to tomorrow (or the next hour) safely and with the least amount of paperwork' (Reiner 1992, 128).

Psychologically oriented researchers have tended to focus on other components of police culture such as sexism, machismo or hypermasculinity, militarism, authoritarianism, and racism (Neiderhoffer 1969; Reuss-Ianni 1983; Benson 2000; Harris 2000). Hypermasculinity or machismo is based on values that glorify male physical strength, competition, and violence. In fact, 'police work has traditionally been coded hypermasculine by the general culture ... The experience of street policing is steeped in a masculine culture of brotherhood that rests on the division between "us" and "them." Although "us" is supposed to refer to honest citizens and "them" to lawbreakers, often "us" becomes simply a mirror image of "them": our guys against their guys ... The hypermasculinity of policing leads to a culture in which violence is always just below the surface' (Harris 2000, 803).

Hypermasculinity is commonly linked to sexism. Studies have demonstrated that although female police officers are not afraid of using force, they are not as likely to be involved in the use of excessive force. Women officers tend to be better communicators and negotiators. It is also said that they are less challenged by defiant suspects and less likely to deal forcefully with such suspects. Benson (2000, 3) notes that instead of dealing positively with women's strengths and recruiting more of them, 'police departments are bastions of what Spillar (in Benson) describes as "open sex discrimination and sexual harassment" and negative attitudes towards female officers.' Very little research seems to have been conducted on the experiences of racial minority women in policing culture.

Militarism

Police organizations have always been known for their militarism, since their structure, rituals, and ceremonies closely reflect military models. In recent times, however, this militarism has been accentuated. For example, police are using maximum force more often than before, and they are equipping themselves with state-of-the-art military equipment. This has helped create an ethos in which they go about their jobs as if on constant battle alert. The 'war on crime' is a common discourse used to rationalize racial profiling. Crank (1997, 214) contends that when police exercise control over concentrated minority communities in urban areas that are also poor and utterly powerless, the war on crime becomes a 'military containment action.' Such action includes frequent racial harassment and interventions with minority populations and the occasional use of deadly force, which the White dominant culture often sees as an effective means for keeping minorities in their proper place.

In the United States, the Watts riots in Los Angeles in 1965, the national wars on crime and drugs, and the transfer of military technology to police services did much to foster this greater militarism. Militarism is also strongly evident in the rigid ranking system of police services and in the strong commitment to leadership. In fact, police departments as currently organized depend on their top leaders not only to provide direction but also to maintain their control over the culture. More than in other corporate structures, the police chief has unprecedented authority – he is literally 'in command.'

Many researchers have written about how police culture incorporates the framework referred to above. However, Janet Chan (1997) has sharply criticized as outdated some of the paradigms used by many scholars in their analyses of police culture and has proposed a new conceptual framework.

Her first criticism of the traditional paradigm is that most research presents cop culture as too deterministic and inflexible. This is shown by the failure of most theories to account for internal differentiations between groups of officers. Heidensohn (1992, 76) appeared to acknowledge this criticism when she asked if cop culture was as 'purely reactive,' as earlier writers claimed (Skolnick, for example).

Similarly, cop culture is often seen as just referring to 'street' cop culture; this ignores 'management' cop culture (for more discussion on this, see Ruess-Ianni 1983). Manning (1993) has suggested that there are three types of cop culture: 'command,' 'middle management,' and 'lower participants.' Chan (1992) detected differences in working personalities between officers with different functions, thus implying that cop culture is a more 'fluid' concept than was previously recognized.

Chan's second criticism relates to the process whereby police officers become socialized into cop culture. Many accounts suggest that cop culture is a one-way process in which individual officers are passive bystanders. This approach, says Chan, is too deterministic and does not account for the fact that ultimately, officers can choose to adopt the behaviours and attitudes suggested by cop culture. According to Fielding (1988, 135), 'one cannot read the recruit as a cipher for the occupational culture.' Chan emphasizes the importance of noting this interaction between the occupational culture and individuals' existing attitudes.

Chan's third point is that cop culture should be viewed within broader societal, political, legal, and organizational contexts. Thus, the culture within a particular police station can be uniquely affected by an external inquiry, a change in organization, or a new piece of legislation. For example, the Scarman Report (1981) expressed concern that the police were in danger of becoming, by reason of their professional status, an elite body set apart from the rest of the community. Lord Scarman wanted to see a shift away from policies dictated entirely by technological advances and towards more traditional methods such as beat policing – a move that would very probably have far-reaching effects on occupational culture.

Chan's fourth and final criticism serves as a summary of her previous three: the dialectic between social environment and policing has been largely ignored, and thus it is impossible to account for changes or variations in cop culture. She proposes a reconceptualization of police culture within three converging perspectives. First, the active role played by individual members of the police force must be recognized. Second, it must be recognized that multiple cultures may exist within a single organization. Third, police culture must be situated within the ever-changing social and cultural contexts of police work.

Chan concludes by stating that not every police officer walking the streets is conservative, racist, sexist, socially isolated, authoritarian, and prone to violence. Being in a policing role and being surrounded by other police officers for long periods of time does make an individual more susceptible to accepting such views (or at least *claiming* to accept such views). Thus she agrees with Skolnick (1996, 42), who also maintained that 'such an analysis does not suggest that all police are alike in "working personality," but that there are distinctive cognitive tendencies in police as an occupational grouping.'

Next we consider the critical issue in this book: police perceptions of people of colour. Racism has often been identified as a component of police culture in the United States, Britain, and other countries. The controversy around racial profiling in Canada (and elsewhere) focuses on the perceptions of police racism as reflected in the *Star*'s series on racial profiling. So the central question is this: Is there racism in police culture? From the fact that we are raising the question, it should be clear that we are not content with the 'rotten apples' theory – that is, with the idea that the problem is merely the individual racism of a few police officers. The problem is in fact fundamental and goes to the very structure of the organization.

Racism is an inevitable consequence of key aspects of police culture. Many features of that culture relate to the distance or difference between police officers and the rest of the population. Characteristics such as isolation and suspiciousness lead directly to a division that comes naturally to police – a division that actually is the defining feature of racism.

Wieviorka (1992, 22) addressed this in his comparative study of policing in England and France:

> Granted, the police complain about the bureaucracy, red tape and administrative rules that set boundaries on their work, and about the weight of hierarchy or any other power; but they are also actors, individually and collectively, acting subjectively with a degree of freedom in which they contribute, if only modestly, to defining the focus and methods of their work. They are neither cogs in some machine that shapes them into racists nor completely autonomous individuals, free of any determinism or institutional constraints, whose racism or powerlessness to oppose racism could be said to come entirely from their own social background and education outside the police institution. They are actors defined by their belonging to systems of action, and this is how we have defined them.

The implication of Wieviorka's observations is that racism in policing is a highly complex and dynamic phenomenon.

One of the seminal studies of policing attitudes in Canada explored how perceptions and assumptions develop in police culture, especially as these relate to racism. In an audit of the Toronto Police Service, Andrews (1992) found that the police had done a reasonable job of ensuring that recruits did not *display* an overt racial bias. However:

> A change occurs after joining the Force. There was significant evidence that many police officers who are constantly in contact with public

develop strong feelings and beliefs as to attributes of individuals, based on factors such as appearance and racial background. These officers would no doubt be offended if their attitudes were described as potentially racist. Nevertheless, the same attitudes can and do produce a bias in behaviour which results in unequal treatment of individuals of different cultural or racial backgrounds.

The power and influence of a given organizational culture on the individuals who work within that culture has been well documented by scholars. For example, 'the racism of police culture is embedded in routine practices such as joking, banter and shared pastimes like off duty drinking, that are not intrinsically racist, but which succeed in excluding ethnic minority officers and reinforcing stereotypes' (Waddington 1999, 290).

Ungerleider (1992) studied two Canadian municipal police forces. He examined the judgments that police make about others and found that of the 251 officers sampled, 25 per cent expressed views that could be categorized as 'irrationally negative' towards visible minorities and as reflecting 'confusion.' He found it 'disquieting' that large numbers of Canadian police officers make irrational judgments about others. We find here not so much symptoms of individual negative attitudes towards others, but rather evidence of a developed culture and value system within police organizations. This model of socialization theory encompasses the notion that changes in the behaviour of police officers are related to their job experiences and to their interactions with fellow officers. Again, Andrews's audit of the Toronto police (Andrews 1992) found strong evidence that police who were regularly in contact with the public acquired deep-seated beliefs as to the attributes of individuals, based on factors such as appearance and racial background. Over time they came to embrace views of particular groups that were consonant with the prevailing notions of the majority of the force. These views tended to be more conservative and authoritarian.

From these findings, we can surmise that the work environment of policing and the ethos of officers both emphasize order, productivity, and efficiency, and also on bonding, cooperation, and secrecy. The 'we' that reflects the police also implies Whiteness and the White world, because Whiteness dominates the police organizations in most of the countries where research has been conducted. The 'they' groups in this equation are outsider communities, especially communities of colour. Canada is no exception here; until very recently, this country's police forces as well as the RCMP were almost solidly White. Inevitably, the rules and regulations of these organizations replicate those of the White hegemonic order. For obvious example, minimum height and weight regulations gave no thought to other groups who might be shorter and thinner – or to women, for that matter. Today, multicultur-alism and ethno-racial diversity are defining characteristics of Cana-dian society, yet the police still reflect the hegemonic order notwithstanding their repeated and sometimes desperate efforts to recruit more women and minorities.

There are a number of reasons why individuals from minority com-munities resist becoming police officers. First and perhaps most impor-tant is the deep conflict that characterizes relations between the police and minority communities. Second, Blacks and other racialized minor-ities lack significant advancement opportunities on police forces – which itself does not send a positive message to minority communi-ties. Third, many people of colour are immigrants or the children of immigrants and thus tend to value other careers over policing. Fourth, it may be that minority officers encounter racism on the job, from the organization and from fellow officers – and the impressionistic evi-dence for this is growing (see chapter 6).

Police tend to negatively evaluate communities of colour. It is part of police culture to hold stereotypic views about Blacks and to view them as prone to criminal activity. This can be blamed in part on the very nature of the policing function: most officers spend very little time interacting with ordinary Black citizens; their only contacts with Blacks are likely to be with suspected criminals or with uncooperative wit-nesses at crime scenes.

John Crank (1997) offers many provocative insights into police rac-ism. He believes, for example, that 'racism is a phenomenon grounded in local police culture … Cultural predispositions are learned and replayed in a process of concrete practice in police–citizen interactions' (ibid., 207). Any predispositions to racism that officers bring to the career cannot but be reinforced by the daily experience on the job. The police are motivated to act by overt differences in skin colour, style of dress, and behaviour, and these are often related to minority groups. Over time, Crank argues, these symbols of cultural difference become 'shorthand for identifying suspicious characters'; they become the obvious way to size people up. Thus, when there is a real or perceived history of certain groups committing crimes, their overt symbols of dif-ference become triggers for police action.

For whatever reasons, there is a general consensus in the literature on policing that racism is part of the subculture. Most explanations rely on two key assumptions: that police racism is part of the broader culture of a particular society, and that profiling based on visible difference of any kind is part of normal police practice. Notwithstanding Chan's cogent criticisms of the static determinism that has characterized so much research on the police, the main conclusion seems to be that police culture and practices predispose police officers towards racism against groups that are visibly different – especially Blacks. This manifests itself in the seemingly 'normal' practice of dividing the world between 'us' and 'them.'

Does Policing Culture Support Deviant Behaviour?

Do the values and norms of policing culture contribute to deviancy within policing? Do elements of policing culture such as the 'siege mentality,' the powerful codes of solidarity, secrecy, and silence, the wide discretion enjoyed by beat cops, and the lack of supervision in everyday policing practices lead to high rates of police misconduct?

Former Calgary police chief Christine Silverberg (2004a) explored this highly contentious issue. In an opinion piece in the *Globe and Mail* she observed that allegations of corruption among police drug squads, videotapes of officers making racist remarks about Aboriginals and Blacks, beatings of people of colour, and suspicious deaths of people in police custody are all grounds for police and public concern. She notes that American research on corruption indicates that corrupt organizations have two critical common denominators: 'First, their officers do not know what the organization's values are, and what their service's overall mission is. Secondly, they have weak organizational systems which tend to breed integrity problems.' She goes on to suggest that 'creating values-based police organizations takes know-how from the top, but it also takes an enlightened governing authority and legislative mechanisms of support.'

In another column in the *Globe and Mail* (2004b), Silverberg discussed the findings of the inquiry into the death of Neil Stonechild in the winter of 1990 (see chapter 3). Stonechild, a seventeen-year-old Aboriginal, was taken into custody by the Saskatoon police and later found dead. In his report, Justice David Wright stated that prevailing attitudes among the Saskatoon police led to an incompetent investigation, years of indifference, and a police service that failed to 'lift a finger to inquire into the merits of the complaints against its members.' In her column, Silverberg wrote that police services structured along traditional command-and-control lines cannot serve communities well. She called for community policing structures that would be 'tough on crime' but that would also place 'less emphasis on hierarchical rules and more on outcomes.' She argued for models that would commit officers to core values and for leaders who would constantly reinforce those values through recruiting, evaluation, promotion, supervision, and discipline. Both Silverberg and Wright call for accountability structures, and for provincial governments to lead the way in developing and maintaining effective mechanisms for holding police accountable.

Earlier in this chapter, we described the propensity for deviant behaviour as part of the dynamics of police culture. Suspiciousness, isolation, and constant exposure to society's underbelly can quite probably be blamed when police involve themselves in deviant activities. But in addition to this, police work by its very nature involves activities that are deviant by common societal standards. For example, police officers engage in undercover work that involves taking on false identities and that is aimed at inducing criminal behaviour. They are often allowed to make promises to criminals – promises they have no intention of keeping. For example, in hostage situations they sometimes promise lesser sentences for criminal behavior in return for releasing the victim(s). Officers are trained to be misleading, ambiguous, and even untruthful during interrogations. There are laws against invasion of privacy, yet police work often involves applying technologies that invade individual privacy. In sum, ethics that deviate from societal norms and values are basic to a number of routine police activities. This suggests, perhaps, why police officers are often charged with misconduct.

Alcohol and drug abuse are common problems among the police. Another commonly identified issue is officers who are 'on the take' – that is, who are accepting bribes, kickbacks, and gratuities from club owners, drug lords, pimps, and other criminals in exchange for turning a blind eye to their activities. Police officers are often accused of perjury on the witness stand and of doctoring their notes. In several high-profile cases of racial profiling (including the one cited in the introduction to this book), officers were accused of the latter.[2]

---

2 In the case of the racial profiling of Kevin Khan, a young Black motorist, Judge Malloy dismissed a drug charge against him, finding that two Toronto police officers had used racial profiling when stopping him and that they had later 'fabricated' evidence. Molloy wrote that 'the evidence is overpowering' that the officers' testimony was 'untrue' (Small 2004).

Misuse of authority is another concern. Yet another is sexual misconduct – specifically, accepting the services of prostitutes in return for let-
ting them ply their trade without being charged. Police too often use
excessive force – sometimes deadly force – and are feared for this reason by minoritized communities in particular (see chapter 3). Some
level of force is necessary in police work, but its overuse (however
defined) is cause for alarm. Police violence is often associated with
demonstrations or riots; since these often take place in public locations,
they often lead to investigations and commissions of inquiry.

Thus, elements of police culture may lead to unethical or deviant
behaviour and even to misconduct and corruption (Kappeler, Sluder,
and Albert 1994). Some researchers argue that because of slipshod
recruitment procedures, the police accept recruits who are especially
vulnerable to unethical as well as racist behaviour; however, it is also
quite possible that police culture lends itself to charges of unethical
and inappropriate behaviour.

One tired explanation of deviant police behaviour is the 'rotten
apples' thesis so beloved by public and police officials everywhere.
The contention here is that a few bigoted or deviant individuals have
managed to pass recruitment screening, or some good men have gone
rotten since joining the force, but that the system overall is above
reproach. The rotten apples view was first propounded by the Knapp
Commission, which in the early 1970s investigated rampant corruption
in the New York Police Department (the movie *Serpico* is based on the
life of the police officer whose whistleblowing led to this commission).
In Britain a famous report on policing by Lord Scarman (1981) also
relied on the rotten apples theory; his recommendations focused
mainly on the shortcomings of individual police officers rather than on
structural and systemic problems. More recently, with allegations of
racial profiling and other forms of misconduct being voiced in Toronto
and other Canadian, American, and British cities, the rotten apples theory has again been receiving heavy play.

In Toronto, starting in 2003 and continuing into 2005, allegations of
police misconduct have been mounting. They have involved many levels of the Toronto Police Service, including two former presidents of
the Toronto Police Association. RCMP investigations over a period of
years resulted in shocking allegations of police corruption – shake-
downs, beatings, and death threats; thefts of jewellery, narcotics, guns,
and cash; a 'tax' levied on drug dealers if they wanted to operate unim-
peded in part of the city; and so on. Jim Coyle (2004a) of the *Toronto*

Star observed: 'Fantino has done nothing to diminish a cultural defensiveness and paranoia fuelled by the bellicose leadership of a police association that seems to see anyone outside the blue tent as an enemy, and all criticism, however valid, as a declaration of war.' A few months later, John Barber (2004) of the *Globe and Mail* observed that Chief Fantino was locked into a permanent state of denial, along with the recently elected community safety minister, Monte Kwinter, who was also brushing off calls for an inquiry into the force with assurances that the chief would catch the few 'bad apples' who continued to infect his command.

Toronto Police Service

Over the past two decades, a long series of task force reports and studies have concluded that relations between the police and the Black community are obviously and profoundly strained. Unfortunately, the key recommendations in most of these reports have focused on a limited range of strategies – for example, changes in recruitment policies, training in race relations and cultural sensitivity, and the establishment of community advisory committees and independent civilian review mechanisms. Stenning (2004) observes that despite calls for the recruitment and promotion of minority officers, their representation has remained substantially unchanged in almost all of Canada's police services.[3] Training in race relations and cultural sensitivity has also failed to create substantive change.[4] These reports alluded many times to the

---

3 As of 2000, racial minorities were less than 4 per cent of sworn officers on the Montreal Urban Community Police Service, approximately 10 per cent of those on the Toronto Police Services, and about 7 per cent of those on the Vancouver Police Service (Stenning 2004).

4 Doreen Guy, a Black officer with the Toronto Police Service for twenty-one years, provides some insights. Guy decided to speak out publicly at a farewell dinner before scores of her fellow officers about her experiences as a Black woman in a racist working environment. Guy said that she was deeply affected by everyday racism over two decades of service to the Toronto Police Service and that senior officers and supervisors on the force had done nothing to stop the racial harassment. She observed: 'I would be paraded for duty and assigned to work with one person, a few minutes later I would be put with someone else. Whenever the person refused the supervisor would put me with yet another person. This would occur three or four times before we would leave the building. There was also the "silent treatment": the officer would resent being in a car with me and would not make any attempt to be civil' (Toronto Police Accountability Bulletin No. 13, September, 2004).

inadequacy of race relations training at Toronto's C.O. Bick Police Academy. Apparently, the amount of time and attention paid to this training has decreased over the years. Also, the academy tends to use police officers as trainers rather than qualified non-police professionals. In any case, training cannot solve the issue of racism; if there is a solution, it will have to be directed at the police culture and its racialized view on the world.[5]

Mechanisms for the independent review of policing practices by civilians have been totally inadequate. Many recommendations have been made over the years, and several organizational structures have existed. Most of them – including the current Special Investigations Unit (SIU) in Toronto – suffer from inadequate resources. More importantly, their powers are constrained by the police culture. Police are extremely resistant to the idea of civilian review; even when a review is conducted by police officers, frontline officers rarely cooperate for fear of being marked as informers or snitches (Wortley 2003). Police unions are also resistant to civilian review; the Toronto Police Association wields enormous power, and uses it whenever attempts are made to regulate police–civilian relations.[6]

So it can be argued that as long as reports continue to limit their recommendations to the strategies of recruitment, training, and civilian review, and as long as they do not even attempt to tackle the core issues of institutional culture, racialized ideology, and racialized norms and practices, there is little likelihood that racism will ever be addressed in any productive way.

The most recent report on the Toronto Police Service was written by a retired judge, George Ferguson, who was appointed by police chief

---

5 Stenning (2004) observes that such evaluations as have been done on training initiatives have shown very modest and in some instances even negative results in meeting the stated objectives. This failure has been attributed to resistance to such training. Also, training in race relations and cultural sensitivity has typically not been integrated with mainstream police training programs; rather, these forms of training are seen as add-ons. Silverberg (2004b) also criticizes add-on, ad hoc forms of race relations training, arguing that introducing these programs into an intemperate environment 'does nothing to change the fundamental structure, systems and processes of the organization that support a discriminatory culture.'

6 In the early 1990s the Police Complaints Commission investigated public allegations against the police. Apparently, it provided a better overview of police behaviour than what is currently available. However, the commission was disbanded by the Conservative government in 1997.

Julian Fantino to lead an inquiry into police misconduct in 2002, after some officers were charged with drug offences. This report was not mandated to deal with racial profiling but only with police misconduct; nevertheless, its findings and recommendations are worth including here, mainly because they highlight the perennial failure to deal with the crucial issue of police culture. Ferguson tabled his report in January 2003, but little was done with its recommendations.

At the time we were writing this book, the Toronto Police Service was facing its worst scandal in recent history, with fourteen officers facing a number of criminal and internal charges in three separate corruption cases. Fantino (since replaced) had already made it clear that he viewed the scandals as the work of a few 'bad apples' among the force's 5,100 officers. In the light of these further examples of police misconduct, Judge Ferguson was asked to continue his investigations, and his mandate was broadened.

The Ferguson Report

Following the mandate assigned to him, Judge Ferguson (2003) in his report dealt with only four issues. Significantly, none of them directly addressed the issue of police culture. His mandate included the recruitment and employment unit; training promotions and transfers; internal affairs; and the use of drugs, alcohol, and other substances. The report makes many standard recommendations on all of these points. It notes that there is an overly militaristic hierarchy in the force that includes automatic promotions and the like, but nowhere does it discuss in any depth the systemic nature of many of these policing issues. Racism and racial profiling are not even mentioned, as neither topic was included in the mandate. In other words, Ferguson's report completely ignores the systemic nature of racism on the Toronto police force. Essentially, the report, with its emphasis on recruitment and selection procedures, harks back to the 'rotten apples' approach to changing police structures. The report is based on the assumption that if only applicants who are above reproach were accepted into the force, misconduct, unethical behaviour, and charges of racism and racial profiling would not arise. There is a brief discussion of the hierarchical nature of the police service but virtually no discussion of police culture and its powerful influence on the socialization of new recruits. In light of Ferguson's inability to review and discuss the culture of policing, little in the way of substantive improvements can be expected if his recommendations are implemented. Simon Holdaway, a renowned expert on police culture in Britain, criticized Ferguson's report for very similar reasons when he was interviewed on the CBC morning show in April 2004.

Conclusions

This chapter has emphasized how the dominant White culture influences the unwritten and largely unarticulated value systems, implicit assumptions, and commonsense understandings of the police. These in turn shape the ethos of the organization. Police officers learn their cultural dispositions as part of an intense socialization process that strongly influences norms and behaviours. The occupational culture of policing requires officers to adjust to a multiplicity of roles, and they must constantly move between different worlds: the inner world of policing; the outer world of diverse publics; the street world; and the world of the station.

Our analysis has identified a number of dispositions that characterize police culture and that as a whole provide a fertile environment for both deviant behaviour and racism. These dispositions include social isolation; a siege mentality; high levels of cynicism and pessimism; and the need to maintain invisibility ('stay low and avoid trouble'). Another prominent feature of police culture is its paramilitaristic, authoritarian, hierarchical structure. Police view codes of secrecy and silence as necessary to protect fellow officers from management as well as the public.

These cultural traits and norms reinforce deep ruptures in the interactions between largely White police forces and racialized communities. These relations are characterized by constant tension and conflict. Much of police work provides significant opportunities for individual officers to exercise discretion in decisions about whom to stop, search, and arrest; this has had a grave impact on many law-abiding citizens. This discretionary power is informed by racially constructed stereotypes that can lead to racially biased practices against those identified as the 'other.'

Our analysis has been sharply critical of police culture. So it is appropriate to end this chapter by reminding readers that this subculture does not exist in isolation from the racialized beliefs, values, and norms of the dominant culture. The cultural dispositions in policing are reinforced every day by the social, cultural, political, and legal institutions and systems within which police officers work and live.

5 The Role of Narrative Inquiry in Social Science Research: Understanding Dominant and Oppositional Discourses

History is the struggle over who has the authority to tell the stories that define us. (Morales 1998, 5)

The quote that begins this chapter suggests that discourse is more than a vehicle for communication and interaction. It is not just a symptom and signal of the problem of racism; it essentially produces and reproduces racialized ideologies (van Dijk 1993). Discursive formations imply forms of social organization, as well as social practices that structure institutions and that constitute individuals as thinking, feeling, and acting subjects (Jordan and Weedon 1995). Discourse represents forms of knowledge. That is, it represents ways of constituting our meaning of the world and of assigning to that world an institutional form and discursive location (Foucault 1980).

This chapter offers a theoretical approach to competing discourses on race and racism – discourses that will be the central focus of the two chapters that follow. Chapter 6 will highlight the dominant discourses identified in the talk and text of some of the key policy-making officials involved in the racial profiling crisis in Toronto. Then Chapter 7 by Maureen Brown will explore oppositional discourses in the form of stories told by African Canadians about their experiences of being racially profiled by police. These two chapters are meant to delineate the conflicting world views expressed by two discursive communities.

Discourse analysis helps identify the schisms between diametrically opposed world views, lived experiences, and social positions. By exploring discursive formations, we can begin to understand the net-

nings and frames of reference that underpin both domi-
ositional discourse.

Rhetorical Strategies Framing Dominant Discourse

Reactions to the *Toronto Star*'s series on racial profiling came from a
number of quarters, including the police themselves as well as members of the government (both provincial and municipal) whose responsibility it is to exert social control. By analysing the discourses of the
White authorities, we can better understand their perceptions of racial
profiling. Deconstructing *their* discourses, we will gain insight into the
strategies they used to rationalize *their* racialized beliefs and values,
their organizational and professional norms, *their* positions of power
and privilege. The *Star* articles provided the public authorities with a
platform for expressing their discursive and rhetorical strategies, the
purpose of which was to counter-balance the findings of the *Star*'s
research on the racial profiling of African Canadians in Toronto.

Several analytic terms will be used throughout the following chapters. These include discursive strategy, rhetorical strategy, hegemonic
narrative, and dominant discourse. To a certain extent these terms are
interchangeable in that they all refer to the discourses cited or
expressed by White public authorities. For the sake of clarity, however,
we will differentiate them here. A discursive strategy is a discourse or
speech act that conveys a particular meaning or value. It is, of course,
based on the concept of 'discourse,' which is a practice that not only
represents the world but also signifies it by constituting and constructing its meanings (Fairclough 1992). Thus, when police chief Julian Fantino claimed there was no racism on his force, this discourse signified
his particular world view of the organization he was representing. The
specific themes embedded in his rhetoric reflected the beliefs, values,
and norms of his organization. Dominant or hegemonic discourse con-
tains the hidden conceptions and underlying assumptions that regulate the norms of social control (Ewick and Silbey 1995). These include,
for example, the notion that there are only 'a few rotten apples' among
the police – or, more tellingly, that the real reason there are tensions
between the police and the Black community is that Blacks commit
more crimes than do other groups. When discursive meanings are produced or reproduced by the media or in other forms of public expression and representation, they become strategies designed to persuade

the public to adopt their point of view. In this way, these strategies become legitimated and naturalized and result in the general belief that racial profiling does not exist – or at least not to the extent that beleaguered minorities claim. The use of rhetoric or symbols to influence other people underlies this persuasive or argumentative strategy. Rhetoric and argument are important tools for those who want to persuade others of a particular point of view.

The techniques of discourse and their strategies are linked to hegemony and asymmetrical power relations in society (Foucault 1980; van Dijk 1998). Dominant discourses are composed of the thoughts, beliefs, attitudes, and public declarations made by public authority figures who are involved in maintaining political order and social control. The dominant discourses in the following chapters emanated from public figures who had specific authority within or over the police. Discourses of this type are embedded in the everyday stories that the dominant elite (the in-group) tells about itself and about the 'other.' Furthermore, these stories are often codified through implicit language – language that itself influences the mindset from which the dominant elite (who are mainly White) observe 'reality.' Dominant discourses are culturally bound, and they construct the way the world is viewed. A key source of hegemonic discourse is systems of cultural representation such as the media.

A dominant discourse has the power to interpret important social, political, and economic issues and events according to its own definitions and constructions. The dominant discourse of elites functions as a medium for society's discussion of particular issues (Karim 1993). These discourses reflect the changing nature of structures of power and are always influenced by the evolving and potentially contradictory combinations of assumptions and world views of the dominant culture's elites.

Dominant discourses or narratives were of particular interest to post-structuralists – in particular to Lyotard (1984, 150), who defined them as 'master narratives or hegemonic stories told by those in power.' Through both their structure and their content, dominant/ hegemonic stories often articulate and reproduce existing ideologies and existing relations of power and inequality in society. Hegemonic or master discourses do more than express existing ideologies; they actually constitute the power and authority that shapes the lives and social relations of people. Hegemonic or master discourse is continuously evolving in order to maintain its position in the face of counter or oppositional narratives.

Dominant discourse carries social meanings, which usually are politicized in the sense that they carry with them a general concept of power that reflects the interests of the power elite. Opinion leaders, including police chiefs, politicians, bureaucrats, lawyers and judges, editors and journalists, advertisers, academics, and business leaders, play a crucial role in shaping issues and in identifying the boundaries of 'legitimate' discourse (van Dijk 1993). Those who have power can isolate, marginalize, and racialize their opponents by defining them as the 'other.' They assign labels that become social markers – for example, 'social deviants,' 'criminals,' 'illegal immigrants,' 'aliens,' 'radicals,' 'special interest groups,' 'troublemakers,' or 'spokespeople who do not represent anyone but themselves' (ibid.).

Social, cultural, economic, and political authority figures play a crucial role in postmodern societies by defining the boundaries of 'commonsense' discourse. They do this by defining their preferred positions as 'self-evident' truths and by dismissing other perspectives and positions as irrelevant, inappropriate, or without substance (ibid.; Gandy 1998). Wodak and Matouschek (1993, 226) described the role of the elite in society in the following way: 'Elites ... may be seen to comprise those who in one form or another dominate public discourse ... Elites are those who initially formulate and evaluate the various issues regarding minority groups. By virtue of their ability to determine an initial set of public discursive parameters, these elites are thus able to formulate an ethnic consensus.'

Elites have practically exclusive access to and control over the most important decision-making institutions in society, including cultural systems of representation: 'Wherever it really counts ... the crucial decisions about inclusion and exclusion are made by the elites. It is therefore essentially the elites who pre-formulate many of the everyday ideological beliefs that have become widespread in racialized societies' (van Dijk 1998).

Oppositional discourses are often dismissed or silenced because the elite have the power to declare which issues are 'credible' and which individuals and groups are trustworthy and reliable. Elites are able to use discourse to frame social problems, and they wield that power to make sure people will understand inequality as the product of individual rather than structural weaknesses (Gandy 1998).

Narratology, or the Stories That People Tell

The stories people tell about their lived experiences are more than mere individual communications; they are embedded in a cultural and ideological context. These stories reflect their existing social relations; and while many stories reflect an individual's experience, taken together they reveal cultural assumptions that transcend the individual. Bell (2003, 4) observes that stories are a bridge between individual experience and systemic social relations. Thus, their analysis can be a potential tool for developing a more critical consciousness about social relations in our society.'

Studies of culture, race, and racism draw from a broad conceptual framework, one that includes elements of cultural studies, discourse analysis, and critical race theory. Each of these theoretical approaches informs our analysis of the stories we present in this book and the meanings embedded in them. There has been a resurgence of interest in storytelling both as a social process and as a tool of research and analysis in many disciplines, including anthropology, sociology, communication, and the law. Through personal and collective narratives, human experience can be explored. When applied to the study of race and racism in society, the analysis of cultural narratives can uncover the myths, assumptions, and presuppositions that comprise the commonsense understandings of this phenomenon (Delgado and Stefancic 2000a; Ewick and Silbey 1995).

Theoretical Perspectives on Narratology

Anthropologists have collected stories from their respondents in the course of fieldwork since that discipline was invented. However, the use of stories as a means to uncover the dominant or metanarratives of societies is relatively recent. This technique entered the social sciences through the influence of postmodern theorists, who were sharply critical of what they called 'metanarratives.' This term, which loosely means 'big stories,' suggests a discursive explanation of how societies function on a grand scale. For example, Marxism and capitalism are metanarrative explanations of how society holds itself together. Grand theories in the social sciences – for example, the theory of functionalism – are also metanarratives in that they attempt to explain how and why societies function over time. Barthes (1973) and Lyotard (1984),

both postmodern theorists, are sharply critical of the 'postmodern condition'; in their view, master narratives are now dominant to the point
that people believe they represent the only valid and true conceptions
of the world. Lyotard argues that all aspects of modern societies –
including science as the primary form of knowledge – depend on these
grand narratives (1984). As a consequence, grand or metanarratives
have become the only real sources of knowledge and power. However,
another dimension of postmodern thinking tends to subscribe to the
view that these metanarratives actually mask the contradictions and
instabilities that are inherent in any social organization or practice. In
any society or organization, there is both order and disorder. Things
work and other things don't work, creating a natural tension. A 'grand
narrative' will mask these tensions by claiming that only order is rational and good while all disorder is chaotic and bad. (Klages, M. http://
www.colorado.edu/English/Engl2012Klages/pomo).

In rejecting grand or metanarratives, therefore, postmodernists, critical race theorists, and critical discourse analysts point to the significant
role played by mininarratives or counter-narrative stories that explain
everyday experiences in the context of more localized phenomena
rather than large-scale universal or global concepts (Bell 1987; Williams
1991; Delgado and Stefancic 2000a; van Dijk 1993; Fairclough 1992;
Ewick and Silbey 1995). These mininarratives – also referred to as oppositional narratives or subversive stories – depend on the situational context in which they occur as well as on the actual experiences of people.
Thus the collection and analysis of stories or oppositional narratives
constitutes a postmodern research method for understanding those stories which challenge dominant discourse and the master narratives.

Narrative inquiry can illuminate the social, political, ethical, and
moral dimensions of life and experience in a way that other research
approaches cannot. The discursive analyses of documented stories can
serve as primary data in academic research, as well as powerful educational and organizing tools. As Davis (2002, 22) notes, stories can serve
as catalysts for movements that lead to social change. The narratives of
oppression provide 'a powerful vehicle for producing, articulating,
regulating, and diffusing shared meaning.' The stories of oppression
are commonly contextualized in personal/individual experiences, yet
they also communicate broader cultural assumptions, beliefs, and habits of thinking that transcend the individual (Bourdieu 1999). In this
way stories link individual experience to broader social patterns. The
stories told about racism draw from and reflect culturally and histori-

cally constructed discursive themes and strategies, which resonate in individual accounts (van Dijk 1993).

Delgado (1995) lists three distinct classes of stories: (1) first-person accounts of negative experiences linked to forms of racial, ethnic, or gender discrimination; (2) dominant discourses designed to reaffirm the common ideology about various social and legal stories; and (3) counter-stories authored by members of out-groups as devices to counteract, or at least raise questions about, dominant narratives.

The narratives expressed within dominant discourses are intended to orchestrate the appearance of unanimity among the dominant group. The hegemonic narrative acts as a metacode that shapes the dominant group's 'mindset'; from this mindset, that group (read 'Whites') observes and interprets the world and develops an understanding of it. These codes exclude or silence other possible interpretations; this in turn serves to justify the dominant group's maintenance of existing social hierarchies based on socially constructed categories of racial differences. Dominant narratives of Whiteness require constant repetition and reiteration in order to maintain their position (van Dijk 1999).

Hegemonic stories such as those identified in chapter 6 are used strategically to reinforce the dominant White culture of the police and the politicians – and the media as well – in relation to out-groups. These stories portray elites in a favourable light and confirm their superior position as natural. In opposition to this, counter-narratives critique and challenge the assumptions, beliefs, myths, and misconceptions embedded in dominant narratives. These stories 'break the silence' and 'bear witness' to the lived experiences of people of colour and other minorities in the face of a hegemonic culture that distorts, stereotypes, and marginalizes that experience (Bell 2003; Ewick and Silbey 1995). Delgado (1995, 64) writes: 'The cohesiveness these stories bring is part of the strength of the out-group. An out-group creates its stories which circulate within the group as a kind of counter-reality.' bell hooks (1990, 9) suggests that the counter-narratives that describe the common psychological understandings of African Americans cut across the boundaries of race, class, gender, and sexual orientation. In the postmodernist deconstruction of dominant narratives, there is a sense of 'yearning' that 'wells in the hearts and minds of those whom such narratives have silenced in the longing for critical voice.'

The use of narrative stories as data has been sharply criticized by those social science 'hard liners' who subscribe to the power of science and scientific methodology (Wallace 2000). Scientific materialism is based on the Newtonian model of the universe, which maintains that if something cannot be measured objectively it does not exist. Those who criticize the use of stories as data maintain that stories merely recount subjectively defined events; furthermore, subjective phenomena cannot be analysed scientifically and cannot therefore be replicated by other scientists. In short, subjective experiential data are unscientific and ought to be ignored. In this dialogue, the old dichotomy between objectivism and subjectivity emerges once again.

Yet there is one field that has argued strongly for this approach and that in fact has used narratives successfully: critical legal theory. That includes critical race theory as it applies to the justice system. Critical race theorists such as Delgado (1995), Bell (1987), and Williams (1991) have written extensively about the use of narratives in law. In fact, they have created scenarios in order to argue legal issues. Nunan (1999) has described examples of this quasi-fictional approach as well as criticisms of it. For example, he quotes a prominent opponent of critical race theory, Richard Posner, who wrote:

What is most arresting about critical race theory is that ... it turns its back on the Western tradition of rational inquiry, forswearing analysis for narrative. Rather than marshal logical arguments and empirical data, critical race theorists tell stories – fictional, science-fictional, quasi-fictional, autobiographical, anecdotal designed to expose the pervasive and debilitating racism of America today. By repudiating reasoned argumentation, the storytellers reinforce stereotypes about the intellectual capacities of nonwhites. (cited in Nunan 1999)

He also maintains that the use of narrative is incompatible with rational analysis because 'narrative is fictional or quasi-fictional, and therefore at best anecdotal, at worst a tissue of lies – not the stuff of reasoned argument' (ibid.).

Nunan, however, maintains that legal storytelling 'is nothing more than a proposal for broadening the narratives available to judges and juries, to help them get (quite literally) to the bottom of things.' Critical race theorists argue that dominant groups (that is, Whites) protect their own interests by constructing social reality through language. Race theorists also stress the importance of counter-narratives by subordinated voices that emphasize social context and personal experience. These storytellers maintain that Blacks have not only different experiences, but also different ways of communicating and understanding them.

Another critic of the counter-narrative approach, Rosen, maintains that 'in its most radical form, the storytelling movement is a direct assault ... on the possibility of objectivity.' However, drawing on strains of literary theory, some critical race theorists claim that no event or text has an objective meaning, that each community of readers must determine how the text will be understood.

In support of storytelling, Nunan points out: 'After all, lawyers in courtrooms tell stories to juries all the time, both to cultivate their empathy by depicting their clients sympathetically through these stories, and to render abstract laws into a comprehensible three-dimensional concrete form, to make the law or rather the lawyer's version of it accessible to a lay audience of twelve. At this level, the call for voices of color is simply a call to expand the horizons of judges, juries, and even legal theorists, in taking account of the lived experiences of hitherto unnoticed people with respect to the law' (ibid.).

Critical race theory maintains that important values such as right and wrong and justice and injustice must be examined from the perspective of those who have suffered. When they are, the actual experiences and traditions of people of colour become a valuable source of knowledge for the justice system. These experiences and traditions are best told through narratives. Nunan answers some of his critics by contending that if justice remains colour-blind it will 'simply sustain a racially and ethnically inequitable status quo, whereas colour consciousness is what is required and this is best achieved through the voice of people of colour telling their stories' (ibid.).

Yet, as already noted, the dismissal of stories as 'anecdotal evidence' is pervasive in public and official discourse. Minority people's accounts of racial profiling by police and of other forms of racism and discrimination are almost always rejected as unreliable in the courts and everywhere else.

But because of their sheer number, stories of racial profiling rise above the criticism that they are mere anecdotes. Almost every study or report that has been published on racism in Canada (see Henry and Tator 2005) has included personal accounts of racism and racial profiling. What critics label as anecdotal evidence is in fact a body of systematic evidence of individual and systemic racism directed against people of colour not just by the police but by all of Canada's social institutions.

We have discussed at length our reasons for using stories in this study because it has long been standard practice for dominant hegemonic authorities to dismiss the counter-narratives of racialized individuals and communities. Counter-narratives almost always contest reality as constructed by dominant discourses. We view narrative analysis as an important methodological tool for understanding human experience in general, and in particular the experiences of people of colour who must deal with race and racism.

Studies of counter-narratives reveal truths about the social world that are often hidden or silenced by more traditional methods of social science and legal scholarship. Critical race theorists argue that oppositional stories can shatter complacency and challenge the status quo. Counter or oppositional narratives express the social relations of inequality that the dominant culture likes to deny, minimize, or degrade. Storytelling is a form of cultural activism; it allows those who have been oppressed and silenced 'to name and reclaim over and over, the connections we are taught to ignore, the dynamics we are told do not exist' (Morales 1998, 5).

The next two chapters demonstrate how dominant discourse can serve as a tool of social control (chapter 6), whereas oppositional discourse can serve as an instrument of social transformation (chapter 7).

6 The Dominant Discourses of Whi Authorities: Narratives of Denial Deflection, and Oppression

> To the extent that Canada presents itself as a raceless state, police atti-
> tudes and actions towards racial minorities will not be perceived as being
> founded on race, but on attempts to be proactive, to maintain law and
> order and to 'serve and protect' the 'citizens' ... from the troublemakers
> and 'misfits' ... of society. (James 2002, 292)

This chapter critically analyses some of the dominant discourses on
race, crime, and policing that were, and continue to be, disseminated
by public authorities and the media in the weeks and months after the
launch of the *Toronto Star* series on racial profiling and the police. We
refer to these discourses as dominant, elite, or hegemonic.

The dominant elite discourses that were used to challenge the findings of the *Star* series on race and crime are highlighted in this chapter.
There were two central themes in these discourses: the denial of racism
and racial profiling in policing; and the social construction of Blacks as
the 'other.' Within these two discursive strategies, other subthemes can
be identified.

Rhetorical Strategies and Narrative Themes Used by the White Elite Authorities

The Discourse of Denial: 'We are not racist – we do not engage in racial profiling'

In a democratic liberal society in which racism is seen as the aberrant
beliefs and behaviour of isolated and dysfunctional extremists, denials

of racism in public discourse – including that of the news media – are always present. These denials are often articulated in the context of doubt that acts of discrimination take place. Also, they are usually followed by claims made by those who profess to be liberal that people of colour and other minority groups are hypersensitive about prejudice and discrimination and that they often see bias where there is none. The assumption is that because Canadian society upholds the values and ideals of a liberal democracy, it cannot be racist, and neither can the country's key institutions be racist, and certainly neither can the media, which play a crucial role in preserving democratic principles. Central to this discourse are positive self-presentations ('I'm not racist'; 'This is not a racist organization'; 'This is not a racist society'). These denials are of course based on a very limited understanding of how racism manifests itself in contemporary society.

Racism is still understood by most people as involving isolated and individual discriminatory acts and expressions of racial bias. By this definition, racists are those who use strongly pejorative words and labels, who physically attack people of colour and vandalize their property, and/or who are aligned with extremist political movements. The denial of racism is part of a defensive strategy that actually *enhances* in-group preservation through positive self-representations (van Dijk 1991). Racism and racialized discourses in everyday and institutional life of a more sophisticated, elusive, and linguistically 'coded' type are poorly understood. Yet these are the most pervasive forms of racism in modern society. The discourse of denial of racism has become so routine at all levels of society that charges of racism – and the very suggestion that racism can influence social outcomes – have come to be perceived as serious contraventions of mainstream values and norms. Ironically, such charges are sometimes regarded as more serious infractions than overt racism.

Immediately after the *Star* published its findings on the racial profiling of African Canadians, the discourse of denial raised its head, in the reactions of those most closely affiliated with policing structures. It was in fact the angry 'knee jerk' response of the police chief, Julian Fantino, that initiated the discourse of denial. The very day the *Star* series began to run, he was quoted as follows in that paper: 'We do not do racial profiling. We do not deal with people on the basis of their ethnicity, their race or any other factor. We're not perfect people but you're barking up the wrong tree. There's no racism … It seems that, according to some people, no matter what honest efforts people make, there are always those who are intent on causing trouble. Obviously this [story] is going to do exactly that' (Fantino, 'We Do Not Do Racial Profiling,' *Toronto Star*, 19 October 2002).

The Toronto Police Association supported Fantino's discourse of denial and went several steps further. Craig Bromell, head of the TPA at the time, contended that 'no racial profiling has ever been conducted by the Toronto Police Service and we question the Toronto Star's interpretation of its statistical information' (Porter 2002). Bromell questioned the *Star*'s methodology and statistical analysis and even urged citizens to boycott the paper by cancelling their subscriptions.

The Toronto Police Services Board, which supervises the police, was the next police-related agency to apply the discourse of denial. Its chair at the time, Norm Gardner, described the *Star*'s findings as 'reckless' and suggested that 'some of the people involved, who are trying to keep on bringing this stuff up ... They make a good living out of social unrest' (in 'Analysis Raises Board Hackles,' *Toronto Star*, 2002). Gardner added that he was confident the police were not using racial profiling. The board's vice-chair, Gloria Luby, agreed with Gardner, noting that statistics can be used to prove anything and that 'police discrimination has not been an issue' (ibid.). The discourse of denial then moved to the political level, with Toronto's mayor, Mel Lastman, insisting that 'the police only arrest bad guys ... I don't believe the Toronto police engage in racial profiling in any way, shape or form. Quite the opposite, they're very sensitive to our different communities' (ibid.).

Within the discursive framework of denial, several subthemes emerged. One of the most striking was what can be called 'the discourse of competing experts.' As part of Fantino's determination to challenge the *Star*'s findings, he engaged an expert in methodology and quantitative analysis. (The *Star*'s analysis was conducted by its own staff, but its methodology, analysis, and general results were reviewed by York University professor Michael Friendly, whose expertise is statistical methodology.) Fantino's expert, Edward Harvey of OISE, was asked to review the *Star*'s methods and analysis. A version of Harvey's report was presented to a meeting of the Police Services Board on 20 February 2003. Alan Gold, a high-profile lawyer, accompanied Harvey and also made a presentation (see board minutes at http://www.torontopolice.on.ca). These two presentations differed markedly in their substance, content, and language. Harvey provided a reasoned and sober discussion of his methods and findings; Gold used highly inflammatory language. His presentation was laced with terms such as 'junk science,' 'illogical,' 'unreasonable conclusions,' 'scientifically unsound,' and 'unfair selection.' He declared the conclusions 'simply false based on the data they had ... The *Star*'s mistakes ... are fundamental, basic and simply embarrassing ... Their whole project ... will enter the junk science hall of fame.' He claimed that systemic racism in the Toronto Police Service 'is not an issue' and therefore 'the *Star*'s completely unjustified, irresponsible and bogus slurs against the TPS must be put down once and for all' ('The *Star*'s Response to Its Critics,' *Toronto Star*, 1 March 2003).

Clearly, Gold had taken Harvey's criticisms and injected them with hyperbole. His approach was also strongly personalized; he was contending that the *Star* had taken a subjective approach to the data, yet his own presentation was also guilty of subjectivity. Gold's presentation was yet another powerful example of the denial of racism in the Toronto Police Service.[1]

Harvey, in contrast, took a far more objective and reasoned approach. Fundamental to his analysis was that the TPS database had not been collected for research purposes and that it contained so many flaws that it was of limited use as a research instrument.

However, no other database on race and the police existed in Toronto, and in any case, social scientists have for many years made effective use of data collected for other purposes. So the *Star*'s research strategy was not inappropriate, whatever Harvey was implying. Such databases must, however, be 'cleaned up' before they can be useful for research, and one of the differences between his study and the *Star*'s was that different 'clean-up' techniques were used. Harvey also argued that comparing Black and White offenders to their respective numbers in the population was an 'overly simple' use of demographic baselines. Again, this criticism had some merit. But Harvey then proceeded to base his detailed analysis on only half the police divisions – specifically, the ones where the 'proportion of the Division's population that is Black is 7% or greater'; he justified this by explaining that the numbers from the other divisions were too small to conduct statistical analysis. Wortley and Tanner (2003) suggested that in so doing, he was neglecting the critical importance of Blacks in predominantly

---

1 Alan Gold (2003) has written a long article about racial profiling and the methodological weaknesses of not only the *Star*'s series but also the general literature on racial profiling.

white residential areas who could be subject to unusual police scrutiny. Wortley and Tanner observe that areas such as the nightclub district and around the Eaton Centre have a mainly White population but also attract many Black visitors. Excluding those areas from analysis would have a significant impact in the data. The *Star*'s publisher, John Honderich, also responded to the criticisms of the research in a detailed statement (Honderich 2003).

The presentations by Harvey and Gold were made at a meeting of the board to which Black community members had been invited to make presentations. They were apparently kept waiting for two hours while the two experts were placed ahead of them on the agenda. *Star* columnist Jim Coyle (2003a) pointed out the seeming unfairness of the process: 'To have black community leaders in attendance at a police services board meeting expecting a chance to make submissions on race relations, then to hold them hostage for two hours of an unannounced presentation denying one of their most publicized concerns, is a large act of rudeness and a big step backwards.'

In hiring his own expert to defend his officers from charges of racial profiling, Fantino was following a time-worn academic strategy: attack the methodology. It is very well known that any and every methodology in the social sciences is open to criticism and even outright attack. There are many methodological schools in these disciplines, and the easiest, quickest, and dirtiest game is to attack the methodology and statistical analysis of a study. Academic journals offer many examples of such efforts. In the case at hand, time and resources that could have been put to better use in combatting whatever problems exist in the Toronto police (and other societal institutions) were being used simply to amplify the denial response. Once again, dominant and elite forces were exerting their hegemonic power in an effort to influence events and silence opposition.

The discourse of the 'battle of experts' reveals yet another important element in the debate. The public, media personnel, and government officials are not familiar with the ideological and theoretical divisions in the social sciences. As with any institution, there are sharp differences in opinion and ideological commitment within these disciplines. These differences are reflected in their perspectives on social phenomena and in their methods of analysis, but they are especially evident in the approaches taken to applied projects. Scholars who are committed to social change – especially with regard to bringing about equity for disadvantaged groups in society – are often more sensitive to the need to conduct research without adhering strictly to the rigid requirements of formal, quantitative methodologies. They recognize that complex social behaviour does not always conform to these requirements. These differences in research perspectives may well account for some of the differences between the two experts in the present case. The crucial point, however, is that results obtained by adhering to more rigid criteria do not necessarily negate those informed by other approaches. Social science research does not lend itself to polarized, 'either/or' approaches.

Harvey's report became a point of contention again two months later, when a coalition of Toronto's Black organizations, the African Canadian Community Coalition on Racial Profiling (ACCCRP) asked once again to make a deputation to the Police Services Board. They came well prepared to respond to Harvey's report. They asked for ninety minutes. The board responded that they had five minutes. The coalition left, declaring that the board was unfit to represent the multiethnic City of Toronto (Vasil 2003).

As the discursive event continued to play out, a new participant - the justice system - entered the discourse. Dee Brown, a former member of the Toronto Raptors basketball team, had recently been convicted of drunk driving. He had appealed the conviction. On 17 January 2002, the *Star* reported that according to Brown's lawyer, his client had been pulled over by the police because he was Black, not because of how he was driving. An Ontario Superior Court judge agreed, and overturned his drunk driving conviction. In speaking to the appeal, the Crown attorney stated: 'I'm not challenging the existence of racial profiling. This is a problem that merits corrective action.'

This statement provoked a strong reaction from the justice system. Several people tried immediately to distance themselves and the system from his words. Ontario's attorney general was quoted: 'It's important to remember that Crown attorneys do not make political statements on behalf of the government. What they say, they say in relation to that case' (*Toronto Star*, 25 January 2003). Noting that the case was still before the appeal court, he refused further comment, except to express his 'utmost confidence' in the police chief.

Police organizations also responded to the Crown attorney's admission that racial profiling exists. The Ontario Association of Chiefs of Police (OACP) wrote a strong letter to Premier Ernie Eves in which they demanded that action be taken against the Crown attorney. The following rather long extract from a statement by Tom Kaye, president of the OACP (31 January 2003), makes it clear that the OACP was not only criticizing the Crown attorney but also expressing its own sense that police forces were being victimized through reverse discrimination:

These unsubstantiated allegations are extremely provocative and disturbing in their intent. We feel that Mr. Stewart's unfounded statements are a blatant attempt to shake public confidence in the professional principles of our police officers ... Our concerns lie in the damage his remarks have had on various aspects of public/police relations, reaping havoc on the ability of police to perform their day to day tasks and obligations in protecting the citizens of Ontario. The OACP has spoken publicly denying the existence of this type of systemic prejudice ... For the aforementioned reasons, the OACP sees no alternative but to demand that immediate and appropriate action be taken in this matter and the Attorney General contend with Mr. Stewart in a manner that would publicly reflect the province's support and confidence in the dedicated police officers that serve to protect Ontarians. (http://www.oacp.on.ca/public)

It seems that both government officials and police organizations were attempting to silence – indeed, erase – the words of a progressive-thinking Crown attorney.

On the heels of this, Larry Hill, deputy chief of the Ottawa Police Department, told a federally sponsored forum that the Ottawa police did in fact conduct racial profiling. When he elaborated on this afterwards, he maintained that systemic forms of racism exist in society, including the police: 'Our members are not racist ... but we are no different than any other organization ... Do stereotypes exist? Yes. Do things happen because we stereotype people? Yes. So if we're going to call that racial profiling, then yes, certainly it occurs in our police force as well as other police services' (Sorensen 2003).

These straightforward remarks were immediately disputed by his chief, Vince Bevan, who released a statement which said in part: 'Remarks made about the Ottawa police, made at the conference this morning by Deputy Chief Hill, were interpreted by some as an assertion that the Ottawa Police Service and its members routinely practice racial profiling in their work. This is not the case' (Harper 2003). Bevan also prohibited his deputy from granting any further interviews on the subject.

In February 2003, the Ontario Human Rights Commission (OHRC) launched a study of racial profiling in policing and in other public sector institutions. The OHRC's objective was to offer those who had experienced profiling an opportunity to express how it had affected them and to raise awareness of the harmful effects and social costs of this practice. They asked people in Ontario who believed they had been targeted by this practice to e-mail, telephone, or write to the commission describing their experiences. The commission received more than eight hundred responses, four hundred of which were specifically related to the issue of racial profiling (OHRC 2003). Later, the commission released a separate report detailing the stories of Aboriginal people who had been racially profiled.

The commission's study was quickly attacked by a number of public officials, including the premier and the public safety minister. Again, the major discourse was one of denial. Premier Eves described the initiative as a 'broad sweeping inquiry without making the complainant accountable or identifiable, for that matter, and giving the person or the other side of the equation that chance to defend themselves, is not in my opinion a very fair or equitable way to administer justice' (Brennan 2003). However, this misrepresented the purpose of the study. The commission clearly stated that its purpose was to gather data and facts, not to administer justice; moreover, the commission's complaint process did indeed allow the other side to 'defend' itself. The premier seemed to be applying the wrong criteria to the commission's review.

On the same day, the public safety minister, Bob Runciman, was quoted as saying that 'the potential is there to do damage. No one has proven that it [racial profiling] exists' (Campbell 2003). He added: 'I don't think anyone has substantiated it's a problem.' He also maintained that the inquiry was bad for police morale and that it encouraged anecdotal evidence.' Meanwhile, Tom Kaye, head of the Ontario Association of Chiefs of Police maintained that it was 'open season on police officers' (Korstanje 2003).

These statements, which seemingly focused on the unfairness of the commission's initiative, were again embedded in a discourse of denial of racial profiling. Thus the validity of a process that apparently was a genuine attempt to collect critical information on the extent of the problem of racism had to be challenged. The criticisms led the commissioner of the OHRC, Keith Norton, to write to the members of government defending his inquiry: 'This is an inquiry; it's not an investigation. We are not investigating anybody ... I also want to make it very clear that the commission is not conducting an investigation of individual allegations of racial profiling' (Brennan 2003).

Nine months later, the release of the commission's report – *Paying the Price: The Human Cost of Racial Profiling* (2003) – unleashed another set of dominant discourses from police authorities. The report documented the human cost of racial profiling on individuals who had experienced it, and on their families and communities; it also pointed to the detrimental impacts on society as a whole. It concluded with a number of recommendations (see chapter 7). The study looked at the issue of racial profiling across institutional sectors, although racial profiling by police was addressed by a significant number of respondents. Among its other things, the commission recommended that cameras be installed in police cruisers across the province.

Fantino immediately challenged the commission's findings: 'To now portray the whole of the police community as a bunch of racists and no goods and unprofessional people that need to be watched at every turn is not in keeping with the trust and support that we know exists in our community … This is totally divorced from the reality of today … We have become, really, the whipping boys and girls of society for all these other issues' (Yourk 2003).

A month later, Fantino filed a Freedom of Information (FOI) request seeking access to deputations made by people alleging racial profiling by the police before the OHRC. He said he wanted the names of respondents who had complained to the commission regarding racial profiling by police so that he could vet details about these complaints. In its report, the commission had used only the initials of the complainants, not their full names (Gordon 2004).

The Discourse of Rationalizing the Status Quo

Another discursive strategy used by police authorities involved the argument that focuses on support for the status quo. Without supplying any evidence, police officials maintained that present-day relations between police and Black communities had never been better. For example, Craig Bromell declared: 'There's many people in the black community who are quite satisfied with policing and law enforcement in the city. The relations are better now than they ever were before. There's no complaining about this profiling' (Porter 2002).

Using a similar argument, the Toronto Police Association released a statement that read in part: 'The Toronto Police Service and our members have never had a more successful relationship with the mosaic of citizens of our city regardless of race, religion, colour or creed' (ibid.).

This same sentiment was echoed by the vice-chair of the Police Services Board: 'My feeling is that we've been getting along very well. Police discrimination has not been an issue. So why should it suddenly become one? Because the *Star* did this research?' Mayor Lastman attempted to justify the present situation by noting that Toronto police officers undergo diversity training courses. He also cited the *Star* as saying that 'the broader policing community has recognized the force to be a leader in civil rights' (ibid.). Even Fantino used the discourse of justification in noting in his first response to the *Star* that 'The *Star* has done this ... at a time when I feel that the relationship with all of our communities is a good one' (Fantino, *Toronto Star*, 19 October 2002).

Most striking about this particular discourse of denial was that the authorities were making assumptions without offering any evidence that things were as good as they were suggesting. It is extraordinary that in the face of massive discontent – which Black organizations and other members of the community immediately and powerfully communicated – the White elite authorities were still able to misread the community and spread misinformation.

The Discourse of Reverse Discrimination

A common rhetorical strategy when discourses clash is the reversal of semantic roles. Here, the perpetrators of prejudiced commentaries and acts were portrayed as the innocent victims of a new form of oppression and exclusion. It was then argued that *minority groups* were engaging in reverse discrimination. In the commentaries of Fantino and other police officials, a strong belief was visible that as a result of the *Star* series, the police had become the victims of reverse discrimination. They had become the objects of prejudice and discrimination; not only that, but their important work in society was being disparaged and undermined. It was even suggested that the police now had to fear for their own safety.

At a summit on Policing, Race Relations, and Racial Profiling organized by the Honourable Lincoln Alexander (former chair of the Race Relations Foundation) to address the issue of racial profiling, TPA president Craig Bromell made a presentation. In a later speech to the TPA (25 November 2002, published in the *Star* on 27 November 2003), he summarized the comments he made there: 'I told them we believe that police have become the target of hatred and we are concerned for our member's safety ... We told them there are self-appointed people taking advantage of the situation and doing nothing but political grandstanding ... We viewed this as an opportunity for certain people who would do anything to convict a cop. This will not happen. Do not paint us in a corner or we will come out fighting' (Bromell 2002).

In another statement following the summit conference, Bromell again declared that the police were being victimized. His observation appeared almost paranoid in its intensity: 'We feel we were sold out by certain people in the room on this issue' (ibid.).

Employing a similar discourse, Fantino often lamented that his force was being unfairly treated. Examples: 'It seems if there is anybody that is stereotyped in this community it's the police.' 'People are getting shot and killed and hurt and we better get our collective act together and stop blaming the police for everything that's going on. We're not the problem here' (Wilkes 2003).

The construct of reverse discrimination and police victimization was the basis for a $2.7 billion class action libel suit by the Toronto Police Association against the *Star* for turning the spotlight on the Toronto police's treatment of Blacks. The association's lawyer, Tim Danson, stated: 'Accusing the members of the Toronto Police Service of racism is a very serious allegation and if such a serious allegation is going to be made, the accusers will be called upon to prove it' (Small 2003). Danson argued that the series contained numerous falsehoods, malicious innuendos and untruthful allegations, accusing the *Star* of 'deplorable, inflammatory, and dangerous bias.' The association claimed that every officer's reputation had been damaged by the *Star*'s series in that the articles implied that 'wearing a uniform, for many, is now synonymous with racism and intolerance ... disgracing the uniform puts the police and public safety at risk' (ibid.).

But in an Ontario Superior court decision that came down six months later, Justice Maurice Cullity noted that there could be no legal basis for this suit because the *Star* articles had not implied that every police officer is racist. He added that 'the whole thrust of the articles is that the evidence suggests that racial profiling occurs and that steps must be taken to identify the causes and remove them' (Tyler 2003). The police association sought leave to appeal this decision to the Supreme Court of Canada; leave was denied.

As this discursive crisis progressed, Fantino and the police launched various initiatives to improve relations with minority communities. These included a series of town hall meetings. But even while these dialogues were taking place, the police chief was complaining that unnamed groups – including, apparently, some officers on the force itself – were 'deliberately undermining Toronto police ... I believe that some people are intent on demoralizing and destroying the spirit of our people ... There are those who have special agendas. They wouldn't like the police no matter what.' Admitting that the police had problems, he added: 'Yes we do have our problems, mostly ... with police being smeared' (Mackie 2003a).

One of the first of the town hall forums called by Fantino was held on 7 January 2003 in a community that is heavily Black. There, a fifteen-year-old girl came to the microphone set up for questions and asked: 'Why should you expect us to respect you when you don't respect us Black kids?' Instead of trying to answer the question, Fantino replied angrily: 'I don't agree with it [the question]. It's totally uncalled for. I don't think it dignifies an answer' (Leong 2003).

The chief was sharply criticized for his reply, not only in the community but also in the media and by various commentators. Later that week, he blamed the media for their biased coverage of the meeting and maintained that they had not covered the many positive things that were happening at the meetings: 'For the main part, all you see is one incident, one situation, one person making a statement, which has then become the focus of the big to-do ... I think the media should be ashamed of itself for having done that ... Some of the media never reported one favourable comment of many that were made there by the citizens who were there, the thank yous that our people got. All we got is a whole lot of the usual attack the police, criticize the police, denigrate what the police do, the racist police and on it goes.' In a final lament, he added: 'At least treat us fairly. Our people are decent, hard-working folks who are trying very hard' (Wilkes 2003).

The Discourse of Political Correctness

This discourse has become a common rhetorical strategy in terms of expressing resistance to social change. The demands of marginalized groups for fairness and equity are ridiculed, discredited, and dismissed by resorting to the term 'political correctness.' This strategy is intended to stifle debate on a wide variety of issues focusing on the inclusion of non-dominant voices and perspectives in public discourse. It has polarized positions with respect to issues of representation, multiculturalism, and equity. Bromell used this discourse often and in a number of ways. The demands of marginalized communities and their particular focus on ending racial profiling and other racialized practices were discredited as political correctness run wild.

In a television interview with CBC broadcaster Evan Solomon on 10 November 2002, Bromell used the term political correctness in describing the actions of the Black community. When the commentator responded that some people don't consider it political correctness to respect citizens and respect minorities, he replied: 'Then if that's what you're saying, then we'll get the call and we'll drive on. We won't talk to that group. Let's see what happens ... Yeah, we'll see what happens. Let's see who's coming to us in two or three months screaming for us to start doing our job again' (McCabe-Lokos 2002).

Bromell then compared Toronto to Cincinnati, stating that officers in the latter city gave up after violence broke out there. He then suggested: 'We're going to sit in our cars and wait until we get the radio call. Crime went up 600 percent. They became, they became your politically correct officers that you're talking about ... We're not going to sit back and have people make changes because of the political correctness. That is not how it's done and it's not going to happen with our members' (ibid.)

The term political correctness had arisen in the Dee Brown case, discussed earlier in this chapter. The Court of Appeal had overturned a drunk driving conviction after the defendant accused the police of racial profiling. In an interview following the appeal court ruling, Bromell described the decision as 'politically correct crap': 'Black drivers can now commit infractions without fear of consequences. Go do what you want. You won: we give up. If that's what the system wants, go do what you want. You won: we give up ... If they're going to be using bullshit excuses like this then so be it ... We're not going to serve our guys up on a silver platter ... It's a complete joke ... Why would you put your career on the line for some crap like this? There's never been any proof of racial profiling' (Coyle 2003b).

The Discourse of Otherness

One of the most powerful forms of dominant discourse within the framework of the denial of racial profiling involves attempts to discredit, marginalize, and silence those members of the Black community (and others) who dare to challenge existing racialized practices of the police. This rhetorical strategy reinforces a 'we–they' polarization. The ubiquitous *we* represents the values and norms of the White dominant culture or the culture of the organization or system (that is, the police, the courts, the media, schools, governments); *they* refers to those who are the 'other,' and who possess 'different' (read 'questionable') values, beliefs, and behaviours. As the following examples indicate, the discourse revolved around the supposedly ulterior motives of those Black community leaders who were criticizing the police and protesting racial profiling.

In this context, the former public safety minister, Bob Runciman, observed: 'I think some folks appear to have a vested interest in seeing this kind of tension continue to exist ... I think that some people make a living off some of this and I think we have to step back and say what do we really want to achieve here. We want to achieve a community that can work together where we have respect for one another. They certainly don't seem to be focused on finding solutions' (Mallan 2003).

Norm Gardner, former chair of the Police Services Board, also employed the discourse of otherness when he observed that some people were trying to 'make a living out of social unrest' ('Analysis Raises Board Hackles' 2002). Bromell made a similar point when he told his association members that 'self-appointed people' were 'doing nothing but political grandstanding' (Bromell 2002).

To summarize, within the broad discursive pattern of a sustained and categorical denial that the police and other public authorities conduct racial profiling, the most powerful and commonly used rhetorical strategy involves trivializing and erasing any perspective that challenges the view that policing practices are fair. Examples of this strategy as cited above have included the following: the attempt to silence the *Star* by hiring a scholar to challenge the newspaper's research methodology; a $2.7 billion lawsuit against the *Star* launched by the Toronto Police Association; calls to reprimand a Crown attorney and muzzle the deputy chief of the Ottawa police for acknowledging that racial profiling happens; the vitriolic responses of political and policing authorities to the OHRC's inquiry into racial profiling; the failure of the Toronto police chief, Julian Fantino, to respond with respect to a young girl's plea for the same; the decision by the Police Services Board to give Professor Harvey two full hours to report but only five minutes for a deputation from the African-Canadian community; and finally, efforts to silence and censure the entire Black community by constantly repeating dominant discourses that carry implicit and explicit messages of denunciation and reprobation.

The Discursive Role of Blackness in Constructing the Other

This section explores the second persistent discursive strategy used by White elite policing officials and politicians: the discourses of Blackness that link race, crime, and culture.

As discussed in chapter 1, the abnormalization of the Black male identified in theories of 'danger and racialization' is relevant to analyses of the discursive role that Blackness plays in the construction of the 'Black criminal.' Rose and others argue that Blackness has historically been used to denote danger in societies: 'Black bodies have (been) supersaturated with meaning ... The dominant and hegemonic narrative attached to Black men in particular, has been one of criminal danger' (Rose 2002, 182). This results in a need for increased surveillance, which ultimately leads to more racial profiling. Moreover, the Black man has been made to embody the internal threat to law and order; it follows that surveillance must be directed against him to ensure that he is contained both geographically and socially in his place (Fiske 2000).

The public's perception is that crime is violent, Black, and male. These constructs have converged to create the 'criminalblackman.' Yet there is practically no literature that exposes the 'criminalwhiteman.' In the media, in research studies, and in everyday discourses there are few if any references to the problem of White-on-White crime (Russell 1998). Whites, and other ethno-cultural groups, visualize crime in Blackface. The virtual absence of discussion of White crime suggests that in our singular and collective minds, 'White' and crime simply do not go together (ibid., 115). Carl James (2002, 203) links the racial profiling and fatal shootings of Blacks to the 'racial imaginary schema' used by police, which interweaves Blackness with 'assumed citizenship, immigrant status and nationality (often Jamaican) ... to inform their perceptions and actions.' He also suggests that the stigmatizing of Black people as a criminal group likely 'to threaten the social order, safety and security of citizens turns them into racialized subjects that are "always under suspicion."' Aboriginal people are subject to the same perceptions and are also 'suspect.' This racialization and criminalization of the Black male – more specifically, Black youth – is thus structured within a social, ideological, and discursive context. In the dominant discourse of White authorities, both gangs and Jamaican culture become coded language for the dangerous 'other.'

As noted earlier, Chief Julian Fantino held a series of town hall meetings with various communities across the city in an attempt at damage control over the contested issue of racial profiling. At one of the first of these forums, which was attended by many Blacks, Fantino commented: 'Race relations is not the only thing happening here. Dwelling on the topic is hijacking the real issues – violence and the gun crisis' (Fowlie and Abate 2003). Implicit in this statement is the assumption that the concerns of the Black community over racial profiling are not real or compelling and thus are not worth serious attention.

Later, Fantino argued that the *Star* series on racial profiling was feeding the problem of racial violence in Toronto. *Star* columnist Royson James responded to remarks made by Fantino on a radio show by suggesting that the police chief was implying that 'black leaders are coddling the black thugs in our city; that the black community ... and is doing precious little to solve the problem of black-on-black violence' (James 2003).

Central to Fantino's racialized discourse was an effort to link Blackness with the out-of-control violence happening in the city. This theme took on epic proportions in the context of waging a 'war on crime.' The police chief lashed out against 'out-of-control' youth who were engaging in violent behaviour involving firearms. He then suggested a number of strategies to address the problem, including the installation of CCTV surveillance systems on downtown streets. As well, Fantino and Bob Runciman, the public security minister, called for a new provincial law that would require doctors in hospital emergency departments to inform police whenever they treated patients with gunshot wounds. Both these strategies would have presented a serious conflict with existing privacy laws. It is somewhat ironic that Fantino and Runciman adamantly rejected the OHRC's recommendation that surveillance cameras be placed in police cars in order to help identify officers who engage in racial profiling; both men argued that such an action would be a violation of the rights of innocent police officers. Yet they strongly supported the installing of surveillance cameras in urban areas, even though many innocent people would inevitably be caught by those cameras.

In various forums, the voice of White public authority focused strongly and consistently on the Black community's failure to act like 'responsible citizens.' This voice argued that the Black community had not demonstrated sufficient concern about the murders of Black men by other Black men – that over the past year it had not cooperated sufficiently with the authorities to combat the soaring rates of violent crime. For example, Runciman suggested that tougher policing was needed because leaders in Toronto's Black community – which includes 300,000 people – had not tried to end the violence. He complained about 'people who don't accept any degree of responsibility for trying to solve the problems and challenges and misunderstandings' about Blacks and the police. When asked if he was talking about people in the Black community, he replied that he was (Mackie 2003b).

In the next stage of 'othering,' the police authorities – including Fantino and Bromell – broadened their rhetoric and employed a discourse of moral panic in the context of the 'explosive' increase in crime, especially violent 'street crime.' Note that in discourses of law and order the focus tends to be on 'street crime' as 'real crime.' This hegemonic conception deletes from serious consideration the crimes committed by the White privileged elite, which cause considerably more damage to society (Wortley 2002; James 2002; Schissel and Brooks 2002).

The linkage between race and crime was visible in the political discourses embedded in the Ontario Progressive Conservative Party platform and campaign strategy in the fall of 2003. The same linkage was made during the Toronto mayoral campaign in November of the same year. There was no specific reference to Blacks and crime in either campaign; that said, the convergence between race, culture, immigration, and crime was a dominant political discourse in both. Implicit messages about the dangerous 'others' were woven into both campaigns. The PCs combined their 'law and order' platform with a discourse of moral panic. The title of one of their policy papers, 'Safe Communities in a Secure Society,' conveyed the message that society was in danger, out of order, in crisis, and under siege. This paper blamed the crisis on youth, immigrants and refugees, and terrorists, among others. The PC platform spoke to the importance of 'bringing good people into Ontario while keeping bad people out.' In one campaign speech, Ernie Eves brandished a loop of barbwire in one hand and a 'get-out-of-jail-free' Monopoly card in the other. 'You can have a little more of this, where criminals should be,' he told his audience, waving the wire strands to symbolize prisons; then he gestured with the Monopoly card to symbolize his preference for tough jails. Eves, like Fantino, was especially critical of the Youth Criminal Justice Act; both argued that the law must be more aggressive and punitive. Yet as Schissel (2002, 121) points out, the Canadian youth justice system is considered one of the harshest in the Western world: 'We lock up more young offenders per capita than any other industrialized country.'

The same theme and message emerged a few months later in the Toronto mayoral campaign, in which the more conservative candidate, John Tory, focused on the problem of out-of-control crime. In his speeches and press releases, Tory often referred to the need for hundreds more police officers to ensure safer neighbourhoods. Significantly, both Bromell and Fantino actively supported Eves and Tory in these two elections. In the waning days of the mayoral campaign, in an interview with a Toronto radio station (CFRB), Fantino spoke again of the impossible obstacles he faced in a city with 'gun-crazed gangsters,' declaring that he had 350 fewer officers than he needed.

Nowhere in the political campaigning or in police authorities' approaches to crime was there any apparent interest in discussing the underlying causes of this violence. In the same radio interview, when the idea of community policing was raised, Fantino observed: 'Community policing, what does that mean? ... Does that mean we're going to go and flip hamburgers all day and watch the gunmen do their thing?' The following day, during a press conference, Fantino demanded an inquiry into the effectiveness of the entire justice system (Slinger 2003a).

Bromell and the Toronto Police Association also actively supported Tory, just as they had supported Eves in the provincial election. He declared that the police would vote for the party that supported law and order, and he warned that if the Liberals won, the police would march on Queen's Park in protest.

The Social Construction of Blackness and Otherness through Dominant Media Narratives

In chapter 2 we argued that public institutions are strongly linked when it comes to the production and reproduction of racialization and criminalization. This is especially true in relation to the media and agencies of social control (Hall et al. 1978; Gray 1995; Gandy 1998; Entman and Rojecki 2002; Wortley 2002; Henry and Tator 2002). The print and electronic media reinforce the image and message of 'otherness' that police officials express in dominant discourses. In this section we examine some of the dominant, hegemonic discourses that emerged in the aftermath of the *Star* series on race and crime. Columnists such as

Christie Blatchford, William Thorsell, Margaret Wente, and Peter Worthington reinforced the stigmatization and racialization of Blacks.

The Discourse of Talking about Race

One of the first themes to emerge during the debate over racial profiling involved a critical discourse on the media itself. Some journalists were criticized for deleting race as a descriptor in stories about crime and criminal activities – specifically, some reporters were criticized for their reluctance to note the race of alleged offenders. For example, in the *National Post* (29 October 2002), Christie Blatchford declared that sometimes race is simply a 'fact.' She began her article with a long description of the slaying of several Black men in Toronto, using highly emotional language: 'a veritable plethora of bereaved parents ... four children left fatherless including a baby girl ... brotherless siblings ...' She then shifted her focus to Fantino's press conference on the killings, noting that police spokespeople did not 'ever volunteer the enormous elephant awkwardly hulking in the corner of the room. That is, the single common denominator the police already had that link all the victims and all but one of the suspects. It is, alas and alack, skin colour.'

Her use of a metaphoric imagery sent a confusing message to readers. Why would a biological construct such as race be described as an elephant? The implicit message here was that the use of racial descriptors was a huge and unwieldy issue.

William Thorsell, the former editor of the *Globe and Mail*, in an opinion piece in that paper in 2002, discussed the issue of identifying race. After a lengthy introduction, he moved carefully and subtly to his main point. He referred to a magazine cover from the 1980s that showed the 'typical contents of a refrigerator in Toronto's Waspy Rosedale ... Cheez Whiz, white bread ... caught the brittle nerdishness of the Haute Wasps perfectly.' He described this media article as 'public racial profiling,' which was permitted then 'but probably wouldn't be allowed today, given how intimidated we have become about discussing the darker [!] sides of any distinctive culture.'

For him to describe that magazine cover, which focused on the 'rich and powerful,' as racial profiling was inaccurate and misleading; it also betrayed a total lack of understanding of how racism works. In representing the issue of racism – or racial profiling, which is the specific form of racism employed by police organizations – as a topic that also relates to the concerns of the rich and powerful, he was completely missing the point: racism is almost always directed at the powerless, and often the poor, in society. Moreover, we strongly question the use of the adjective 'darker' in this context; clearly, Thorsell was referring to the Black community and to some of the criminal activity alleged to be occurring in certain elements of it. 'Darkness' here played out on two levels: it implied not only the subject of his discourse – Black people - but also their alleged deviant, murderous behaviour.

Thorsell ended his piece by reiterating his main point: that 'troubling and dangerous' differences within communities need 'illumination and public discussion.' On a related subject, he commented that identifying a community in trouble – this time he specifically mentioned the Innu in Labrador – is not evidence of racism. He ended his column on a facetious note: 'Have you been called a racist recently? Just say no.' This dismissive ending seemed to be suggesting that issues such as racism are really not that important; a 'no' is all that is required.

Both Blatchford and Thorsell tackled the issue of political correctness, although neither used that term; rather, they challenged the 'sensitivity' to racial descriptors that had arisen in some sectors of society. In the following days and weeks, the debate over racial profiling shifted from the findings and implications of the *Star* series to embrace the subtler and more intrusive discourse of 'blame the victim.' Specifically, the Black (more to the point, Jamaican) community was not taking any responsibility; crime had become racialized ('Jamaicanized'); the issue as the media and others saw it was now 'Black-on-Black crime.'

The Discourse of the Jamaicanization of Crime

Peter Worthington was one of the first columnists to feature this issue. He began his column in the *Toronto Sun* (29 October 2002) by suggesting that while we all wait for the arrest of those who had shot and killed 'black guys ... lets look at the details.' The columnist wondered whether these victims were 'average black youths that the *Toronto Star* thinks are being unfairly profiled by police.' Then he answered his own query: 'Dunno.' Each time he asked a question, he answered it himself: 'Dunno.' Thus: 'How typical was ... better known as Peanuts, shot dead at age 21, the father of a two year old, a six week old and a three week old? Three different mothers of his children? Again, "dunno." Peanuts half brother (different father?) was wounded in the leg, for no reason says his mother describing Peanuts as always smiling. He cared for people, had dreams of big things in life ... Smokey was gunned down. Smokey was unemployed ... [and] leaves a three month old daughter ... Two excellent boys according to their father were shot ... Kevin leaves three children ...'

It seems that Worthington's main purpose was to draw attention to negative aspects of Jamaican culture. By constantly inserting the numbers of children these young men had left behind – children who had nothing to do with their fathers' deaths – he was telling his readers that these young men were not upstanding citizens minding their own business and getting shot. They were, in fact, unemployed gang members who had fathered too many children. (Later in the article he would refer to the importance of gangs in the Jamaican community.) This was argumentation in reverse – that is, saying one thing and conveying an entirely different meaning. He maintained that 'colour is not the issue here or in most black-on-black crimes. Culture is the issue. Jamaican culture.' He emphasized this point later when he singled out other communities of colour: 'It is grossly unfair for people from Nigeria, Ghana, South Africa, Trinidad, Barbados, etc. to be stopped by police because Jamaicans give them and other blacks a bad name. Who can blame non-Jamaicans for feeling resentful?'

Yet he provided no evidence that 'other Blacks' resented Jamaicans. He concluded his article by arguing strongly for racial profiling. He wondered aloud why it was 'profiling to keep a record of which part of society criminals come from.' He concluded that profiling is necessary in order to fight crime and that it is 'part of normal daily life.'

On 29 October 2002, *Globe and Mail* columnist Margaret Wente wrote a column on the same subject. In it, she touched on the silence around the subject of race as well as the Jamaicanization of crime. She described the murder of several Black youths on what she called 'Bloody Monday' and the press conference the police held about these murders. She called attention to the fact that Fantino had not mentioned the race of either the victims or the suspects. While Fantino did not answer the questions, Wente did in the following way: 'The answer is that all nine victims were black. All but one of the suspects is black too. What hung unmentioned in the air is something everyone knows so well it scarcely bears repeating. Violent black-on-black crime is a serious problem in Toronto.'

Using her freedom as a journalist, Wente noted the racial backgrounds of the dead. She acknowledged that our society (including leaders in the Black community) is conflicted about the keeping of race/crime statistics, and she made passing mention of the *Star*'s findings on police profiling. However, her focus in this article was on Black-on-Black crime. Again citing the *Star*, she described the facts 'about black crime in Toronto [as] rather grim' and noted that Jamaicans were disproportionately represented: 'What everyone knows but no one says in polite company is that the guns-and-drugs culture is heavily Jamaican, and it's spinning out of control.'

Continuing along these lines, she concluded that 'racial profiling has a context' – that racial profiling may be wrong but there are reasons why it happens. She argued that it had become a necessary strategy for the police because 9.5 per cent of charges laid for violent crimes were being committed (supposedly) by the 2.4 per cent of Toronto's population who were born in Jamaica.

What Wente did not point out was that non-Jamaicans – that is, White Canadians and members of other ethnic communities – must therefore commit 91.5 per cent of violent crimes. Clearly, White-on-White crime is not a sufficient provocation for allegations of racial profiling, but Black-on-Black crime – specifically, 'Jamaican on Jamaican' – is.

In a 2002 column (24 November) in the *Toronto Sun*, Tom Godfrey played on the same discursive themes – that is, Black-on-Black crime and Jamaican-on-Jamaican crime. The piece's title, 'Jamaica's Bloodbath May Spread to T.O. Cops Say,' was an attempt to reinforce fear and apprehension among readers. Its opening line alluded to a bloody gang turf war that would soon be 'felt on the streets of Toronto.' Godfrey sought to lend authenticity to the argument by adding that he was quoting a Jamaican official.

In a *Globe and Mail* article on 2 November 2002, Peter Cheney described the clubs in various parts of Toronto that cater mainly to Blacks. Many murders of young Black men have taken place in or near these clubs. A few paragraphs into this lengthy piece, he noted that Black leaders saw the killings as largely a consequence of the disadvantage and prejudice faced by young Black men; but besides that, they added, these Blacks were victims of a police force that typically failed to protect them. From that point on, however, the article proceeded to quote people who contended that the crimes were the result of a dysfunctional community. The 'blame the victim' discourse was obvious. For example, one of the club owners was quoted as saying that it had nothing to do with dysfunction: 'If people knew what was going on they'd be amazed, its like there's a war going on.'

Here, Cheney was resorting to hyperbole by proxy: these were not his words, but he had chosen to quote them. The tensions or conflicts between victims were being referred to as a 'war.' After describing some of the murders, the article noted that the clubgoers came from neighbourhoods that share 'dismal demographics': high unemployment, endemic poverty, and broken homes. Alleging that 'society has stayed clear of any discussion of whether race plays a role,' Cheney cited statistics from the *Star*'s series to show that Blacks and specifically Jamaicans were overrepresented. (Other *Star* statistics on police profiling were not presented.)

Continuing the discourses of blaming the victim and Jamaicanization, and using the familiar journalistic strategy of evidentiality, Cheney quoted a 'well-known' White criminal lawyer who had often defended Black clients: 'What we're seeing here is not black crime ... It's Jamaican crime. The guys committing all these shootings aren't Somalis. They're not Kenyans. They're Jamaican. The Jamaican-Canadian community has to start taking responsibility for its young men.' In drawing from these other origins, both the source and the journalist were presenting themselves as unprejudiced in that they were not criticizing all the groups in the Black community but only one section of that community.

Cheney made sure to use other sources of evidence. For example, he quoted Dudley Laws, chair of the Black Action Defense Committee, who acknowledged that there was a problem but attributed the killings to an 'overabundance of guns and drugs and a lack of employment ... The music culture is awful now.' But the article quickly went back to the lawyer, who told Cheney: 'This is a violent culture ... Canada has inherited Jamaica's crime problem.' The article concluded with another quote from the club owner, who was worried about his business: 'People see our name in the news, and they're afraid ... They think they're going to get shot.'

On 10 February 2003, Chief Fantino visited Jamaica. According to the *Sun*, the chief had accepted an invitation from that country's security minister to visit the island on a fact-finding mission to better understand the dynamics of its horrifying murder rate, which was among the highest in the world. While he was there, his activities were closely followed in Toronto's print and electronic media. Radio and TV stories presented numerous vivid accounts of poverty, degradation, slum life, ghettoization, and crime, and described an armed military and a strong police presence in the high-risk areas of Kingston. The emphasis throughout was on violence, guns, shootings, and murders.

Also noted was the security surrounding embassies and other official areas. Fantino praised the efforts of Jamaican officials and police to maintain some degree of social control in a country that had been over-run by violence. Overall, Jamaica was presented as the murder capital of the world.

Even the *Star* found itself caught up in the web of 'othering' and 'Jamaicanization' in relation to Fantino's visit to Jamaica. Scott Simmie, one of the reporters who had worked on the *Star*'s racial profiling series, was sent to Jamaica to report on the poverty, despair, and vio-lent crime in that country. He wrote (24 November 2002) that the 'plague of guns and violence' in Kingston had become 'white noise in pockets of the impoverished ghettos that demarcate the capital.' This very long article described a country whose urban areas were a huge ghetto controlled by 'dons.' Simmie interviewed police and other offi-cials in Jamaica, who reinforced this negative picture of the country. It is ironic that the same newspaper that spearheaded the discursive event that placed the racial profiling of Blacks on the public agenda was also responsible for reinforcing a negative discourse on the Jamai-canization of crime.

Summary of Media Discourses

These articles reflected a number of recurring themes, including con-flict, tensions, violent behaviour, shootings, killings, guns, weaponry, and drugs; they also highlighted social problems such as poverty, unemployment, and substandard housing. Jamaica and Jamaicans were strongly implicated in all of this. The articles, while attempting to be explanatory and analytic, on the whole used strongly hyperbolic and stereotypic language that left readers with a strongly negative image of Jamaican culture and communities. Throughout these media discourses on the Jamaicanization of crime, almost nothing positive was said about the country. There was no reference to Jamaica's vibrant art, music, literature, and cuisine. There was no mention of the strong communities and loving intergenerational relationships that are still a vital part of Jamaican life. What was largely ignored is that Jamaica is a relatively stable democracy with a Westminster-style parliamentary government. On the media's part, this was classic one-sidedness: the emphasis was entirely on negatives; the more positive aspects of Jamaican society were ignored.

The journalists cited here were all writing in response to the crisis evoked by the *Star*'s series on racial profiling. Drawing from their own racialized ideologies, these columnists developed hegemonic narratives that resonated among the ideologically conservative segments of the community. The journalists cited above showed little understanding of the pain and humiliation experienced by the victims of racial profiling. Instead, they saw such events and situations through a White gaze – that is, through the lens of their White experiences, interpretations, and understandings of the world. Other columnists did write features in support of the victims of racial profiling; that said, the press leaned heavily towards is own dominant White interpretation of events.

We are told that the discourse of political correctness is the reason why race has been deleted from discussions of criminal activity. But then we are told that the deviant activities of groups within racial minority communities must be fully exposed by identifying the role of race. When the heavily racialized discourse of Jamaicanization is constantly raised, the audience – even people who may not share a writer's negative views – is led to believe that Jamaicans commit more crimes than other groups. Given that there is so little positive coverage of Jamaican communities in the mainstream media (see Henry and Tator 2002; Benjamin 2003; Wortley 2002), this race-driven discourse can only strengthen the linkages among crime, Jamaicans, and racial profiling.

Afterword

The Impact of Racial Profiling on Black Officers in the Toronto Police Service

While we were completing this book, there was a startling breakthrough: revelations came to light about racial profiling inside the Toronto Police Service itself. In October 2003, at the height of the racial profiling crisis, while Chief Fantino was still in a state of total denial that racial profiling was happening, he authorized a focus group of thirty-eight Black officers, led by four of the service's most senior Black officers. The group came together to discuss what it was like to be a Black officer on a force that was facing allegations of racial profiling. They also discussed how racial profiling influenced their own professional and personal lives.

The documents and notes generated by this focus group were obtained by the *Star*; overall, they demonstrated that racial profiling was consistently experienced on the force. In fact, most of the focus group's participants said that they themselves had been inappropriately stopped while off duty. Three said they had been stopped more than once in a single week. There was a strong consensus within the group that racial profiling was a serious problem and that the Toronto Police Service would have to deal with it internally if anything was to change.

On 8 November 2003, a police-only conference was held on 'Policing a Diverse Community.' The sponsors were the International Association of Chiefs of Police and the Ontario Association of Chiefs of Police. The four senior Black officers presented an 'edited' version of the focus group's findings, as they felt that the information that had been shared during group discussions was too shocking to deliver unedited. They began by declaring: 'We know racial profiling exists.' Two weeks after the conference, a complete version of the presentation was presented to the senior levels of the Toronto Police Service. A few weeks later, Fantino met with the focus group and heard their comments first-hand. He promised that specific allegations would be investigated by the force's Professional Standards body. No action was ever taken. For the next sixteen months, Fantino continued to deny that the Toronto Police Service conducted racial profiling.

The results of the internal consultation were not made public until 31 March 2005. The publication of these findings was linked to a racial profiling incident involving one of the few Black senior officers on the Toronto police. On 20 February 2005 a Black police inspector was sitting in the compound of the yard of the police station in Toronto waiting for his turn to fill up at the gas pump when a uniformed junior constable approached him and asked for identification (the inspector was not in uniform and was in an unmarked police car). After the inspector showed the junior constable his identity card, he wondered out loud whether the constable would have challenged a White police officer in the same circumstances. According to the inspector's lawyer, this was yet another example of the sort of differential treatment he had experienced one too many times in his career: 'It was the straw that broke the camel's back.' Incredibly, the constable felt that the inspector had acted inappropriately and laid a complaint against him before the force's disciplinary body. A meeting was convened, attended by the inspector and his lawyer as well as the constable and representatives from the police association. Other senior officers were present and decided that there were no grounds for the constable's complaint. After the meeting, the two shook hands, and the inspector believed that this was the end of the incident. Later, however, the union demanded that the inspector apologize to the constable. This led to the 'outing' of the Black officers' focus group, which had been held sixteen months earlier. When questioned by the *Star* in March 2005, Fantino said he couldn't recall whether any incidents raised by the officers had led to formal complaints. Also, he was not sure whether any investigations had been launched. But he was quick to reassure the reporter that he considered his approach to the issue of racial profiling to be 'exemplary.'

In the focus group documents, the following manifestations of racism within the force were identified:

- 'Differential enforcement activities.'
- Derogatory comments directed at Black officers and civilians. Black officers were reluctant to report these, fearing ostracism by fellow officers.
- The stereotype that Black motorists in expensive cars received extra attention was confirmed by Black officers.
- Apathy among senior officers regarding racist behaviour. This included the protection of 'rotten apples' and ineffective or non-existent remedies for racism on the job. In one instance, an officer allegedly referred to Black citizens riding bicycles as 'chimps on bikes,' and the acronym 'COB' was used on one of the in-car computer screens.
- White officers who hold the stereotype that Black officers are lazy.
- The perception among Black officers that they are not allowed the same margin of error as White officers.
- A lack of change in the overall climate despite a zero tolerance stance taken by Fantino.
- The belief among Black officers (who wanted to defend the organization) that nothing could be done externally until internal issues were dealt with.
- Racial misconduct. All of the officers in the focus group had either experienced or witnessed it.
- Being stopped for insufficient reason while off duty. Most of the focus group members felt they had been subjected to this. Half a dozen said they had been stopped more than twelve times in a year, and three said they had been stopped more than once in a one-week span.
- Overreliance on racial profiling. Most of the officers stated that racial profiling (as opposed to criminal profiling) was a poor policing tool.
- Systemic racism on the force. Most of the officers saw strong indica-

tors of this and contended that it reinforced the practice of racial profiling. The same systemic racism led to barriers to promotion.
• Reluctance among police to face the realities of policing a diverse
community.

In the summary to the conference notes, the senior Toronto officers
emphasized (a) that Black officers had the best interests of their organizations and communities at heart and (b) that racial profiling was a
product of racism and the organization's culture. They spoke of the
importance of addressing the root causes of the problem, rather than
adopting measures to mask the symptoms (Mascoll and Rankin 2005).

Conclusions

The discursive crisis over the *Star* series on race and crime offers critical insights into the ways in which dominant racialized discourses are
used to deny that racial profiling of Blacks takes place and to deflect
attention away from the general issue of racism in policing. The dominant narratives examined in this chapter included statements articulated by powerful public figures who were responsible for maintaining
social control and who had specific authority within or over the police.
Dominant discourses also emerged from the media. All of these discourses were based on the denial of racism. The White gaze is also an
important feature of these discourses, and draws on the constructions
of Black people as the deviant 'other.' White officials used an invisible
coded language to distinguish and divide 'them' from 'us.' The discourse of moral panic contained symbolic images and ideas also
encountered in the text and talk of the White elite; these reflected the
widespread perception that civil society was descending into a state of
lawlessness and disorder.

A defining aspect of hegemonic discourses is that dominant narratives become 'public transcripts,' which then legitimize the position
and power of the dominant White elite; these transcripts also ensure
that counter-narratives go unheard. From the perspective of the dominant narrative, the stories framed by the experiences of the Black police
officers and the Black community had to be censored and silenced. In
the next chapter, Maureen Brown analyses some of the oppositional
discourses and counter-narratives that have challenged 'the official
story' of racial profiling.

7 In Their Own Voices: African Canadians in Toronto Share Experiences of Police Profiling

MAUREEN BROWN

> Stories reconfigure the past, endowing it with meaning and continuity, and so also project a sense of what will or should happen in the future.
> (Davis 2002, 12)

Narrative is one of the most powerful tools available to paint a multi-dimensional portrait of a community's experience. I found this especially true as I interviewed African Canadians in the Greater Toronto Area for a study on racial profiling by the police. The study was commissioned by the African Canadian Community Coalition on Racial Profiling (ACCCRP), an ad hoc group formed in the wake of widespread allegations that police single out Blacks for negative treatment. Youth and adults, city dwellers and GTA residents, wealthy suburbanites and inner-city poor – all told me that from their own experience, they believed firmly that the police use race as a factor in determining who is likely to commit or has likely committed a crime. All of these people spoke of their anger, pain, and loss of innocence, as well as their haunting fear that as Blacks, they could not expect the same treatment or benefit of the doubt as others receive in this society. Their stories, taken together, sketch a group of people forged by soul-searing experiences that only they, the tellers, can truly appreciate.

The following points guided the study:

1. African Canadians believe that as a group they are singled out by police, who stop and question them as they go about their business. They complain of police body searches, verbal abuse, name calling,

and the apparent assumption that if they are driving a 'nice' car, it could well be a stolen car.

2. Racial profiling is *not* the problem of a single police service. Respondents were drawn from across the GTA, and at least one of them told of being stopped by the Ontario Provincial Police while he was driving on the highway.

3. Racial profiling as a societal issue needs to be chronicled. We cannot manage what we cannot measure, nor can we deny what we have not documented.

One African-Canadian police officer told me that racial profiling is not an academic issue. 'When you experience it,' he said, 'you know it.'

Through their stories, the respondents were challenging society to think about the experiences that African Canadians have with the police, and to let those experiences serve as a catalyst for increased police accountability, which they believed would strengthen the Black community's confidence in the law enforcement system. *In Their Own Voices* did not set out to 'prove' that racial profiling exists, nor did it examine the motives of individual officers in their encounters with African Canadians.[1] The report avoided the question, 'Does racial profiling by police happen?' Instead, through narrative, it explored this question: 'What is it about the experiences that Blacks are having with the police that can leave them often feeling disrespected, targeted, and victims of racial profiling, also known as racially biased policing?' In their responses, people shared stories that offered a glimpse of the unease that many African Canadians feel when their sons, daughters, and spouses go through the door. Even for the most ardent supporters of the police, the issue was not whether their loved ones stood a chance of being unreasonably questioned by police, but rather how these incidents should be regarded and handled.

The Interviews

The respondents entered the study through a variety of doors. Community organizers and municipal recreational workers paved the way for me to interview youth. Also, I randomly interviewed people at local basketball courts and other hangouts, and well as participants at

---

1 For a copy of *In Their Own Voices* and its companion report, *Crisis Conflict and Accountability*, contact the African Canadian Legal Clinic in Toronto.

conferences. Many interviewees saw profiling as an inseparable part of being Black. The point of these interviews was not to establish through numbers the extent of racial profiling of African Canadians. Rather, it was to show what profiling — or 'racially biased policing' – looks like through the eyes of African Canadians who have experienced it.

Getting to the Truth

Sceptics will challenge the oppositional narratives I present in this chapter by asking one of two questions (or both): Are the interviewees telling the truth? And are these just 'a few' people who 'occasionally' have negative encounters with maverick police officers? The answers to both questions should interest all sectors of society, from community workers who advocate on behalf of profiled community members; to faith groups who, increasingly, are weighing in on the issue; to law-makers charged with maintaining our social fabric of justice and equity. The stories should be of particular interest to police services. If in the course of their duties ('to serve and protect'), police are using race as a factor in determining 'criminality' or 'criminal propensity,' and if these practices are being 'unintentionally systemically facili-tated' by police organizations and by society – a belief held by the Association of Black Law Enforcers (ABLE) and many others – we should all *want* to hear the voices of community members whose expe-riences differ from what police services contend. And we should be prepared to accept the validity of these voices.

The stories I heard during the interviews were consistent among themselves; they were also consistent with stories from jurisdictions beyond the GTA. Still, to make sure I was not 'putting words in peo-ple's mouths,' I invited the respondents to share positive experiences with the police as well, if they felt that these more appropriately defined their experiences with the police. Some did share positive experiences. Some – very much the minority – even offered narratives that others would read as profiling, but which they saw as profes-sional, by-the-book police work. I felt it was important to include *all* voices, since the dominant discourse is not exclusive to Whites.

Perception versus Reality

A powerful weapon sometimes used to challenge narratives about racial profiling involves the old 'perception versus reality' argument.

Are African Canadians really being profiled? Or do they merely *perceive* that they are? Interestingly, some experts see nothing wrong per se with describing one's life experiences as a function of perception. The question, though, is 'Whose perception is to be believed?' For that matter, 'Whose perceptions enter the public "transcript" that we all take for granted?'

The interviews suggested a simple answer: 'Perception *is* reality.' This does not mean that every perceived act of profiling is in fact so. The trouble with perception, though, is that it plays a significant role in interactions between African Canadians and the police. Perception affects *both* sides of these encounters. It seems that police, like other members of society, are affected by popular notions of what to expect from African Canadians just as much as African Canadians are affected by popular notions of what to expect from police. The result is a lethal brew of fear, posturing, suspicion, and distrust that can ratchet even a simple encounter up to levels that lead to arrest, resistance, a criminal record, and 'confirmation' that police dislike African Canadians and/or that African Canadians are 'predisposed to crime.' Perhaps the best way to demonstrate how this can happen is through the following scenario involving Marlon, Tariq, and Officer Smith (these people are composites based on my interviews).

The Stories

Marlon, Tariq, and Officer Smith

Parents, friends, and his own experience have taught Marlon that the police are his friends and that he should feel free to approach them. He therefore has no second thoughts when Officer Smith approaches him as he walks home from a party and asks him for his name and identification. He does not react 'with attitude' when the officer asks him to empty his pockets and his backpack. In fact, he does not even question what Officer Smith means when he says that this is a 'routine check' and a 'routine pat-down.' The term racial profiling does not cross his mind.

Officer Smith has a job to do – a job he loves and of which he is proud. He has chosen his profession because he believes in an ordered society. But he also finds fulfilment in helping lost children, protecting seniors from muggers, raising funds for charity, and protecting the community from dangers seen and unseen. Officer Smith has no particular philosophy about African Canadians as a group. What he does have is an 'instinct' for crime and, from experience, a gut sense of the types of people likely to commit particular crimes.

Tariq did not have the upbringing Marlon did. Actually, he did, but his experience led him to change his view of the police by the time he was fifteen. A bright, perceptive young man, he loves his high school law course and plans to become a lawyer. So when Officer Smith approaches him and a couple of his friends one night and orders them up against the wall for a search, he has many questions, which he asks the officer: 'Why are you doing this?' 'What did we do wrong?' 'Don't you have to have reasonable and probable grounds to stop us like this?'

Officer Smith is in no mood to engage in a social science lesson with a fifteen-year-old. 'It's a routine pat-down,' he replies, adding, 'You people think you're bad, don't you?' Reluctantly, Tariq submits to the search. His friends seem undisturbed as they do the same. Later, they laugh the incident off. They have seen and experienced this type of treatment before. They actually scold Tariq for talking back to The Man. 'Don't do that next time,' they admonish him. The Man does not like to be challenged. It's the quickest way into the back seat of a cruiser and onto the path away from law school. Tariq's questions turn to anger, especially when other friends at school to whom he recounts the incident react with the same kind of 'so where have you been' attitude his friends demonstrated that night.

Are Marlon and Tariq victims of racial profiling? In the term proposed by a Joint Working Group of the Toronto Police Services Board, were they targets of 'racially biased policing'? Was Officer Smith merely doing his job, or was he a racist maverick who under cover of a dark uniform engaged in the uncommon act of racial profiling? Does it matter what label society places on the exchanges that night? Should we be concerned about Tariq's growing anger? about Officer Smith's policing methods? about Marlon's blitheness? about the acceptance on the part of Tariq's friends that they live in a society in which they have no right to ask why they are being randomly searched by a police officer? Who is the victim, and who is the villain?

Strangers in a Foreign Land

Perception (or misperception), whatever its source, serves as a great divide when racial profiling is discussed. Many of the respondents believed they were on the losing side of that divide. From their perspective, they may often be viewed as a threat to society, but it is the police, they said, who are equipped with guns, batons, Tasers, and two-way radios. It is the police who can easily summon an army of scout cars for back-up, and who have a powerful union and – most critically – the public's good will. For African Canadians who see things this way, police racial profiling is merely an extension of society's desire to keep them in their place.

Their reactions to police, then, are woven into the overall landscape of their lives. They filter police behaviour towards them through 'lenses' such as those used by a group of youth who put together a recent African-Canadian submission to the UN Rapporteur on Race in 2004:

> I am The African Canadian Youth ... feared by some, reviled by others, misunderstood by even many who try to help me, regarded with hope by those who believe I can Rise. The first thing you need to know about me is that like all other Canadians I am offered protections under the laws of this country. As a matter of fact, the Government Official will show you the policies, programs [and] initiatives that she will say are designed for youth. I am a youth and in her eyes there is nothing stopping me from reaching out and taking my share of the pie. Even my parents sometimes chide me for not taking my share of what [African-Canadian author Cecil Foster] says is, in the eyes of an immigrant generation, 'a place called heaven.' And when I marvel at the gleam of Corporate Canada; when I see the Good Life in TV ads; when I hear of scholarship programs and opportunities to travel and[of] an offer of a second chance under the *Youth Criminal Justice Act*, I see why to some this is a place called heaven. But there is another side of Paradise that you need to visit. This side is not included in The Guided Tour. It's not on the map. As a matter of fact, were it not for me and for those who fight on my behalf, you wouldn't even know it existed. It's our own little family secret ... our Secret Garden of weeds, underbrush and Unacknowledged Spaces.

A Deep and Complex Rage

Forever seared in listeners' minds is the broken voice of an African-Canadian businessman as he described to a joint ACCCRP-OHRC focus group the treatment he received at the hands of security personnel and later the police after a seemingly simple act of returning merchandise went horribly wrong. It's difficult to watch a grown man cry. It's gut-wrenching to watch a tall, distinguished-looking African-Canadian businessman hang his head as he tries to fight back tears. 'They've broken me,' he says softly. 'They've broken me.' What the businessman described that day was not just a debatable act of racial profiling – debatable as in 'Was I treated this way because I'm Black, or because I deserved it?' He was placing the treatment meted out to him by law enforcement officers in the context of shattered expectations of how a person *should* be treated in such an incident. He was echoing Tariq's disillusionment with the vision of courtesy one normally expects when one is angry while dealing with the police, though not necessarily rude.

The businessman was expressing the same feelings as held by Dudley, who agreed to be interviewed for *In Their Own Voices* only after much persuasion. Dudley had buried the memories of the night he was accosted by a police officer while he and his friends were leaving a nightclub. He told his story hesitantly, brushing away the memories as one would an invisible fly. Dudley's calm exterior belied a deep and complex rage, which nevertheless seeped out through his words and through his body language. His rage was deep because he had tied his experiences with the police to other disappointments in life – disappointments he attributed partly to his status as a Black man in society, and partly to his failure to listen to his mother and to the bad choices he had made as a result. In Dudley's eyes there were few socially acceptable ways of expressing how he felt. His rage was complex because at twenty-seven, his encounters with the police were colliding with the dawning reality that he would never be an NBA star. Dudley had no marketable skill, and he felt like a failure.

The respondents placed clear responsibility for police misbehaviour at the feet of the police services themselves – although some felt that those who feel targeted 'must have' done something to attract police attention. At the same time, interviewees on both sides of the fence saw solutions in the form of a partnership among the police, African-Canadian youth, local African-Canadian communities, and society at large. The stories were sometimes heart breaking. Some reflected wilful acts on the part of police officers. Others suggested that 'how things are done' has a unique impact on African-Canadian communities – a clear reflection of the 'unintentional systemic facilitation' that ABLE speaks about.

The African-Canadian respondents *did not* expect police to overlook it if they were carrying drugs when stopped. They *did* expect that – as per the law – they would be stopped only if officers had reasonable and probable grounds to believe they were carrying drugs. They knew that if the licence plates were missing from their car they could be stopped and that once stopped they could be asked for ID. They *did not* expect that while they were walking along the street, the police would pull up and ask for ID as part of a 'routine check.' They *did not* deny that African Canadians had their share of lawbreakers among them, as with any other subgroup in society. They *did* wonder what others – who are not stopped and searched as often – have in *their* backpacks and cars as they pass smugly by. In the end, the respondents sought fair and equitable treatment, not special treatment.

Anatomy of Profiling

What does profiling look like? What does it feel like? Is it deliberate? Is it circumstantial? Is it an element of good policing? Does it yield the desired results? To help locate the many stories, I took the liberty of naming the categories of profiling-related behaviours – often in terms used by the speakers.

Use of Force

A mother of three in her thirties submitted a written account of what she considered police use of excessive force. The incident involved a group of Black youth. She believed that the use of force was triggered by the police's perception that a young Black man had perpetrated the incident. From what she had seen, they were wrong. Merlene normally did not get involved in these kinds of issues. Horrified by what she had witnessed, however, she offered to testify on behalf of a fifteen-year-old African-Canadian boy after she saw him arrested and beaten.

> At around 10:30 pm, my husband and I pulled into the parking lot of a [fast food] restaurant, located [outside Toronto]. On entering the lot, I witnessed a group of 20–30 youths, surrounding a security guard, due to a fight, which had happened earlier on. A black youth in particular, was persistently going after the security guard, in a bullish behaviour. A young girl and another black (male) youth were trying to prevent the situation from getting worse.
>
> We continued to stick around and observe the confrontation. I became

afraid of what the outcome might bring, so I called 911 and reported, 'We've been in the lot for about 8-10 minutes, and there seems to be no backup in site' [sic]. During the 911 call sounds of sirens were evident and I ended the call. When the youth who was going after the guard heard the sirens he ran off, which led to a foot chase by the guard north on [an adjacent road] where the youth disappeared.

From then on things turned for the worst. The security guard was seen afterwards, running west of [the Road], followed by a black youth holding a piece of 'iron pipe'. The youth confronted him in what appeared to be a non-harming manner. We continued to observe. By then the police cruisers, started surrounding the area. At least four police officers came to the guard's rescue, one of whom jumped the youth [Grant] from behind and pinned him face down, in an arresting gesture. Grant did not appear to be resisting arrest or even had the chance of fighting back. He did, however, say to the officer 'What are you trying to do, aren't you going to read me my rights.' By then, he was handcuffed, still facing downward.

All of a sudden the officer drew his baton and started to severely beat Grant with it. In the midst of all this, the security guard did try telling them, that 'he (Grant) was not the one causing the fight.'

I stood steps away from the situation, watching the officer making the arrest, in amazement. I distinctly, stood there, saying out loud, 'I cannot believe what I'm seeing. This is so not right and unfair. It's wrong, I cannot believe it.' One of the officers turned in surprise and shone his flashlight at me. He pointed to the piece of pipe in his hand and said 'Ma'am, he was trying to hit the security guard with it.' I said to the officer, 'I did not see that and it's wrong, the way you are hitting him.' The arresting officer pulled Grant up, walked him across the street to the parked cruiser, and put him in the back seat. The security guard was standing around with total loss of control.

In Merlene's view, the police had acted in a racially biased manner. Why did they not ask her for a statement even after she told them she had seen the incident? Why was Grant's mother prevented from speaking to him, especially given that he was underage? Why did at least some of the officers not try to gather information that would have helped them find the earlier aggressor? And, most critically, why did the police beat the boy after he was handcuffed?

Merlene's story was not unique. One family services worker in an inner-city neighbourhood watched the police take a young Black male off a bus. It was in the middle of winter, she told me, and the youth's coat somehow came undone. He had been travelling with his little sister, who began to panic and scream when she saw what was happening to her brother. The police, the worker said, threw the youth face down on the frozen car, where they held him for a prolonged period, despite his pleas to let him put his coat on. As his sister continued crying and trying to help her brother, the officer, she said, grabbed the child roughly and held her up from the ground.

In another account, a woman – also a community recreational worker – watched from her ground-floor apartment while officers chased a young teen across a parking lot. They caught up with him and began to search him. They pulled a small quantity of drugs from his pocket and then felt something else inside. They threw the boy to the ground, handcuffed him, and began to search his pockets. Then they began to slam him into the ground. While they were doing so, an asthma inhaler rolled out of his pocket. She told me the officers kept slamming the boy until she and others ran out of the apartment telling them to stop. She shouted at them: 'We've seen too many of our young men die like this.'

A twenty-nine-year-old mother of four named Patsy gave a similar account. One morning, the police detained her for leaving her children overnight without proper supervision, following a message that the children were not in school. Patsy admitted that she had been wrong to leave her children while she went to the doctor and her husband went to work:

> When I got to the station they told me to explain myself. [I did]. Then they locked me in a room by myself and turned the air conditioning on really cold … Then they take me to this [other room]. They chain my feet and they chain my hands behind me and one of my hands was sick and I said to them that my right hand is not well, it broke or slipped out. They tighten the cuff really tight and they start to push me really hard for no reason at all. I [hadn't] killed nobody.
>
> It was in November and the way that I [was] frightened I didn't wear a jacket and my husband take my jacket for me and they tell him that I'm OK. I told them that I am cold. And you know what they do? They take a blanket that they use to cover the dog with and give it to me. I said no, this [is] full of dog hair. They said, 'Well, we have nothing else for you.' I said can I get one from my house and they said no.
>
> They were really rough with me. The only name [they didn't call me]

was 'Gal.' They were shouting and getting really upset. They hold my head down and push my head into the corner. I said, 'I'm a lady you know' and they said, 'So?' They deal with me like a nobody ... [And] they write on the report that I am mentally ill. So if anybody wants a report on me that's what is stuck in the report.

Regarding another incident, Patsy said she called the police after a teacher grabbed her daughter, leaving deep scratch marks around her neck. When the police arrived, they told her the 'teacher had the right to do whatever they want to do':

I said, 'What?' I am not telling you a lie, I was cussing when they said that ... I was really not satisfied with [how they treated me] and I went back over to the station ... They said, 'You know what, get out ... This is not the reason why police station is here.' That's what they said. I don't care [if the police recognize me from this story]. A stoppage have to be done.

Tagging and Clocking

'Tagging' and 'clocking' take many forms. The first is The Look.

Youth know the power of The Look. Anthony was a recent scholarship winner on his way to studying in the United States. He described himself as having been there, done that. He said he had engaged in robberies, fights, and thefts, been expelled from school, and spent time in jail ... all before he turned eighteen. In the focus group, Anthony sounded more like a motivational speaker than a delinquent.

'A Look,' he explained,

will start a war between two communities ... Two people from different [inner city communities] come to the mall. Eye contact will start a beef between the two people. When they go outside the mall they will want to fight. Then a whole gang comes in. Then another gang ... Just that look. It's powerful ... The first thing that comes to my mind will always be the negative.

When it comes to the police, he said, The Look is a game of chicken: a war of nerves to see who will blink first. If the youth blinks, the police feel they have something to hide, or that they are giving attitude.

Banks, fifteen, supported this: '[The police] will look at you, clocking you. Like they expect you to do something.' Anthony continued:

It's a daring look. A dirty look that that expects you to react negatively. Because obviously, if I smile at you you're going to smile back at me. If I give you a grudge look you're going to give me one back. Obviously if you do that [to the police], they [the police] are going to come and do something to you. These days The Look is the most effective weapon of all. It makes me feel bad … because I know I am not [a bad] person.

Anthony likened the feeling generated by The Look to how he felt in jail, when bars, orders, and rules governed his every move:

I'm caged up. This world is like a cage because you can't move freely. There's people telling you when to leave, [where] to go, how to do [things]. To tell you the truth, sometimes I feel real bad knowing that I'm paying the price for someone else's bad deeds.

Then, Anthony said, there is The Trap:

You go by certain parking lots and you'll see ten squad cars. And if you pass they will question you, they'll want to tag you, they'll frame you, put stuff on you, try to set you up.

According to the respondents, The Trap usually involves establishing a strong presence in a conspicuous part of a neighbourhood, such as a parking lot. There the police wait. And wait. According to the police themselves, they're waiting to see if criminal activity will take place. According to the youth, they're waiting for some kid to lose nerve – or, in the officer's interpretation, display guilt – and run. It's downhill from there as The Chase begins. Once The Chase is on, most young respondents told me, they don't care if you're guilty or innocent. You run. They run and the police chase.[2]

The Pat Down is humiliating to innocent people going about their business. Many of younger respondents in different parts of the GTA talked about having their pockets and personal belongings searched at random by the police while they walked home. For some, The Pat Down is a part of tagging or clocking – almost a regular part of life.

Tom, eighteen, had lived in his 905 community for only a couple of

---

2 As indicated in many interviews, the reason some youth run is that they try to avoid any kind of engagement with the police, or because they feel the police will harass them in some way.

months when he had his first Pat Down. He had just arrived from a Caribbean island in the middle of winter to join his parents. He was in high school and working two part-time jobs. One morning he was waiting at a coffee shop across from the building where he worked. While waiting for his building to open, he huddled against the cold, pulling his hood around his face. Suddenly a police cruiser pulled up and the officers asked him what he was doing there. His explanation was not good enough for them, and before long he was draped over the hood of the cold cruiser being searched and patted down. Tom had no ill feelings towards the police, even though the experience was intimidating and humiliating.

Name Calling and Intimidation

Kofi was walking to a suburban mall with friends when a police car drove by. The officer, he said, called out to him: 'Get out of the road, nigger.' Another time, he was accompanying a relative to a hearing at the courthouse when the detectors went off. All the youth were wearing metal belt buckles, and those had triggered the alarm. All checked out clean. His relative's buckle was shaped like a gun. An officer told him to take the belt off. The youth asked him, 'Why? It's a belt.' He said he couldn't remove his belt or his pants would fall. 'They tried to beat him up for no reason,' Kofi said. 'The officer went to his car, got his .45 and cocked it for no reason. They grabbed him, pulled him up [off the floor], put him in the elevator. My cousin said the police cocked guns on him and all that.' His cousin was later charged for 'DTP' – disturbing the peace. 'It was kind of stupid.'

Routine Checks

> Luckily, I stay two steps ahead of [the police]. But does that mean that everybody has to stay three steps in front of the police? It's not fair. (Dwayne, twenty-one)

Of all police behaviours interviewees questioned, The Routine Check seemed most controversial. The term came up often, especially among inner-city youth when they told me the reason police gave for searching and or questioning them at random. Older interviewees – including a retired police officer – also shared stories of being checked:

When [the police] say it's a routine check. Like let me see your driver's licence ... Or that you fit the description of somebody. If you are speeding those are legit arguments. (Lawrence, retired police officer, mid-fifties)

Me and my friend were just walking home from school and got pulled over by the cops. They pulled their stuff on him, like 'Freeze! Freeze!' They said he fit the description of someone that was making gunfire, because he was tall, Black, and had a white shirt on ... They handcuffed him and put him in the backseat. (Nick, seventeen)

Sometimes I'll be walking by myself ... or with a group of people ... Near my house or in my neighbourhood when out of the blue, for no reason they'll be driving their cars and stop us and they'll be asking us for ID [or if you're packing a weapon]. I don't know for what reason. It takes place in broad daylight or any time else ... They just want to harass you 'cause they're bored probably. (ibid.)

Whenever they check my information they always find ... everything up to date. So then that's the only excuse they can give me. They say they have a right to stop us and give us a routine check. 'That's my job,' one officer said to me ... when I asked him why did he pull me over ... Most times [my friends] don't even want to see [the police]. If they see a police officer coming they make a left, or a right, because it's just not worth it to them, you know. They don't have time to be held up by them for no reason. [My White friends] say they can get away with anything ... We talk about it all the time.' (Herman, mechanic shop owner)

Herman's White friend has 'that edge ... He doesn't try to use it over us; he just uses it to his advantage because he knows he can get away with it.' White friends, he says, drive around with expired licence plates: 'Ten day passes expired for month ... and they just keep driving.'

The Description

They gave him some BS excuse about him stealing shoes ... said he fit the description of somebody they thought stole shoes from the mall. (Nick, seventeen)

In an inner-city neighbourhood, the police stopped Bryan and his friends and took their names down 'for no reason.' When officers in the same neighbourhood stopped Sam and asked his name, he refused to tell them, asking instead: 'Am I under arrest?' The officers left him alone. According to Sam: 'When you know your rights they know they can't do anything to you. The only thing they can do is catch you some other time and try to beat up on you or whatever.' Others, like sixteen-year-old Simon, give the police a name ... but not their real name. Sometimes, he says, 'I tell the police my Mom says not to talk to strangers and I just walk off. Why should I tell them my name? They write [our names] in their little notebook. They ask us if we have criminal records.'

Kevin, seventeen, said he 'avoids' the police when they patrol his neighbourhood: 'They usually pick on people in a big group.' He felt, however, that the police are justified in randomly interrogating youth. Sangster, seventeen, agreed that the police are justified in asking youth personal questions, but added that they sometimes go overboard:

Sometimes they get mad. They get out of their car and harass people because they don't want to answer their questions. They think they are bad and they'll just check them for no reason. They don't [even] introduce themselves because they say that they are cops and they have the higher authority. No one enjoys being searched but what are you going to do when the cops have you in a corner and searching you? You can't do nothing. If you complain they are normally going to win 'cause they are going to lie on you. They have power because if they suspect you to be doing something bad they can put you in jail for twenty-four hours.

Is there a generic profile of the African-Canadian criminal? The pattern of these stories tended to be either no description given, or a description so universal it could fit half of African Canadians in an urban setting:

I was walking in a plaza and they [the police] pulled up on me and said I fit the description of somebody and asked me for ID. So I said no. I know my rights. They can't tell me nothing. I took classes about that at school. They ask me for my name and I tell them, 'No – am I under arrest?' And he doesn't say nothing ... When you know your rights you actually know what you can do and what you can't do. You also know what they can do and what they can't. (Claude, sixteen)

I was chilling [on the street] and there was a drug raid. Ten minutes after the raid since there was me and two friends the cops came. [He and his friends were crossing a school parking lot at night] They did a 360 in front of us and pulled their guns and said, 'Do you know what happened with the drug raid' ... Start feeling up our pockets. They found a bag with sugar in it from my candies and were, like, 'This is cocaine! Get down! Give us your names!' It was horrible. They put us up against the wall. We were like, 'It's sugar. Smell it.' He smelled it and he was, like, 'Do you know those people over there? Why are you looking over there?' We were, like, 'We're walking home.' He was, like, 'You're lying to us. Give us your names, your student cards and all this stuff,' 'cause they thought we were dealing for the guy. They let us go and then they made up a weird excuse that we were loitering and next time they catch us they would give us a ticket. (Shabbah, fourteen)

I was walking home from school and they [the police] pulled up and started harassing me for no reason ... said I fit the description of someone they were looking for. After that they fling me in the car, banged my head into the car trunk. One of them searched me and one used his thing [nightstick] and hit me in my head. I told [a community worker] and she told me to file a complaint but I never did. I don't like causing problems so I just left it alone. (Mica, late teens)

I'm not going to cooperate with them. When I see them and they ask me for help I say no and go about my business. Or I just ignore them. Some of my friends know them because they [the police in their area] beat them up before. A group of them come around here ... drive around and try to pick on the kids. We know all their names, so when we see them we have to run from them like we are criminals. Even when we are playing ball and we see them, we just drop the ball and run. What kind of life is that? That's not the life I want to live. I have no charge or anything like that. But I have to run because they are going to beat me too. I don't want to get beaten by any police. (ibid.)

Power Play

Several interviewees described a kind of unspoken power play with police:

As a Black man – God bless my Mom and the people I have around me — [racial profiling] doesn't phase me for I know no man can keep me down. I've got confidence in whatever happens to me 'cause I know, listen, they have nothing on me. In a sense I do feel some remorse though because I have served the system before as a cadet. I raised money for the police when they were trying to get their choppers for Toronto. I have pictures with [the Lieutenant Governor]. I felt a little bit of betrayal. (Dwayne, twenty-one)

Police told my friend that they are the biggest gang in the city ... 'cause just like a gang, they could stop you. Nothing you can do about it 'cause if you take one down, there's always going to be someone else to replace them. (Justin, eighteen)

During one discussion, Joseph stared off into the distance, seemingly unconcerned about his friend's spirited wish that the police would just 'go away' and leave them alone. 'I hate them,' Joseph finally said out of nowhere. 'I wish I could snuff one of them.' Joseph is fourteen years old.

In the same neighborhood, Sam said he was standing on his ground-floor balcony talking with a group of friends. Six officers in unmarked cars who patrol the area around the apartment buildings came over to check out what was being discussed:

He said to me that because I'm on the balcony that's my side. But if I jump over my balcony I'm on his side, I'm in his world. So I said, it's your world? He's like, 'Yes.' I'm like, who's ruler? He goes 'Us.' So I'm like, so what if there's nobody to rule? Who you gonna rule? So he didn't have nothing to say. He just kept quiet. So I said, 'Just shut up and get out of my face.'

Shielded by his balcony rail, Sam felt the balance of power shift – for the moment.

Power play between African-Canadian residents and the police in their neighbourhoods reflects the community's fine line between its desire to protect personal privacy and its desire to maintain community safety. Some community workers, for example, felt they needed to protect youth at play in the local recreational centre from random probing by police; the centre's managers had to put their foot down on police attempts to randomly walk in and scan the young participants. The workers were worried about crime in their area, but they were just as worried that the centre would no longer be seen as a safe place for youth to hang out away from criminals and from police questioning.

Breaking the Spirit

From the perspective of the respondents, breaking the Black person's spirit was the ultimate expression of police power:

> It's like they want someone to go to jail or something. They're hating on African-Canadian people. (Julius, thirteen)

> They ask stupid questions ... like you know of any African-Canadian people who sell drugs. I said I don't rat on my friends. (Cruise, twelve)

> When they have African-Canadian people in the back [of the cruiser] they wind down the window so everyone can see their face. (Omar, fourteen)

> Right now African Canadians are trying to take over the world in sports and everything. It's like they [the police] feel threatened. (Gill, fourteen)

According to fourteen-year-old Joyce, her twenty-year-old brother has not been the same since the day police blocked him off with their cars while he was walking with his friends. They asked him if he knew a fifteen- to nineteen-year-old wearing an outfit similar to his. They told him he looked familiar. Her brother, she says, decided to give the police 'attitude' for asking these questions. The resulting showdown landed the young men in jail for a week. Her brother now refuses to leave the house, and has grown rebellious at home.

(Note: Use of Joyce's story was not to condone her brother cursing the police and giving them 'attitude,' but to illustrate the rage and sense of invasion some African Canadians feel when police ask what in other situations would be seen as a valid question as part of an investigation. We saw this anger among other interviewees – and not just those from inner cities. Those who experience this rage say they are reacting to what they see as police assumption that 'they all look the same.')

Where Profiling Happens

'Walking to the Store to Buy Bleach'

> One Sunday I was going to the store to buy bleach. Two cop cars were coming into our complex. You would not think that a cop car could drive

where I thought this car was going. So as a concerned tenant with children I kind of did a [double take]. Upon doing so the police officer [who sat in the car] called out, 'Hey you.' I'm thinking that as a [grown] woman going to the store he couldn't be talking to me. So I kept on my merry way. Then I heard 'Hey you' again ... I turned around and saw two cops sitting in their cruiser directing me over. I walked over and said, 'Can I help you gentlemen?'

One said, 'What are you doing?' I said I'm going to the store to buy bleach. They started to interrogate me, asking a lot of questions. I asked them for their badge number, because I'm not no fool. I know the law. I asked them for the number of their car and their response was, 'Look at the side of the vehicle.'

I was so disgusted that day, I thought to myself, how could they treat someone like me – who was just going to the store to buy bleach – in the manner that they did? I thought about all of the incidents and all the stories I had heard from the youth. The youth kept saying, 'You just don't understand.' That day, believe me, I understood as a female. Before I even got home with the bleach I stood at the side of the building and I just upchucked. I was so disgusted. I threw up at the thought of how I felt and [of] all the young men who have complained before me. (Daisy, forties)

On Your Own Property and in Your Neighbourhood

A few weeks ago I was at my boy's house ... We were play fighting with his cousin. I guess a few people from their houses down the street called the police on us. Police came to the house and said that we were trying to kidnap the kid. They were putting on their gloves trying to frisk us. (Tim, sixteen)

I was at my house [apartment] ... A bunch of us chillin' and about [three] undercover cars see us and thought we were planning something ... [They] came and make a big scene at my house ... saying my friends are drug dealers, whatever. I live with my parents ... and I almost got kicked out of the house. One of my friends started arguing with them and the police said to him, he's lucky he had his kid in his hands or he would see what would happen to him ...

The police told him to put his kid down and come over the balcony. But we told him no, don't go, because they looked like they wanted to beat him up because he was telling them to leave ... They said they had a hint that something was going to happen ... because of the way we dressed ...

and that something is going on in the building and they assumed it's us. After that they said they are going to make it a project every day. From that day, every day you see them. They drive past in their car, they peep in my house. (Micah, nineteen)

In Front of Your Apartment Building

In one neighbourhood, African-Canadian community workers described the 'very good relationship' between the landlords, the security companies, and the police. They felt, however, that while this might indeed be necessary in order to control those who threaten the community with drugs and other illegal activities, the three-way relationship should in fact be a four-way one that includes law-abiding members of the community. Failure to do this, they said, makes the community feel suspect and under siege, as well as victimized by the illegal activities themselves. Pat, a community organizer, pointed out that 'there are a lot of good kids – there are also a few bad apples, but there are more good kids than bad apples.'

The African-Canadian parents at the focus group knew that the police have no choice but to respond to calls from the security guards who patrol the area. They added, however, that when police arrive they don't feel they are listened to equally when their version of events differs from that of the security officers.

We are not all bad apples. People turn us into bad apples. We don't do nothing. They just label us to do stuff. You go to get a job you can't even get a job because they're going to look at you. (Coby, eighteen)

On the Street in Plain Open View

Winston, twenty-seven, is a government employee who lives on the outskirts of Toronto. He has had many encounters with the police, such as in his neighborhood and in front of a coffee shop, where he was taken to the washroom and searched. He admits to having done 'foolishness' as a teenager that landed him in jail, but says he has put that behind him.

I was walking [along a major street in a downtown area] with my girlfriend, who was pregnant. [My girlfriend is White.] She asked me to carry her bag for her while she did something because the bag was too heavy ...

I got stopped [and] police asked for my identification and I refused to [give it to them]. I asked the officer what was the problem. He told me that he doesn't know me. I'm like, 'Well that's good. I don't know you either. But you don't see me coming after you for your ID.'

He got more and more intense but I refused to give him my ID. My girl-friend told him it was her bag that I was carrying and she had her ID in the bag. But [the officer] said that was irrelevant, he wanted to see *my* ID … He said I fit the description of a purse snatcher, which was pretty lame to me.

We started exchanging words … He started choking me and calling me all words in the book … He called me a nigger. He called me a piece of shit. He called me an f—ing liar. When I showed him my ID that still wasn't good enough for him. He still continued to choke me. There were people passing by and saw everything but I couldn't get anybody's name to testify on my behalf. [The officer] kept asking me, 'What are you going to do now, mouthpiece? … I love when I catch you guys like this' … meaning us niggers.

Before he choked me he called for back-up … I told him if I was a purse snatcher I would be running …

He must have been a rookie cop as he looked younger than me. He was just basically abusing his power because he had a badge and a gun … I said I am a fellow [government] employee. I might not be up in rank as he is but I am a government employee … 'You treat me like shit, I'll treat you like shit.'

What goes around comes around. It all boils down to respect. If you talk to someone in a pleasant tone or manner you will get a response in a pleasant tone or manner nine times out of ten …

Driving

Inner City Youth

Coby had this story to tell:

I was coming from my friend's apartment [waiting for my friend, who had just gone to the store]. The cops came behind me and turned on their siren and the car wasn't even moving˙…

They were, like, 'Step out of the car.' I stepped out and gave them my G1 … He goes, 'Go around to the back of the building.' We went and then he goes, 'So where's the weed?' Then he goes, 'As a matter of fact I don't want the weed ... [I] just want to know if you have crack on you or if you have a gun.' I go 'What? No!'

[Another time] I was driving with a licensed driver. I made a left turn. There was another car behind me, then the light turned yellow. The cop came down on me and told me to step out the car.

Coby did, and the officer told him he had run the red light. Coby replied that this wasn't possible, that if anything the car behind him (driven by a White person and *not* stopped) would have been the one that did:

Then he called his supervisor. They looked at the car and at our address and then they go, 'You guys shouldn't be dressing like that. Now when I drive I don't even drive with a hat because they always pull us over. They go, like, 'Why are you guys wearing hats? Are you in a gang? You guys have any tattoos?' I go 'No.' 'You guys been in trouble with the law?'

The police ordered Coby and his friends to step out of the car so they could search it. They asked them if they had guns in the car. Again no. The police searched his friend's bag – to find out, they said, if he had guns in it. After they searched the car, they asked, 'So where are you guys going?' They told the police. The police then told Coby that they knew he was at a particular nightclub on a night when there was a shooting. Did he have any information about the shooting? '[The officer] goes, "If you give me information I can rip up the ticket and let you go." He had me standing like that in the road.'

Businessman

Herman, twenty-seven, has gotten so fed up with being questioned by police while driving his own vehicle – they always ask where he got the money to buy the car – that he now drives only a vehicle registered in his mother's name: not that this helps, because now the police question him on whose car it is and, when told, on whether his mother knows he has it. His mother holds a high-level job in a financial institution. He feels that questions like these are meant to 'antagonize' him. He describes the car he had before as 'kind of flashy [with] a lot of stereo in it.'

I was driving my friend's truck. He's a white guy. So [in seating arrange-ment] it's African-Canadian guy, White guy, and [in the back] African-

Canadian guy, White girl. When they pulled us over they asked me for information and the African-Canadian guy in the back for information. Nobody else ... The White guys had no seat belt on.

Herman felt his rights were being violated by these random stops, which he described as now 'second nature.' He recently got stopped three times in one day: once because he was using a ten-day permit (he says he was within the ten-day range); and once because the officer said he had run a red light – a claim Herman denied. He was not charged. The third time was a 'routine check.' His brother's girlfriend, who is White, was shocked when her boyfriend was recently randomly stopped. 'She couldn't believe it! ... She was like wow!' (I later interviewed the woman, who confirmed the story.)

African-Canadian Police Officer

I was driving along a suburban road going east. A police car was going west. The policeman just looked over at me and he made a U-turn and stopped me. The car that was ahead of me stopped because he saw what was happening. The [officer] approached me and asked for my driver's licence. He said, 'Do you realize how fast you were going?' I said I was driving the speed limit. He said no, I was going 90 kilometres. I said to him, 'How could I be going 90? How fast was that car ahead of me going?' He said, 'I don't care how fast he was going, you were going 90.' So I said, how do you know I was going that speed? He said he had me on radar. I said, 'Let me see your radar.' I went over to the car and he had 30 km on the radar. The speed limit was 60. I said, 'Listen, I know how radar works as I have done radar work before, so tell me what you mean by the 30 on the screen there.' He asked me where I worked. I told him I was a police officer.

He said, 'Let me see your tin [police badge].' I said, 'No, I'm not going to show you my badge because I don't want you to change your mind because I told you this. 'I told him that if I was going faster than the speed limit I would be flying past the man ahead of me ... He gave me back my licence. He didn't say anything else.' (Andrew, early fifties)

In the Suburbs

Paul is a twenty-three-year-old suburbanite whose father holds a high-level job in a multimillion-dollar firm. Few law enforcement officers will miss Paul's steely sarcasm when, after stopping him while he's driving his late-model BMW – a gift from his dad – or his father's current-model Cadillac, they proceed to ask him whose car it is. *Well, officer,* he thinks, *you have the papers in your hand, whose car do you think it is?* But Paul is too polite and well raised to swear at or insult the officer. His rock-solid self-esteem leads him to impatience rather than rudeness. He's got a fledgling business to run. But his disdain is palpable.

Paul lives in an upscale neighbourhood. In his driveway one will find a current-model Mercedes 500 series, a current-model Cadillac Escalade, a Mercedes 350 series, and a late-model BMW. Paul wears a curly hairdo that befits the artist he is. His father asked him once to wear a hat while driving – he was worried the police would target him because of his hair. Paul refused: 'I explained to him that if I was going to get pulled over because of the way I looked, then that's unfortunate. I guess I will have to sacrifice my time by getting pulled over, as opposed to conforming to society.' An articulate young man, Paul carried himself during our interview like someone for whom symbols of wealth hold no awe. Paul gets pulled over often when he's driving one of his parents' cars. He says he has no problem with this, since a check of the licence plate always shows it is registered to a female or to a male in his fifties. He figures that the 'mature' way to handle such stops is to comply. He finds it interesting, though, that police think they have to check the plates of the car he is driving as he passes by.

At the Store

> Five of us ... went to the store to get some firecrackers. The store owner [who was at the back of the store] called [the police] ... because he thought we were making trouble. We went outside. [The police] said we took firecrackers ... The firecrackers were over the counter, so none of us could have [taken them]. They tried to charge all of us for mischief. (Chris, sixteen)

Filing Reports

Coby went to the local police station to complain that the security guards had posted his picture when he had done nothing wrong: 'They were like, oh I can't expect better because the building I live in is a drugs building and it's all drug dealers who live there. So basically, he's telling me that I'm a drug dealer.'

In Search of Drugs and Guns

Research on racial profiling in the United States and Britain shows a link – especially in the United States – between profiling and the 'war on drugs.' Government and police organizations link the proliferation of street-level drugs (and the guns that enforce the drug trade) to Black communities. For them, this justifies – and sometimes directs – a 'by any means necessary' approach to combatting the drug trade. In their narratives, however, the African-Canadian respondents felt strongly that the 'by any means necessary' approach was encouraging police officers to target and harass anyone who fit their profile of a drug dealer.

> Me and Coby were walking home one night and we see a police in the corner just standing. We were wearing hoods. The police officer ran up on us with his gun drawn ... We just stood up, 'cause we were thinking he was going to do something to us. He's, like, 'Assume the position. Spread your legs.' He searched us. He told us they were looking for someone in the area. They all stood up [a] next man at the back with their guns and he was pleading for his life, saying, 'You guys are going to shoot me! You guys are going to shoot me!' (Freeway, late teens)

> Me and my friend were walking with our coach. Police said there were kids with a gun. They tripped me and my friend and put shotguns in our backs. We weren't the guys but we're Black and they said two Black kids [had the gun] ... After, they let us go 'cause the coach talked to them. That's why I hate police. I don't talk to them. They're racist. They only go after Black people. Life goes on though. (Hawk, twelve)

> I was walking about six o'clock and like four undercover cops came up to me and said, 'Oh, regular pat down strip search.' They put their hand in my pockets going up and down [my body], pulling my pants against my body checking to see if I had any drugs. (Shabbah, fourteen)

Impact of Profiling

In its report, *Paying the Price*, the OHRC (2003) provides extensive documentation on the impact that racial profiling has on those who experience it. The report quotes criminologist Scott Wortley: 'To argue that racial profiling is harmless, that it only hurts those who break the law, is to totally ignore the psychological and social damage that can result from always being considered one of the "usual suspects."' *Paying the Price* captures the gamut of emotions among victims, from fear, guilt, and resentment to humiliation. It documents changed dress and behaviour patterns and mistrust of all institutions. African-Canadians' stories reveal all of these. The impact on Blacks of being profiled is unique, however, because of society's perception of Blacks as a group – that is, because of the 'public transcript.' It is important to understand this if one is to grasp the significance of the respondents' accounts.

When African Canadians feel they are being profiled by police as antisocial wrongdoers, the sting is all the more sharp because they see themselves portrayed the same way on television, in books, and in movies. They become confused by what author John Wideman describes as society's 'deadly ambivalence' towards Blacks. Blacks are rewarded when they fulfil the machisimo and physicality that make them sports heroes and hip-hop and fashion icons, yet they are frowned on when they insist on being treated as 'just one of the guys.'

A Sense of Injustice

> You can't really do anything about it because as hard as it sounds, it's the white man's world. Things may probably change in the future. (Claude, sixteen)

In the interviews, this sense of despair went hand in hand with a sense of injustice – with a feeling that this was not fair, but what are you going to do?

> We were playing ball one day and there were some white guys. They were smoking and drinking beer. [The police] walked right past the white guys and came to us. They only made them pour the beer out. They didn't even ask their name or nothing. Most times when they see [Black] people with alcohol, they confiscate it or take them in. They're going to harass you more. [Black] people are always at a disadvantage. White people get off easy. (Steve, twenty-four)

Lack of Cooperation with Police

> Sometimes there'll be some nice cops who say 'Hi, how're you doing.'

They tell you to go home or whatever the case may be. If they say how is your day or whatever [I'll react politely]. Be nice to me and I'll be nice to you. (John, fifteen)

One time we were parked in the school parking lot waiting for someone. It was pretty late. The police came by. These guys were nice. They didn't give us any hassle. They just asked us for ID and told us next time if we want to wait we should wait outside, not inside the school parking lot. We were loitering in the parking lot. We didn't know we were not supposed to be there but he told us. We said all right and ... moved. (Justin, seventeen)

Fear of Wearing the Clothes One Likes

The younger respondents had conflicting views about whether they should refrain from wearing the ubiquitous 'do-rags' and baggy pants – an urban uniform of sorts. Some felt that wearing these attracted police attention and, by extension, targeting. Others felt they should, like everyone else, be free to wear whatever they want.

I know for a fact that if I walked around in some tight jeans and some weird shirt [and] funky colours in my hair nobody would harass me. Everybody would look at me like I'm a fruit. But as soon as you put on a baggy jeans [sic], hats and stuff ... once you have a bandana on, they're jumping at you ... They haven't learned that these are just clothes. They just do it regardless.

You could be a straight A student, never been in trouble, that's how you like to dress. They still harass you, doesn't matter what you wear. (Jacob, seventeen)

I could be walking gangsta and you could be walking in a suit. I could have a book bag coming from summer school. You could have a briefcase with drugs in it. Who knows? But somehow how they target it is through the bandana, the shoes, the jacket. This is what attracts the cops. That's like their mission. (Anthony, eighteen)

Eighteen-year-old Sylvia lives in what would be considered one of Toronto's 'inner city' districts. A walk through her neighbourhood reveals low-income housing, a mall, and – farther up on the same major artery – attractive apartment buildings and single-family homes.

For the interview, Sylvia wore a pale-blue baseball-style shirt and Phat Farm footwear – a kinder, gentler version of the urban streetwear that is so popular around her neighbourhood mall. She asserted that she couldn't imagine a situation in which she would have a negative encounter with the police: 'I'm pretty reserved.' What would she do if a police officer stopped her?

> One thing I wouldn't do, I wouldn't start yelling at them. Not to general-ize, but sometimes African-Canadian people overreact and want to put on our accents. I know that white people [consider] that ignorant, so I wouldn't do that. Even today I was speaking to somebody, and they said, 'You sound very Valley.' I was like, well you know what, I speak English. I'm from Canada.
>
> I think that African-Canadian people feel like they have to be hard. To look hard. They are walking like they have 100 pounds on their shoulder. The do-rags right above the eyebrows to make them look fierce. They have to be angry. Sometimes [Black] people are trying to be ghetto. They are proud to be ghetto. They're proud that their life looks hard 'cause then they can say, 'I survived this' or 'I survived that.' They are talking about reality. Well, my reality is I am going to university. [My friend's] reality is that, you know, 'I'm just going to chill.'

Screech and Jersey are youth outreach workers in an inner-city neighbourhood. Jersey agreed that youth attract attention with their dress, but so do Black men in suits, such as a friend of his, who on his way to work was rudely interrogated by the police even though he was wearing a badge from the corporation for which he worked. He says he himself has had the same experience while dressed fairly conserva-tively.

> It makes you feel like a bloody criminal. (Winston, late twenties)

Restricted Freedom of Movement

In doing their jobs, law enforcement officers enter the shadowy world of criminals, criminal intent, guilt by association, and plain association whether with a neighborhood, an apartment building, a mode of dress, a way of speech, or even a look. Policing is often a combination of crap-shoot, instincts, gut feel, and good investigative work. It is as much an art as it is a science. It's a world in which 'profiling' helps increase the odds of landing one's target, be it a pedophile, an international arms dealer, a sniper, or a small-time street dealer. The African-Canadian respondents, however, made little distinction between being profiled because off their race, or because they were perceived as possible criminals. Several youth told me they had been 'banned' by police – although most of these cases involved security guards – from visiting friends in certain apartment buildings. A ban under the Trespass Act means the person cannot come onto that property unless able to 'prove' the purpose of the visit. The respondents repeatedly mentioned banning as a sore spot. Proving the legitimacy of a visit might involve anything from carrying a letter of invitation (we were told of one such incident in a public housing complex) to being questioned or having security follow the visitor to the apartment.

When six detectives took Winston down – 'with six Glocks pointed in my face' – in a coffee shop next door to the men's hostel where he was staying, it was clearly a case of mistaken identity. However, like Winston, African Canadians find it difficult to adopt an 'oh well' attitude to these kinds of incidents. To them, it is racial profiling.

> There is no difference between racial profiling and police [trying to sift out the bad guys]. There are kids around here who have the hairstyle or the clothes but who never ever did a bad thing. You got people who are innocent churchgoers who have the hairstyle because it's the in thing and they do get pulled over ... There's bigger crime being committed ... but the police waste their time with nonsense. (Winston, late twenties)

Loss of a Place to Play or to Dream

The feeling of being treated differently by police even before doing anything wrong was common among the respondents. Speaking with reference to African-American men, John Wideman captured this sentiment: 'Black boys are cheated out of the sheltered, precious space of play, of making forgivable mistakes' (*Essence* magazine, November 2003).

Sarah is a bright, articulate sixteen-year-old, the type of normal-looking teenager one would not expect to have strong feelings about the police. But she does:

> We all went to the talent show and we were at [a transit stop]. I guess some other people – two guys – tried to steal from the store. Why is it that

every time we coloured people have gatherings ... Over thirty policemen came [and started to shout] 'Everybody out!' Hitting them, Tasering people. Some people had to go downstairs and they had to go outside the station. They said we were loitering, but we were waiting for our buses to go home. Some people were just minding their own business ... I thought, 'Gee, this is not slavery times, man. Grow up.' Honestly, equality is a part of the Charter of Rights. We all deserve that. I know they are just doing their job, but sometimes they get out of hand when they see a lot of [Black] people around. They need to settle down ... Not all Black people do crime.

Twenty-one-year-old Dwayne symbolized the dream to which many others aspire. Dwayne's pants were loose fitting but not ankle grazing. His ebony skin and handsome features glistened against the white tank shirt he had just donned after playing basketball. To many, Dwayne compares favourably to twenty-seven-year-old Dudley. Both grew up with single mothers who tried their best to inspire them to 'do something with their lives.' Dudley played basketball after school, and Dwayne joined the cadets, through which he had the opportunity to travel to places outside of Ontario and even Canada. Dudley left school as soon as he turned sixteen. Dwayne is in his third year of university. Dudley spent his leisure time 'chillin' with friends; Dwayne raised money for charity and worked a part-time job. Dudley, twenty-seven, has no idea what he wants to be when he grows up; Dwayne, a business major, intends to start his own company. Dudley speaks with the voice of one who feels beaten down, and he has stopped trying to make sense of his situation. Dwayne is forceful and articulate and lives on the basis that nothing and no one will take his dignity: traits that Black males are warned will get them in trouble with 'the system,' because they are so easily interpreted as aggressiveness, arrogance, and disrespect. Dudley's hand curls into a fist as he expresses contempt for the police; Dwayne quotes Bob Marley's song about running away to live to fight another day. According to Dwayne, his fight will not be a physical one.

Notwithstanding the sharp differences between them, Dudley and Dwayne share one painful feature: they have both repeatedly been stopped and questioned by police. The experience has left Dudley barely willing to talk; when he finally does, he recounts only two incidents on tape. The others he captures as 'lots of things,' and only when the tape is switched off do these 'things ... incidents' come stumbling out. The number of incidents is not astronomical, but his anger is growing with each one. Dwayne's incidents took place while he was driving his 'souped up' car. He can well afford it; he bought his first car when he was eighteen from his own summer and part-time money. Most of Dudley's encounters have taken place while walking around his inner-city neighbourhood. Since he has no steady job, one assumes he can't afford a car. He rides a bicycle.

In our society, the freedom to play and dream can also include the freedom to jog and get in shape in preparation to attend an American university on a track scholarship. Community worker Irene saw this dream crumble for one of her young charges:

> [He would] run in the night time. Two officers in a car pulled up on them [the young man and his running partners], shined the light on them ... on a regular basis. They [police] pull into the community asking people for ID, roughing people up for no apparent reason. These people are in a Metro Housing complex. There is no community centre ... no basketball court, schools won't give them a permit anymore to run programs over there. There is nowhere for people to go more than to sit out around in the community.

No Right to Make Forgivable Mistakes

To many young African-Canadian men in particular, the notion that society will allow them, in John Wideman's terms, 'forgivable mistakes' elicits a cynical look or a hearty laugh. For Winston, it means that every time the police stop him and run his name through their computer, he is up for a search, although his legal problems ended a long time ago.

> One time I was stopped because I fit the description of a Black man with his hair in a braid, six feet tall. I had nothing on me but they put the handcuffs on me after they ran my name through the computer. They said it was for their own safety. They went through my pockets to see if I had ... any drugs, any contraband or any sharp objects. The only thing I had on me that was sharp was a pen in my pocket and my house keys ... *It makes me feel like I can't do nothing right.*

'Unintentional Systemic Facilitation'

In its public position on racial profiling, the Association of Black Law Enforcers (ABLE) points out that profiling occurs, and furthermore, that it is being unintentionally supported by systems which allow 'ineffective policy, training, mentoring and control mechanisms.' According to one retired African-Canadian officer, sometimes the support is not altogether unintentional, although good internal checks and balances have proven effective in correcting the behaviour of individual police officers.

> Systemic support means that a certain [senior officer] will target certain groups. Then you have that group that will do everything this person says. [Others] don't participate: but they won't report it. They don't want people to say, 'What are you trying to do?' Or if they are targeting Black people they will say, 'What, are you a nigger lover or something?'
>
> [Senior police brass] will be defensive [about accusations of profiling]. He will want to defend his guys for people to say, 'Oh yes, he's defending us.' He may not want to look bad, like he doesn't know what is happening ... Fairness will have to be seen to be taking place.

Solutions

The solutions the respondents proposed to racial profiling ranged from hiring more African-Canadian police officers, to urging police to stop harassing African-Canadian youth so that they can become more positive towards policing as a career. Many urged increased positive interaction and dialogue between police and communities – for example, on Saturday mornings in school gymnasiums. Others believed strongly that the African-Canadian community would have to be a key partner in helping 'bring lawbreakers to justice' (as one police officer put it).

Some recommendations – for example, to create positive outlets for youth – were often beyond police control, but spoke to the need for police to work more proactively with others in creating positive community environments. Overall, the respondents felt that the police should be more holistic in their perceptions of African Canadians – especially youth. This would reduce stereotyping and negative expectations. This recommendation, though, led to a number of 'chicken or egg' conversations about who should take the lead in showing respect. Most felt that the police should; others – by far the minority – felt that African Canadians needed to reduce their own negative expectations of the police.

Another general consensus was that more positive treatment by police would likely raise the level of cooperation as police went about their business in the community. The reverse, as expressed by one young man, was an attitude among youth: 'You treat me like shit, I treat you like shit.'

Interviewees also advocated the following:

- More training in communication and self-management: 'I have heard that police are told to go with their gut instincts. But if you have a racist cop and he goes with his gut instincts every time ... then we are going to have a lot [fewer] urban African-Canadian youth. Because he's going to figure that everyone of those people has a gun ... It's very sad to think that the very people that are supposed to be saving you are the very people you're afraid of.'
- More exposure to everyday African-Canadian community life to help reduce suspiciousness and distrust.
- More effort on the part of the police to know African Canadians as human beings.
- More effort by the police to understand the unique pressures that African Canadians – especially youth – face and how these pressures (such as racism and stereotyping) can affect encounters with institutions.
- More effort by African Canadians to 'use the system' (for example, to make complaints) and to 'know the law.' This was especially recommended by an African-Canadian police officer:

Ignorance of the law is no excuse not to obey the law ... We are not back home anymore. This is not your home, this is your children's home. The system will mess with you only if you are ignorant. (Member of the Association of Black Law Enforcers)

8 From Narratives to Social Change: Patterns and Possibilities

Culturally and institutionally embedded attitudes and practices provide not only a context, but a catalyst for racial profiling. (Oman 2003, 4)

The series in the *Toronto Star* on race, crime, and racial profiling provoked a discursive crisis that reverberated across the country, with profound implications for society – specifically, for minority/majority relations in Canada. More than three years after the first article in the series was published, the debate over racial profiling in Toronto continues to rage.

We have tried to probe beneath the surface of everyday discourses related to racial profiling as reflected in the dominant discourses of White politicians, the police, and other public authorities, including the media. The crisis that has erupted as a result of the *Star* series has the power to disrupt existing racialized ideologies and to challenge widely accepted myths about the intersection of race and crime. It also provides an opportunity to 'deconstruct' racism – specifically, to decode the message of the Black body (the criminalblackman) as a product of the White gaze and the White imagination (Fanon 1967). Although the book is framed around an discrete set of current phenomena, it is important to emphasize – as Charles Smith does in his chapter – that the issues addressed by the *Star* series and the responses that series has produced have their roots in the broader historical and contemporary struggles of Black and Aboriginal people to be treated as full and equal citizens of a democratic liberal society. The past several decades have been marked by expressions of distress, alarm, and fear in Black and Aboriginal communities about police surveillance, harassment, and brutality. Dozens of studies have been conducted, task forces have been commissioned, and inquiries have been held. Consistent and compelling recommendations have been made to address the issue of biased treatment of Blacks and other racialized communities – and then generally ignored.

The heated debate over racial profiling reflects the deep chasm between the dominant White political, cultural, and social systems, and those communities which are the objects of their dis-enabling and marginalizing effects. Charles Smith's overview of racial profiling in Canada and Maureen Brown's interviews with Black youth from across the GTA, combined with the findings of the OHRC inquiry, the Quebec task force, the Canadian Race Relations Foundation Report to the UN Commission on Human Rights, and numerous other studies suggest that many in Canada's Black communities live in an almost constant state of crisis; the same can be said of Aboriginal communities across this country. Racial profiling has profound psychological, social, and economic consequences. The refusal of politicians, bureaucrats, and policing authorities to acknowledge its impact on the lives of Black people has further increased their individual and collective despair, vulnerability, and marginalization.

We have approached the topic of racial profiling through a series of texts and narratives that reveal the power of White ideologies. The crisis the *Star* series provoked took the form of a highly charged and conflictual set of public discourses across a broad spectrum of public spaces, including newsrooms, courtrooms, government agencies, and academic forums. The subject of the racial profiling of Blacks by police was hotly debated in the meeting rooms of the Police Services Board and the Toronto Police Association and well as in town hall meetings organized by Chief Julian Fantino. It was the focus of a series of conferences sponsored by government and non-government agencies. It was the catalyst for numerous public events organized by social agencies and by community and youth organizations. The actual experience of racial profiling and the denial by White authorities that it happens succeeded in uniting – however briefly – a highly diverse Black community, whose members forged a community coalition of more than fifty-seven organizations. The African Canadian Community Coalition on Racial Profiling (ACCCRP) played a leading role in articulating the Black community's collective voice on the issue of racial profiling.

The *Star* series and the responses to it from the White public authorities provide crucial insights into how racialized discourse is used to deny and deflect attention from the general issue of racism in policing. Throughout this book we have maintained that racial profiling is a manifestation of 'democratic racism,' whereby racial discrimination 'cloaks its presence' in liberal principles and values such as the preservation of the public good and the social order. Concerns about ensuring public safety and social order then conflate with notions of the threat from the dangerous, deviant 'other.' Blackness, maleness, and violence converge to foster a representation of the 'criminalblackman.' Yet no comparable 'criminalwhiteman' exists (Russell 1998, 114). Similarly, as Hall (1997, 51) observes: 'The body of the criminal is *produced* within discourse, according to the different discursive formations ... The conception of the body ... as a sort of surface on which different regimes of power/knowledge write their meaning and effects.'

Canada presents itself as a colour-blind society – a common dominant discourse in democratic liberal but racialized states. One result is that police attitudes and practices are not seen as grounded in race. The discourse of colour-blindness ('We never noticed his skin colour') is offered as a confirmation of White innocence and as proof that racism is not at play in a given set of actions. Instead, racialized practices are couched in terms of maintaining law and order and protecting citizens from society's troublemakers and criminal elements. According to the White authorities, the fact that the targets of the White gaze are often Blacks and other people of colour should not be interpreted as racial profiling, but rather as a reflection of the effort to prevent crimes before they take place.

The White gaze is central to the construction of the Black male body as the site of danger and deviance. The criminalized 'other' is represented as a serious threat that must be contained, by coercion if necessary. However, it is important to emphasize that it is not just the police who mark, stigmatize, and attempt to control Black bodies; the nexus of race and crime is reinforced by lawmakers, immigration officials, the courts, the media, educators, researchers, filmmakers, advertisers, and many others.

The Theoretical Approach of This Book

This book has tried to engage the sometimes acrimonious debates between theoretical models. Regarding questions of knowledge, methodology, and the role of politics in academic life, we agree with Cottle

(2000) that the clash of frameworks can be a positive force, in that it can help address issues of critical concern to society. It can also help push the boundaries of research into new and productive areas. 'Critical' race theory and 'critical' criminology, and the 'critical' analytical approach that is central to cultural studies, are all appropriate frameworks for studying the highly charged issue of racial profiling. Each of these theoretical perspectives addresses the constructs of ideology and hegemony, representation and misrepresentation, normality and abnormality. Each acknowledges power and powerlessness, domination and resistance, and the dialectical nature of knowledge, truth, and 'common sense.'

The theoretical approaches employed in this analysis offer an alternative to traditional empirical models of society. Newer approaches based on critical theory, cultural studies, and other postmodern frameworks suggest that quantitative data can never be sufficient to understand the subjective nature of experience. In this analysis of racial profiling, we have tried to uncover and reconstruct a 'pattern among the instances' (Fiske 2000, 53). We have attempted to expose the pattern of racialization by police of Blacks (and by extension, other racialized communities) – a pattern that reaches beyond individual specific cases of racial bias and discriminatory treatment by police. For example, it can be stated that racial profiling is a real, lived experience based on the hundreds of narratives offered by Blacks. These narratives emerged from a number of sources: the *Star* series; the Toronto Police Service's own database (recently released); Maureen Brown's findings; the OHRC's inquiry into racial profiling; countless task force studies; and, finally, the many other studies documenting the racialization of Blacks, Aboriginal people, and other ethno-racial communities (Wortley 2005; Wortley and Tanner 2003; Barnes 2002; James 2002; Razack 1998; Henry and Tator 2002, 2005). Blacks in Canada (and there are almost half a million of them) are likely to experience some form of racial profiling while driving, walking down the street, shopping in malls, and attending school. They encounter it in the attitudes and behaviour of lawyers, judges, and other courtroom officials; and in media representations, both print and electronic.

Racial profiling has been described as a point of entry for analysing how Blackness becomes equated with deviance and for measuring the social cost of linking Black skin with criminal activity (Russell 2004). The manifestations of racial profiling and racialized policing examined in this book reach well beyond law enforcement. The processes of racialization and racial profiling are deeply embedded in the interlocking discursive spaces and structures of lawmaking, immigration, criminal justice, education, the media, and the various vehicles of cultural production and representation. In this context, we have said that racism in other institutions has an impact on policing culture, and that society's collective beliefs, values, norms, and practices influence the interactions of individual police officers with people of colour – especially Aboriginals and Blacks. Along with many other scholars, some of whom are cited throughout this book, we believe that individual and systemic racism are reciprocally related, and that society's beliefs, norms, and values are inevitably those of the policing culture as well. Racism is embedded in the practices and administrative structures of police services, politicians, government agencies, and other public authorities. In all of these, Blackness serves a signifier – a structure of social meanings – and as a consequence, Black people are dealt with as a 'problem' population. However, the lived dimensions of racism cannot be reduced to administrative procedures and practices that respond to particular conceptualizations of Blackness. If we are to understand racism, we must also consider the micro level – that is, the boundary between lived experience and administrative manifestations (Knowles 1996).

Systemic racism is visible in the lack of systems of accountability, not only within policing structures but also within the governing bodies that oversee policing at the municipal and provincial levels of governance. If there is to be change, these levels must be part of it.

From the evidence offered in this book, it would seem that as a whole, the police lack democratic notions of accountability either to the political ideal that all individuals should be treated with fairness, respect, and equity or to the ideal that they must be accountable to all the communities they serve. Moreover, the absence of independent civilian complaints procedures makes deviant behaviour more likely than otherwise within police forces themselves.

Our chapter on the police analysed some key elements that sustain a racialized police culture (or subculture). Most explanations of the link between police culture and racial profiling rely on two basic assumptions: that police racism is part of the broader culture of a particular society, and that profiling based on visible difference of any kind is part of normative police practice.

Despite Chan's (1997) cogent criticisms of the static determinism that has characterized much research on the police, the main conclusion of many critical scholars appears to be that police culture and practices predispose police officers towards racism against groups that are visibly different – and especially towards those whose bodies are Black. This is mainly because the everyday practices of policing involve a view of society that essentially divides the world between 'us' and 'them.'

An analysis of police culture exposes features that strongly influence the relationship between Blacks and the police. As Crank (1997, 207) notes: 'Racism is a phenomenon grounded in local police culture ... Cultural predispositions are learned and replayed in a process of concrete practice in police-citizen interactions.' Racialized predispositions are reinforced by the day-to-day experiences of officers. The police are motivated by symbols of overt difference such as skin colour, style of dress, and behaviour – symbols that are often related to minority groups. Over time, these symbols of cultural and racial difference become a routine approach to identifying suspicious characters. If there is a real or perceived history of certain groups committing crimes, their overt symbols of difference become trigger points for police action.

Another pertinent feature of police culture relates to the significant levels of individual acts of criminal deviance found within policing agencies, not just in Canada but in other jurisdictions such as Britain, the United States, and Australia. This issue has received significant attention in the literature as well as in recent media accounts (Silverberg 2004a; Duffy 2004; Coyle 2004; DiManno 2004). The seeming prevalence of these deviant behaviours raises fundamental questions about the extent to which the norms, values, and rituals of police culture may be contributing to unlawful policing practices – for example, by sanctioning abusive practices in police interactions with minority communities and other powerless groups in society.

Over and over again, members of the Black community have raised incidents of police brutality and physical and verbal harassment. These narratives were shared in the *Star* series, the OHRC study, the Brown study, and countless other forums. This suggests that something about police culture encourages deviant practices such as constant micro- and macro-aggressions against Black and other racialized minorities. Clearly, the physical abuse of so many Blacks in Toronto and Montreal, and of Aboriginal men in Saskatoon, Winnipeg, Toronto, and other regions of the country – sometimes to the point of death – is a strong indication that racial profiling has serious consequences.

In her analysis of the Rodney King assault by Los Angeles police officers in 1992, Butler observes that within a 'racist interpretive framework, King's beating represents a reading of "the black body" [as a] source of danger, the threat of violence and ... an intention to injure' (in C. James 2002, 291). She also notes that as the 'police are structurally placed to protect Whiteness against violence, the violence of the police cannot be read as violence, because the Black male body ... is the site and source of danger, a threat, the police effort to subdue this body, even if in advance, is justified regardless of circumstances. Or rather, the conviction of that justification rearranges and orders the circumstances to fit that conclusion' (ibid.). Butler also makes the critical point that eyewitness accounts of the 'visual evidence' are scrutinized in such a way that it is difficult to establish 'the truth' about police brutality, because 'no black person can seek recourse to the visible as the sure ground of evidence.' The 'visual field' is itself influenced by the racism prevalent in modern society. ·

As a participant in a Black community forum on racial profiling, Carol Tator listened to dozens of examples on this point. The forum was organized by the ACCCRP following the release of the two studies (2004) commissioned by that organization: Charles Smith's *Crisis, Conflict and Accountability*, and Maureen Brown's *In Their Own Voices*. Participants in this forum included many of the young Black respondents interviewed by Brown, as well as their families and other members of the Black community who had experienced racial profiling by police. During the forum, even more stories of police harassment and brutality were told. A common theme in these narratives was that eyewitness accounts of the events being narrated were denied and resisted by policing authorities. Near the end, one frustrated participant turned to David Mitchell, one of the founders of the Canadian branch of the Association of Black Law Enforcers (ABLE), and pointedly asked him what members of the Black community could do to establish 'the truth' about these incidents of racial profiling and police brutality. Mitchell's answer was very succinct: 'Carry a video camera wherever you go.'

Smith's chapter documented the history of police use of force and violence against Blacks. Dozens of research studies and public inquiries have documented that racial profiling and police abuse of minorities have been going on for decades. A great deal of research also points to patterns of unequal treatment in the criminal justice system and to racial differences in arrest and imprisonment rates (Commission on Systemic Racism in the Ontario Criminal Justice System 1995).

The Construction of Different Realities through Dominant Discourses and Counter-Narratives

The ideological and sociocultural foundations of racial profiling are visible in the White dominant discourses on the Black community. Chapter 6 analysed the rhetorical strategies that are incorporated into the talk and text of the White elite – police officials, politicians, journalists, and so on.

Discourse analysis is a useful tool to deconstruct the coded language of dominant discourses and hegemonic narratives. 'Racism as discourse' has to do with how the White powers-that-be give voice to racism. We have consistently maintained in this book that these hegemonic discourses are embedded in the collective beliefs and values of the broader society; from there, they find their way into the administrative structures of policing.

Racialized discourses operate invisibly and unconsciously in the ongoing arguments and diatribes of police chiefs (Julian Fantino), police union presidents (Craig Bromell), and former members of the Toronto Police Services Board (Norm Gardner). They were echoed in the rhetoric of mayors (Mel Lastman), government ministers (Bob Runciman), and provincial premiers (Ernie Eves). The hegemonic discourses of these people were marked by the stereotyping, essentialization, inferiorization, and the criminalization of Blacks. The dominant stories – told mainly by White Anglo males – provided a deep pool of familiar and reassuring myths, which then circulated throughout White institutional spaces. Through constant repetition, these messages over time became incorporated into the collective belief system of White dominant culture.

In the dominant ideologies and discourses of White police and political figures, and in much of the media, Blackness – more specifically, the Black body – has acquired a number of core social meanings. This is reflected, most obviously, in the rhetorical strategy whereby Black men and youth are viewed as a problem people who require constant surveillance. The dominant discourses identify individuals as dangerous and deviant members of a distinct racial group and then apply these same stereotypes and misrepresentations to the entire Black community. In much the same way, Aboriginal people are also seen as problem people who require excessive attention by police and other public authorities. Toni Morrison (1997, xxviii) has argued that these processes of racialization lead to entire races being represented as needing 'correction, incarceration, censoring, silencing.'

Discourse as a Vehicle of Social Change

Official stories amount to a 'public transcript' that reinforces and legit-imates the authority and power of dominant elites (Scott 1990). A pub-lic transcript or dominant discourse is meant to orchestrate the appearance of a consensus among members of the White dominant group. The language of 'we' and 'they' seeks to identify those who belong to the in-group and to relegate the rest to the margins of society.

However, as the Brown study and the OHRC report make clear, and as African-Canadian responses to the *Star* series have brought to light, another form of storytelling is also extraordinarily powerful. The counter-narratives offered by Blacks, both as individuals and collec-tively, demonstrate how – as bell hooks (1990) has observed – the mar-gin of 'otherness' can be a site of resistance, possibility, and empowerment. That margin can be the catalyst for 'radical perspec-tives from which to see and create, to image alternatives, new worlds' (ibid., 150). These processes of resistance against racial profiling are emerging in Canadian Muslim communities as well.

Marginality itself becomes a strategy for constructing and positively affirming one's own identity as well as a renewed sense of collective identity. This latter identity allows, for example, racialized communi-ties to challenge representations that its members are a 'problem peo-ple.' Furthermore, those who have no choice but to negotiate both margin and centre are well placed to deconstruct dominant discourses and systems of representation (ibid.).

Members of racialized, minoritized communities are finding ways to create counter-narratives that challenge the public transcript. These personal accounts confirm their experiences and bear witness to the reality of racial profiling; at the same time, they offer a different world view, a counter-reality. This kind of storytelling is a form of cultural activism: 'It's a struggle for ... our capacity to see ourselves as human when we are treated inhumanely' (Morales 1998, 4). These stories enable oppressed people to 'name and reclaim, over and over, the con-nections we are taught to ignore, the dynamics we are told do not exist' (ibid., 5). Thus narratives should be seen as a critical tool for empower-ment and change.

The power of oppositional discourse as a tool for challenging racial profiling has been demonstrated in the campaigns against racial profil-ing in the United States. Victims' stories, communicated largely through the media, did much to foster public awareness of racial profiling, including in the White community; this led to changes in laws (Oman 2003). Narratives of injustice can expose complex arenas of social conflict and the fissures under the surface of institutional policies and practices – fissures that would otherwise be invisible to White people (ibid.).

Oppositional narratives contained in the responses to the *Star* series – both in the media (Black and mainstream) and in conversations in various public and private spaces – have brought the issue of racial profiling into sharper focus. Similarly, the narratives of racism in the criminal justice system as told by Canada's Aboriginal people, and as recounted in the dozens of public inquiries in Ontario, Nova Scotia, Saskatchewan, Manitoba, and British Columbia, have also revealed deep schisms in Canadian society.

The duel between dominant and oppositional narratives has raised to prominence some key factors that will have to be considered if racial profiling and other manifestations of racism in Canada are to be controlled. That dominant and counter narratives are now contesting each other underscores the fact that every community interprets ideas, images, words, and actions differently; all of these carry meanings with them that only make sense in the context of particular life histories, experiences, and sociocultural contexts. Many scholars (Bell 1991; Delgado 1995; Ewick and Silbey 1995; Davis 2002) maintain that the study of both hegemonic and counter-hegemonic stories is a highly valid approach to studying social conditions and can be an important catalyst to social change.

Indicators of Social Change in Relation to Racial Profiling

There are a number of indicators that racial profiling has finally been placed on the Canadian public agenda. Some of the encouraging signs of change are discussed below.

Ontario

Ontario's political order changed after the Fall 2003 elections, which brought a new premier for the province and a new mayor for Toronto. These new politicians have influenced the agenda as it relates to racial profiling. As noted in chapter 6, the discourse of moral panic over law and order featured strongly in the political campaigns of the more conservative candidates. They lost (Eves at the provincial level, Tory at the municipal level) to centrist or leftist opponents (McGuinty and Miller, respectively). Clearly, Ontario is abandoning the neoconservative/ neoliberal politics that had dominated for nearly a decade. Toronto's new mayor, David Miller, is a former city councillor with a solid record for supporting diverse ethnoracial communities and for addressing issues of oppression, including racial profiling.

In this new political environment, a more proactive response to racial profiling is more possible than it used to be. Efforts from some quarters to extend Fantino's contract as police chief were stopped by more progressive forces, and several forward-looking individuals have taken seats on Toronto's Police Services Board – these are hopeful signs of change. Also, almost every public official who engaged in the discourses of democratic racism (denial, blame the victim, reverse racism, and so on) is no longer in a position of strong influence, although a few are now opposition members of Parliament. There is one major exception: Fantino has recently been appointed the province's Commissioner of Emergency Management.

The Toronto Police Services Board has two new board members. Alok Mukherjee and Hamlin Grange are both highly skilled and well respected. Both are persons of colour, with strong connections to many ethnoracial communities, and both have been involved in police and racism issues over almost three decades. In an apparent effort to address some of the basic weaknesses of Fantino's approach to policing, the police board recently appointed Bill Blair as the new chief. Blair is taking a more open and collaborative approach to leadership and policing. He has strongly advocated community-based policing and civilian review mechanisms. More importantly, he has committed himself to addressing the problem of racial profiling: 'The only way to fight the problem of racism in our service is by addressing it as part of the organizational culture ... The analogy of a few bad apples quite frankly does not work ... I don't think it explains it and it doesn't enable us to address it organizationally' (Friesen 2005).

Within a few months of the provincial election, the new attorney general, Michael Bryant, announced that the Liberals would be proposing legislation to reinstate a civilian review process (the Tories had dismantled the earlier one). The new agency will likely follow the model established by an NDP government in the early 1990s; that is, it will be an independent body with the power to investigate public complaints against the police and to hold disciplinary hearings.

In the fall of 2003, Kingston became the first city in Canada to require police to record the race and ethnicity of everyone they stopped. That city's police board, following an order issued by its chief, Bill Closs, unanimously approved the plan. Policing authorities such as Tom Kaye, the head of the Ontario Association of Chiefs of Police, immediately attacked the initiative, arguing that it would discourage officers from questioning minorities 'even if they are guilty of a crime.' Despite this resistance, the Kingston police launched a research study (Foster 2003).

In May 2005, the Kingston police released the findings of this pilot research project (Wortley 2005). Within hours, Closs made an emotional apology to his city's Black and Aboriginal communities because some findings in the study suggested racially biased policing. Within days, however, the report's methodology was being called into question.[1] Also within days, the chair of the Toronto Police Services Board, Pam McConnell, stated that she fully expected a 'made in Toronto' version of the Kingston study within eight months (Rankin 2005).

This book has referred often to the OHRC's engagement with the issue of racial profiling. In establishing a provincial inquiry focusing on the human costs of racial profiling, the commission was recognizing that profiling is indeed a human rights issue and that the practice contravenes the Ontario Human Rights Code. Its project was timely and important, because it 'connected the dots' between the huge body of evidence showing that racism exists and the lived experiences of hundreds of men, women, and youth. Somewhat ironically, the commission itself felt the power of the dominant discourse to deny, deflect, and silence those who dare name racism and speak out against it. Immediately after releasing its report, the OHRC was attacked by a number of White public authorities, including Fantino, the presidents of the Toronto Police Association and the police chiefs' association, and many journalists. The critics savaged both the commission's findings and the process it followed. Thus, one of the unexpected outcomes of

---

1 Ron Melchers at the University of Ottawa has argued that Wortley's research is fundamentally flawed because the census data on which it is based do not give an accurate picture of the population that would likely be stopped by the police. He also considers the number of Blacks tracked in the study too small to be useful in drawing any conclusions. Thomas Gabor also dismisses much of the evidence of racial profiling in Canada as baseless and inflammatory. In turn, Wortley has defended this research methodology. See Wortley and Tanner, 'Inflammatory Rhetoric? Baseless accusations? A Response to Gabor's Critique of Racial Profiling Research in Canada,' *Canadian Journal of Criminology and Criminal Justice* 47(3):581–609.

the inquiry was that the commission raised the level of *its own* awareness regarding the nature, extent, and impact of racism in Ontario. As
well, the OHRC experienced some of the perils of challenging hegemonic discourse. The inquiry also led to a new and important initiative
within the commission itself: the development of a new OHRC policy
document on race.[2] The new policy provides a more substantive
framework for how the OHRC approaches the issue of race and racism
in all aspects of its work (OHRC 2005).

Quebec

In Quebec – especially in Montreal – the police have often been
accused of racial profiling. Some recent developments, however, indicate that they are at least beginning to accept that some officers do
engage in racial profiling. In 2004, Montreal police chief Michel Sarrazin sent out a memo to all officers stating that racial profiling is officially against police policy and will not be tolerated. More recently,
Quebec judge Juanita Westmoreland-Traore dismissed charges against
a man after ruling that he had been a victim of racial profiling by the
police (Riga 2005). In addition, an assistant director of the Montreal
police department admitted in a front-page article in the *Montreal
Gazette* that because they see some Black people 'doing wrong,' when
police see a 'black guy in a Lexus, they assume he's in a gang. We're
trying to break that' (Beaudin 2005). After prolonged pressure from
racially profiled communities, a task force composed of community
groups, government officials, police, and human rights advocates was
formed to investigate the problem of racial profiling and to develop an
action plan. The police department agreed to establish a system by the
end of the year to identify police officers who are prone to racial profiling. They added that they were building contacts with minority communities and that all precincts were going to have to develop
community activities to encourage more interaction, especially with
youth. However Dan Philip, president of the Black Coalition of Quebec, noted that 'the police can't be the oppressors and the ones who
sensitize people on oppression' (Rocha 2005).

---

2 The new policy document on race is *Policy and Guidelines on Racism and Racial Discrimination.* Also see a special issue of *Canadian Diversity/Diversité Canadienne* (December
   2004), which includes papers addressing the issue and need for such a policy.

National Initiatives

Another sign of change is that in August 2004, the Canadian Bar Association called on federal, provincial, and municipal governments to adopt laws 'with concrete measures' to identify and stamp out the practice of racial profiling. It also called on judicial councils to educate all judges about racial profiling. David Matas, who chairs the association's racial equality implementation committee, explained that the purpose of the resolution was 'to get people aware of the problem and get them committed to do something about it' (*Toronto Star*, 'Racial Profiling on Agenda,' 3 August 2004).

On 18 November 2004 a private member's bill (C-296) was tabled by MP Libby Davis. The bill would compel enforcement agencies to maintain policies and procedures designed to eliminate all forms of racial profiling (http://www.ndp.ndp.ca).

In 2005, Multiculturalism Canada established an anti-racism program, which includes a permanent network to address the issue of racial profiling and to educate and retrain police officers to be more 'culturally competent.' William Beahen, a twenty-five-year RCMP veteran, has been appointed executive director of the Law Enforcement Aboriginal Diversity Network (LEAD). Beahen has acknowledged that racial profiling does happen and that all police must do better at grappling with the country's growing multicultural population.

One of the most important outcomes of the contestation over racial profiling has been the mobilization of the Black and Aboriginal communities. For example, the Association of Black Law Enforcers (ABLE) has become increasingly proactive in its response to racial profiling. In 2003 the association presented its official position, titled 'Racial Profiling in Canada.' Among other initiatives, it recommended the following: the development of a specific policy and training program to address racial profiling; the installation of cameras in all frontline police vehicles in Ontario; and the inclusion of definitions and circumstances relating to vehicle stops in the policing adequacy standards (ABLE 2003). Members of ABLE have participated in many community and government initiatives, during which they have consistently presented a forward-looking perspective on how to build and maintain positive relations between police and the Black community.

Another positive sign is that in Toronto and Montreal, diverse Black communities are combining their resources. In Montreal in June 2005, a recently formed group called Mothers United Against Racism held a press conference to protest against the racial profiling of their sons. The group is supported by the Centre for Research Action on Race Relations (CRARR) and by youth, civil rights, and social development agencies.

In Toronto, after the publication of the *Star* series, and the collective denial by White public authorities that racial profiling exists, members of diverse Black communities formed a coalition. The African Canadian Community Coalition on Racial Profiling (ACCCRP) has drawn together more than fifty-seven organizations and leaders from the Black communities and is playing a leading role in articulating that community's collective voice on the issue of racial profiling. One of the coalition's first undertakings in response to the *Star* series was to organize a press conference, at which it validated the Black communities' perception that racial profiling is a serious issue with a long and painful history. It also criticized the decision by the Toronto Police Service to commission yet another study on race relations instead of engaging in a more action-oriented dialogue with Toronto's Black community. In 2003 the coalition, with the support of the Canadian Race Relations Foundation and the Federal Department of Multiculturalism, contracted Charles Smith and Maureen Brown to conduct two research projects. Their findings are presented in chapters 3 and 7 of this book.

The Role of the Media

The media have come under strong criticism for their role in the construction of Blacks as criminals. Our analysis of the media's coverage of the *Star* series, and our earlier research on the media's representations of race and crime (or Blackness and crime), reveal a deep reservoir of racialized ideas, images, and discourse (see Henry and Tator 2002).

On the positive side, we believe that the *Star* series was profoundly important; its analysis of racial profiling was careful, powerful, and long overdue. Furthermore, the paper has demonstrated a commitment to the issue; it has stayed with the story and continued to monitor and report on new developments. It is worth noting that the *Star* did not back down even in the face of a $2 billion libel suit launched against it by the Toronto Police Association.

The Role of the Courts and Public Inquiries

Since we began writing this book, there have been many court cases and inquiries in which racism has been an element. These have been cited in various chapters. In almost every instance, there has been a stronger recognition by the courts that racial profiling exists and that it may have played a part in the specific case being addressed. Yet it is disappointing that despite compelling evidence that the police abuse their discretionary power, there have been almost no clear determinations of police misconduct that could lead to the dismissal of officers. On the positive side, the decisions rendered have generated a growing body of case law related to racial profiling.

This book has focused mainly on the racial profiling of Blacks in Toronto. So it is worth reminding readers that countless members of other ethno-racial groups have been profiled by police. Racial profiling has a huge impact on Aboriginal people and has been a factor in a number of deaths in that community. While this book was being written, the judicial inquiry into the death of Neil Stonechild in Saskatoon ended. Justice David Wright's findings in that inquiry went further than most. In his report, he observed that the 'self-protective and defensive' attitudes of policing authorities resulted in an incompetent investigation, years of indifference, and a police service that failed to 'lift a finger to inquire into the merits of the complaints against its members.' In part as a response to the Stonechild Inquiry and to the deaths of so many other Aboriginal men, the Saskatchewan government is changing the law that deals with complaints against the police. That province's Police Amendment Act (2005) – if passed – will establish a Public Complaints Commission, to include First Nations and Metis members. This body will have full authority to oversee all complaint investigations (http://www.assembly.sk.ca/hansard).

Also at this writing, in Ontario, the Ipperwash Inquiry is investigating the events that led to the shooting of Dudley George by the Ontario Provincial Police in 1995. A small group of Chippewa, including women and children, occupied Ipperwash Provincial Park in May of that year; three days later the OPP moved in, their guns firing, and George was killed. Mike Harris, Ontario's premier at the time, resisted holding an inquiry, but one was called in 2003 by Dalton McGuinty, the Liberal premier who had just replaced him.[3]

Extremely important in this context are the findings of the LeSage Report (April 2005), which deal with concerns in Ontario about the

---

3 The mandate of the Ipperwash Inquiry, led by the Honourable Sidney Linden, is to inquire into and report on events surrounding Dudley George's death and recommend ways to avoid violence in similar circumstances. See Peter Edwards, *One Dead Indian* (2004), for a detailed analysis of the events at Ipperwash.

lack of a strong process for civilian review of complaints against the police. For the past nine years, Ontarians with complaints about police brutality, racism, and other misconduct have had to file their complaints with the police forces themselves. LeSage, a former Chief Justice of the Ontario Superior Court, has urged a massive overhaul of the province's 'flawed' police complaints procedures. He notes that 'there is an understandable reluctance to file complaints regarding those in authority by going directly to the authority' (LeSage 2005, 62). He has recommended a return to an independent, civilian-run process of the sort that was eliminated almost a decade ago by the Harris government.

The reflections of Christine Silverberg, one-time chief of the Calgary Police Service, and a police officer for twenty-nine years (fifteen of them in leadership positions), offer another perspective on new directions for policing organizations that would address systemic issues such as racial bias and differential treatment. After the release of Stonechild Report, Silverberg (2004) made a number of observations that are relevant to police services everywhere in Canada. She stated that if police forces are ever going to reflect and value Canada's diversity and regain the public's trust, they will need stronger leadership, and they will also have to change their management style: 'Police services structured along traditional command-and-control lines emphasize elaborate rules and regulations – a model that simplifies police tasks, erodes police officer discretion, and minimizes the importance of decision-making based on core values ... Serving communities starts with a values-based policing approach.' She then made the important point that community-based policing models are fundamentally different from command-and-control models. Law enforcement agencies must emphasize hierarchies less, and outcomes more. This will take more than a few weeks of training; it will require continuous support and reinforcement throughout the stages of recruitment, evaluation, promotion, supervision, and discipline. 'If we want ethical behaviour,' she maintained, 'we need a climate that fosters such behaviour.'

Whether we are transforming individuals, institutions or governments, we have to face the issues head on, and those issues include racism. It is not useful to debate whether such issues exist; we have to acknowledge that they do and then look at their many dangerous dimensions.

Silverberg went on to observe: 'It means acknowledging that racism is not just an overt act of discrimination, or even a series of such incidents, but rather the use of institutional power to deny or grant whole groups of people rights, respect and representation based on their skin colour.'

Silverberg's observations can serve as a template for the structural and cultural changes that police services will have to embrace across the country.

Final Reflections

We have analysed the events flowing from the *Star* series on race, crime, and policing in order to illuminate a far deeper crisis – one that has had a profound impact on Black communities in the Toronto region. We have also tried to show how this crisis is linked to similar ones affecting other racialized communities in Canada, including Aboriginal people, people of Middle Eastern origin, and other people of colour.

Racial profiling is not simply the sum of individual actions of 'a few bad apples.'[4] Nor is it exclusively the product of dominant White values, beliefs, and norms as they are reflected in police culture. Nor is it simply the result of outmoded, hierarchical, and militaristic approaches to the policing of crime. Rather, racial profiling is an aggregate of all of these factors. It is a reflection of the racism that crosses all institutional spaces. This web of institutions includes legislatures and bureaucracies, the criminal justice system, the media, schools and universities, and the vehicles of popular culture. All of these in concert reinforce racism in the mainstream White culture as well as in police culture.

Clearly, no single definition of racial profiling can capture all of the overlapping and conflicting meanings that are generally included under the term 'racial profiling.' This term refers to a number of sometimes very distinct practices; of these, the most relevant for our study has been the police practice of using race as an indicator of criminality. Racial profiling, whether it involves law enforcement specifically or the general perception of race as a dangerous 'abnormality' in diverse public spaces (borders, courtrooms, schools, malls, street corners, and so on), results in particular categories of people being classified as in

---

4 John Barber (2004) of the *Globe and Mail* argues that the often cited 'bad apples' theory never had any basis in fact: 'It's a sham designed to resist system-wide reform of police forces that have developed bad habits and contaminated cultures.'

need of surveillance (Russell-Brown 2004; Fiske 2000). The negative and often oppressive policing of Black, Brown and Red bodies is cloaked in the discourses of democratic racism; from the White dominant cultural perspective, this sort of policing is seen as natural and 'normal.'

The stereotypic constructs of the 'criminalblackman' (Russell 1998), 'Black-on-Black crime,' 'driving while Black,' deviant and drunk 'Indians,' and Muslim 'terrorists' begin in the White families and communities that socialize Canadians, in the schools that educate them, in the media that inform them, in the cultural media that entertain them, and in the systems of governance that shape Canadians' sense of rights and entitlements. This does much to explain why, even though White people commit crimes every day, we never hear the discourse of White-on-White crime.

A central premise of this book is that the strategies for addressing structural and cultural racism in all sectors – including the policing and criminal justice systems – have been impeded by the invisible but deeply embedded ideology of democratic racism. Resistance to changes in the status quo is reflected in the discourses of denial, deflection, and disparagement. This resistance manifests itself in myriad other discourses of democratic racism such as colour-blindness, 'blame the victim,' reverse racism, moral panic, and racialized 'otherness' (Henry and Tator 2005).

Clearly, then, the problem of racial profiling by the police cannot be solved simply by providing a day or week of 'race relations' or by offering more 'cultural sensitivity' programs in police colleges. Furthermore, although it is imperative for law enforcement agencies to recruit many more Blacks, Aboriginals, and other people of colour, this alone will not transform the racialized beliefs, norms, and practices that continue to define the dominant culture of policing. For racial profiling to ever stop or even be controlled, police forces will have to reinvent themselves – that is, discard their paramilitary, patriarchical, hierarchical, closed, and racialized systems. This will not happen until the White racialized culture of other social systems changes as well.

We have written this book not to prove that racial profiling exists – that was done long ago by the many other scholars, cited throughout this work. Evidence of racial profiling is found in the countless stories of those who have experienced it directly, and in the stories of their families and communities, which also pay the price for it. Nor has it been our intention to recommend specific policy changes; many studies and reports have already done that, and done it well. Rather, we have attempted to deconstruct the underlying processes of racialization on which so much policing is based; to expose the multitude of meanings attached to the construct of racial profiling; and to unravel the coded language and racialized discourses that associate Canada's people of colour with deviant and dangerous 'otherness.' Ultimately, the stories of suppression of basic civil and human rights, and the narratives of daily large and small aggressions against Blacks, Aboriginals, and other people of colour, reveal the huge social and psychological costs to society. Racial profiling exists in Canada, yet it does not keep its citizens safer from violence, because *it is an act of violence itself* – an act that challenges the ideals and core values of a democratic liberal society.

Racial profiling by police is 'the canary in the coal mine.' It alerts us to the reality that insidious and systemic racism exists in all our supposedly democratic institutions.

Glossary

anti-racism Measures and mechanisms designed by the state, institutions, organizations, groups, and individuals to counteract racism.

bias An opinion, preference, prejudice, or inclination formed without reasonable justification, which then influences an individual's or group's ability to evaluate a particular situation objectively or accurately; an unfounded preference for or against.

Blackness Refers to the image of the Black male as it is constructed across a broad spectrum of representations, including public, social, and cultural spaces (e.g., media and film, law and justice, bureaucratic and political systems). The negative and stereotypic concepts of the Black male body, which define Blackness as dangerous, deviant, and inferior, were historically constructed under colonialism, but persist as threatening images in contemporary society. Blackness as a racial determinant is the visible sign that leaves Black people vulnerable to individual and societal racism.

critical criminology An approach in criminology that makes use of a conflict framework of neo-Marxism, feminism, political economy, or critical theory. A critical criminological perspective locates the origins of crime within the structure of class and status inequalities and asymmetrical power relations. The law, and the ways in which crimes are defined and punished, are seen as part of a system of social inequality.

critical discourse analysis (CDA) A multidisciplinary study of language use and communication in the context of cultural production that studies how social power, dominance, and oppression are produced, reproduced, and resisted by text and talk in political, cultural, and social arenas. CDA is a tool for deconstructing the ideologies and dominant discourses of the White elite, including the media, policing officials, judges, and educators.

critical race theory (CRT)   A theory that emphasizes the validity of personal experience in order to understand the deep-seated and systemic forces of inequality in society. The stories and experiences of victimized people – which are usually dismissed as biased and subjective – are in this perspective accepted as empirical reality.

cultural studies   The study of cultural practices, of systems of representation and communication, and of the relationship between culture and asymmetrical power relations. Cultural studies uses an interdisciplinary approach that draws from anthropology, sociology, history, semiotics, literature, art, theatre, film criticism, psychoanalysis, feminism, and Third World studies, among others. This approach is used to critically examine the dominant culture and the role that mainstream cultural institutions and the media play in legitimizing, producing, and entrenching systems of inequality. Cultural studies emphasize the roles played by both 'high' and popular culture in the transmission and reproduction of values. It also examines the processes of resistance whereby women, people of colour, and other marginalized groups are challenging hegemonic (*see below*) cultural practices.

cultural racism   A form of racism that is deeply embedded in the collective ideological systems of a society. It represents a tacit network of beliefs and values of the sort that encourage and justify discriminatory actions, behaviours, and practices.

culturalization   The practice, involving coded language, of using cultural differences of the 'Other' to explain the inadequacy, inferiority, and cultural deficiency of non-Western, non-White cultures. These cultures are commonly viewed by the dominant Anglo-European culture as static and monolithic, dangerous, and deviant.

culture   The totality of the ideas, beliefs, values, knowledges, and ways of life of a group of people who share a certain historical, religious, racial, linguistic, ethnic, or social background. For others, culture is a signifying system that utilizes knowledge and symbols; through these, a social order is communicated, reproduced, and experienced (Williams 1976; Grossberg 1992). Manifestations of culture include art, laws, institutions, and customs.

deconstructionism A term first used by philosopher Jacques Derrida, referring to a body of ideas associated with poststructuralism and postmodernism. This language-based analytic method is applied mainly to linguistics, literature, and philosophy; it seeks to 'deconstruct' or unpack the ideological biases and traditional assumptions that are inherent in history and defined as 'truths.' Conventional understandings of gender, race, ethnicity, and other variables have especially lent themselves to deconstruction.

democratic racism An ideology that enables a society to justify and maintain two apparently conflicting sets of values. One set consists of a commitment to a democratic society motivated by egalitarian values of fairness, justice, and equality. Conflicting with these liberal values are attitudes and behaviours such as negative feelings about people of colour, which can lead to differential treatment or discrimination against them. Democratic racism is sustained and reinforced by variety of myths and misconceptions; together, these lead to a pattern of denial of racism in liberal democratic societies.

discourse A socially developed language or system of representation that makes and circulates a coherent set of meanings about an important topic. These meanings serve the interests of that part of society within which the discourse originated. They are then naturalized as 'common sense.' Discourse – often referred to as 'discursive practice' – is thus a social act that may promote or oppose the dominant ideology. Any account of a discourse or a discursive practice must include its topic area, its social origins, and its ideological focus.

discrimination The denial of equal treatment and opportunities to individuals or groups with respect to education, housing, health care, employment, services, goods, and facilities. Discrimination may be based on race, nationality, gender, age, religion, political affiliation, marital or family status, physical or psychiatric disability, or sexual orientation.

dominant discourse/discourses of democratic racism The ways in which society gives voice to racism are often subtle and even invisible because mainstream society's discourses are often contextualized in the framework of democratic liberal principles and values such as colour-blindness, equal opportunity, tolerance, and merit. Within mainstream discourses are planted unchallenged myths and assumptions. Dominant discourse is a powerful tool for social control and hegemony by the White elite.

dominant/majority group/culture   The group in a given society that is largest in number or that successfully shapes or controls other groups through social, economic, cultural, political, or religious power. In Canada the term has generally referred to White, Anglo-Saxon, Protestant males.

equity   The rights of individuals to an equitable share of the goods and services in society. To ensure equality of outcome, equity programs treat groups differently when the situation in society precludes equal treatment. Equity programs are more inclined to give priority to collective rights over individual rights.

essentialism   The practice of reducing the complex identity of a particular group to a series of simplified characteristics which serve to deny individual qualities. Also, the simplistic reduction of an idea or process.

ethnocentrism   A tendency to view events from the perspective of one's own culture, with a corresponding tendency to misunderstand or diminish other groups and regard them as inferior.

Eurocentrism   A complex system of beliefs that upholds the supremacy of Europe's cultural values, ideas, and peoples. European culture is seen as the vehicle for progress towards liberalism and democracy. Eurocentrism minimizes the role of Europeans in maintaining oppressive systems of colonialism and racism.

harassment   Persistent negative expressions (be they attitudes, beliefs, or actions) towards an individual or group, with the intention of disparaging that person or group. Harassment can include name calling, jokes and slurs, graffiti, insults, threats, discourteous treatment, and written and physical abuse.

hegemony   A central concept in cultural studies, first used by Gramsci in the 1930s. It refers to the ability of the dominant classes to maintain power over the economic, political, and cultural life of the state. The concept of hegemony is often encountered in analyses that seek to show how everyday meanings, representations, and activities are organized and normalized as part of a natural order of domination and subordination.

identity   A subjective sense of coherence, consistency, and continuity of self, rooted in both personal and group history.

ideology   A complex set of beliefs, perceptions, and assumptions that provide members of a group with an understanding and an explanation of their world. Ideology influences how people interpret social, cultural, political, and economic systems. It guides behaviour and provides a basis for making sense of the world. It offers a framework for organizing and maintaining relations of power and dominance in a society.

inclusion   A situation that exists when disadvantaged communities and designated group members share power and decision making at all levels in projects, programs, and institutions.

institutional/systemic/structural racism   Racism that consists of policies and practices, entrenched in established institutions, that result in the exclusion or advancement of specific groups of people. It manifests itself in two ways: (1) institutional racism – racial discrimination that arises when individuals carry out the dictates of others who are prejudiced or of a prejudiced society; and (2) structural racism – inequalities rooted in the system-wide operation of a society that exclude substantial numbers of members of particular groups from significant participation in important social institutions.

Jamaicanization   A term that emphasizes the social and cultural problems of Jamaicans in Canadian society and their inability to fit into Canada because of their 'different and deviant' cultural values and norms. Jamaicans are perceived to belong to a 'violent culture' from which they cannot escape.

mainstream   In the context of anti-racism, the dominant culture and the political, social, educational, cultural, and economic institutions through which its power is maintained.

marginalized   The status of groups who do not have full and equal access to the social, economic, cultural, and political institutions of society.

moral panic/discursive crisis   A public campaign in which some person, group, or series of events is constructed as an imminent threat to 'normal civilized society,' or 'our way of life,' if not 'our very lives.' Public opinion is mobilized through agencies of social control such as the media, the police, and the courts in order to challenge and remove the threat. The country or city is described as in crisis and under siege.

oppression   The domination of certain individuals or groups by others through physical, psychological, social, cultural, or economic force.

Otherness   Used in reference to certain racialized groups in society – Aboriginal people, people of African or Caribbean origin, and so on. These people are categorized as the 'Other' – that is, as possessing 'different' (i.e., deviant or undesirable) values, beliefs, and norms. The rhetoric of 'Otherness' is pervasive and can be found in the everyday discourses of the media, politicians, policing officials, educators, and other public authorities.

people of colour   *See* **racialized minorities**

postmodernism   A philosophical system that arose in the arts in the early twentieth century as a reaction to modernism. Later it influenced the social sciences by asserting that social and cultural reality – and social science itself – is a human construction. It emphasizes the subjective nature of knowledge and experience. As a philosophy and discourse, it challenges authority and power relations, questions traditional values, and critiques conventional understandings of 'truth.'

prejudice   A mental state or attitude of prejudging – generally unfavourably. Those who are prejudiced attribute to every member of a group characteristics falsely attributed to the group as a whole.

race   An approach to classifying humankind according to common ancestry. It is based on physical characteristics such as skin colour, hair texture, stature, and facial features. As a concept, race is purely social and has no basis in biology. Yet as a social construction, race significantly affects the lives of people of colour.

racial discrimination   Any distinction, exclusion, restriction, or preference based on race the purpose of which is to nullify or impair the recognition, enjoyment, or exercise of human rights and fundamental freedoms in any aspect of public life.

racial incident   An incident that involves (a) an element of racial motivation or (b) an allegation of racial motivation. Racial incidents may involve verbal abuse (such as banter, jokes, name calling, harassment, teasing, or discourteous treatment), defacement of property, or physical abuse.

racial profiling   A phenomenon in which certain criminal activities are attributed to a group in society on the basis of skin colour or ethnoracial background; as a result, individual members of that group are targeted. Their physical attributes are being used as markers for criminality. In this book, racial profiling is viewed as involving the same processes as racism in all its forms (individual, institutional and systemic).

racialization   Often used interchangeably with racism. It involves processes whereby race is attributed to particular social practices and discourses (e.g., the phrase 'the racialization of crime' means that criminal activity is often associated with Black people). Racialization is also associated with processes whereby ethno-racial populations are categorized, constructed, inferiorized, and marginalized.

racialized (racist) discourse   Refers to the ways in which society gives voice to racism – through its explanations, narratives, myths, codes of meaning, accounts, images, social practices, and so on. These serve to establish, sustain, and reinforce oppressive power relations.

racialized ideology   The concepts, ideas, images, and institutions that provide the framework of interpretation and meaning for racial thought in society. It creates and preserves a system of dominance based on race. It is communicated and reproduced through agencies of socialization and cultural transmission such as the media, schools and universities, religious and legal doctrines, symbols and images, art, music, and literature.

racialized minorities   A group of people who because of their physical characteristics are subjected to differential treatment. Their minority status is the result of a lack of access to power, privilege, and prestige in relation to the majority group.

racism   A system in which one group of people exercises power over another on the basis of skin colour. It involves an implicit or explicit set of beliefs, erroneous assumptions, and actions based on an ideology of the inherent superiority of one racial group over another. It often manifests itself in organizational or institutional structures and programs as well as in individuals' thought and behaviour patterns.

reflective practice Critical thinking and rethinking about issues that are often taken for granted. Also involves deconstructing feelings, events, situations, and experiences by peeling away the various levels of meaning attached to them over time.

representation The process of giving concrete form to abstract ideological concepts (examples: representations of women, workers, Blacks). Representations include all kinds of imagery and discourse and involve constructions of reality taken from specific points of view. Representation is a social process of making sense within all available signifying systems: print and electronic media, speech writing, video, film, books, and so on.

stereotype A false or generalized conception of a group of people that results in an conscious or unconscious categorization of each member of that group, without regard for individual differences.

text Includes not only books, plays, and poetry, but also media representations, films, and visual art forms, as well as codified laws, judicial decisions, and public policies.

Whiteness A social construction which has created a racial hierarchy that has shaped all the social, cultural, educational, political, and economic institutions of society. Whiteness is linked to domination and is a form of race privilege invisible to White people, who are not conscious of its power. Whiteness, from a cultural studies perspective, is description, symbol, experience, and ideology.

Table of Cases

Atwater v. Lago Vista (1996), 533 U.S. 924
Christie v. York, [1940] S.C.R. 139
Plessy v. Ferguson (1896), 163 U.S. 537
R.D.S. v. Her Majesty the Queen, [1997] 3 S.C.R. 484
R. v. Brown (2003) 64 O.R. (3d) 161
R. v. Calderon and Stalas (2004), C 38499 and C. 38500 (Ont. C.A.)
R. v. Gladue, [1999] 1 S.C.R. 668
R. v. Golden, [2001] 3 S.C.R. 679
R. v. Khan (2004), 244 D.L.R. (4th) 443 (Ont. Sup. Ct.)
R. v. Ladouceur, [1990] 1 S.C.R. 1257
R. v. Parks (1993), 15 O.R. (3d) 324
R. v. Peck, [2001] O.J. No. 4581 (Ont. S.C.J.)
R. v. Richards (1999), 26 C.R. (5th) 286
R. v. Simpson (1993),12 O.R. (3d) 182
R. v. Spence, [2004] 1 S.C.R. 76
R. v. Williams, [1998] 1 S.C.R. 1128
Robinson v. U.S. (1973), 414 U.S. 218
Terry v. Ohio (1968), 392 U.S. 1
Whren v. U.S. (1996), 517 U.S. 806

References

Alexander, K.A., and A. Glaze. 1996. *Towards Freedom: The African-Canadian Exerience.* Toronto: Umbrella Press.

'Analysis Raises Board Hackles.' 2002. *Toronto Star.* 20 October.

Andrews, A. 1992. 'Review of Race Relations Practices of the Metropolitan Toronto Police Force.' Report prepared for the Municipality of Metropolitan Toronto.

Anthias, F. 1998. 'The Limits of Ethnic Diversity.' *Patterns of Prejudice* 32(4):6–19.

Apple, M. 1993. 'Constructing the "Other": Rightist Reconstructions of Common Sense.' In C. McCarthy and W. Crichlow, eds. *Race, Identity, and Representation in Education.* New York: Routledge.

Armstrong, F. 2005. 'Academic Assails Racial-Profiling Results.' *Kingston Whig-Standard.* 20 September.

Ashenfelter, D. 2000. 'State Cops More Apt to Search Black Men.' *Detroit Free Press.* 21 July.

Association of Black Law Enforcers. 2003. 'Official Position on Racial Profiling in Canada.' Toronto: Author.

Aylward, C. 2002. *Canadian Critical Race Theory and Praxis: Racism and the Law.* Toronto: Faculty of Law, University of Toronto.

Backhouse, C. 1999. *Colour-Coded: A Legal History of Racism in Canada, 1900–1950.* Toronto: University of Toronto Press.

Bahdi, R. 2003. 'No Exit: Racial Profiling and Canada's War against Terrorism.' *Osgoode Hall Law Journal* 41(2/3):293–317.

Bain, B. 2000. 'Walking While Black.' *Village Voice*, April 26–May2.

Barber, J. 2004. 'Enough with the "Few Bad Apples."' *Globe and Mail.* 24 April.

Barnes, A. 2002. 'Dangerous Duality: The "Net Effect" of Immigration and

Deportation on Jamaicans in Canada.' In Chan and Mirchandani, eds., *Crimes of Colour.*

Barthes, R. 1973. *Mythologies.* London: Paladin.

Bell, D. 1987. *And We Are Not Saved: The Elusive Quest for Racial Justice.* New York: Basic Books.

– 1992. *Faces at the Bottom of the Well: The Permanence of Racism.* New York: Basic Books.

– 2000. 'Police Brutality: Portent of Disaster and Discomforting Divergence.' In J. Nelson, ed. *Police Brutality.* New York: Norton.

Bell, L. 2003. 'Telling Tales: What Stories Can Teach Us about Racism.' *Race, Ethnicity, and Education* 6(1):1–28.

Benjamin, A. 2002. 'The Social and Legal Banishment of Anti-Racism: A Black Perspective.' In W. Chan and K. Mirchandani, eds., *Crimes of Colour.*

– 2003. 'The Black Jamaican Criminal: The Making of Ideology.' PhD thesis, Ontario Institute for Studies in Education.

Benson, R.W. 2000. 'Changing Police Culture: The Sine Qua Non of Reform.' Rampart Scandal Symposium, Loyola Law School, Los Angeles, 14–15 September.

Berger, P., and T. Luckmann. 1966. *The Social Construction of Reality: A Treatise in the Sociology of Knowledge.* New York: Doubleday/Anchor.

Blatchford, C. 2002. 'Sometimes Race Is Simply a Fact.' *National Post.* 30 October.

Bobb, Merrick J. 2002 (March). 'Racial Profiling.' Research Paper, Los Angeles Police Assessment Resource Center.

Bolaria, B.S., and P. Li. 1988. *Racial Oppression in Canada,* 2nd ed. Toronto: Garamond.

Bourdieu, P. 1999. *Language and Symbolic Power.* In A. Jaworski and N. Coupland, eds., *The Discourse Reader.* London: Routledge.

Bowling, B. 2003. 'Disproportionality and Discrimination in the Use of Stop/Search Powers by the West Midlands Police Service.' Report, West Midlands, U.K.

Branswell, B. 2005. 'How Blacks See Encounters with the Police.' *The Gazette* (Montreal). 13 February.

Brennan, R. 2003. 'Norton Defends Profiling Inquiry.' *Toronto Star.* 22 February.

Bromell, C. 2002. 'No Racial Profiling Is Being Done.' *Toronto Star.* 27 November.

Butler, J. 1993. 'Endangered/Endangering: Schematic Racism and White Paranoia.' In R. Gooding-Williams, ed., *Reading Rodney King, Reading Urban Uprising.* London: Routledge.

Calliste, A., and G. Dei, eds. 2000. *Anti-Racist Feminism: Critical Reader and Gender Studies.* Halifax: Fernwood.

Campbell, C. 1995. *Race, Myth, and the News.* Thousand Oaks, CA: Sage.

Campbell, M. 2003. 'Runciman Must Defend His Stand on Racism Issue.' *Toronto Star.* 25 February

Canadian Diversity/Diversité canadienne. 2004. 'Racial Discrimination, Racism, and Human Rights.' Special issue 3(3).

Canadian Press. 2004. 'Saskatoon Police Officers Suspended.' 26 October.

Carmichael, A. 2004. 'Vancouver Police Chief Defends Law That Allows Starlight Tours.' *Canadian Press Wire,* 21 January.

Carrington, B. 2002. 'Race, Representation, and the Sporting Body.' Paper submitted to the CUCR's occasional paper series, May 2002.

CBC. 2005. 'Province Creating New Police Complaints Agency.' 10 May. http://sask.cbc.ca/regional/servlet/View?filename=police-complaints050510

CBC News. 2004. 'Tape Reveals Racist Police Comments at Ipperwash Standoff.' 21 January.

Chan, J. 1997. *Changing Police Culture in a Multicultural Society.* Cambridge, UK: Cambridge University Press.

Chan, W., and K. Mirchandani, eds., 2002. *Crimes of Colour: Racialization and the Criminal Justice System.* Peterborough, ON: Broadview Press.

Chapman, R., and J. Rutherford, eds. 1988. *Male Order: Unwrapping Masculinity.* London: Lawrence and Wishart.

Cheney, P. 2002. 'Blacks Dance to Deadly Beat in Toronto's Clubs.' *Globe and Mail.* 2 November.

Chevigny, P. 1995. *Edge of the Knife: Police Violence in the Americas.* New York: The New Press.

Christmas, B. 2001. 'Aboriginal Solutions, Aboriginal Issues.' Speech to the Criminal Justice Association of Canada, 22 June, Halifax.

Clancy, A., M. Hough, R. Aust, and C. Kershaw. 2001. 'Crime, Policing, and Justice: The Experience of Ethnic Minorities – Findings from the 2000 British Crime Survey.' Home Office Research Study no. 223. London: Home Office.

Cloud, J. 2001. 'What's Race Got to Do with It?' *Time Canada,* 31 July.

Codjoe, H. 2001. '"Public Enemy" of Black Academic Achievement: The Persistence of Race and Schooling in the Experience of Black Students.' *Race, Ethnicity, and Education* 4(4):344–75.

Colby, S.F. 2001. 'Stopping a Moving Target.' *Rutgers Race and the Law Review* 3:191.

Collacott, M. 2002. 'Canadian Immigration Policy: The Need for Major Reform.' Vancouver: Fraser Institute.

Commission of Inquiry into Matters Relating to the Death of Neil Stonechild. 2004. *Final Report.* Regina: Queen's Printer.

Commission on Systemic Racism in the Ontario Criminal Justice System. 1995.

Report of the Commission on Systemic Racism in the Ontario Criminal Justice system. Toronto: Queen's Printer.

Cottle, S., ed. 2000. *Ethnic Minorities and the Media: Changing Cultural Boundaries.* Buckinghamshire, UK, and Philadelphia, PA: Open University Press.

Covington, J. 1999. 'Racial Classification in Criminology: The Reproduction of Racialized Crime.' *Sociological Forum* 10:547–69.

Coyle, J. 2003a. 'Fantino Blew a Chance to Restore City's Confidence.' *Toronto Star.* 22 February.

– 2003b. 'Bromell Huff and Puffs and Blows His Credibility.' *Toronto Star.* 19 April.

– 2004. 'Fantino and Police Deviance.' *Toronto Star.* 29 January.

Crank, J. 1997. *Understanding Police Culture.* Cincinnati, OH: Anderson.

Davis, J., ed. 2002. *Stories of Change: Narratives and Social Movements.* Albany: State University of New York Press.

Dei, G., and A. Calliste, eds. 1996. *Anti-Racism Education: Theory and Practice.* Halifax: Fernwood.

– 2000. *Power, Knowledge and Anti-Racism Education: A Critical Reader.* Halifax: Fernwood.

Dei, G., L. Karumancheryani, and N. Karumanchery. 2004. *'Playing the Race Card': Exposing White Power and Privilege.* New York: Peter Lang.

Delgado, R., ed. 1995. *Critical Race Theory: The Cutting Edge.* Philadelphia: Temple University Press.

Delgado, R., and J. Stephancic, eds. 2000a. *Critical Race Theory: The Cutting Edge.* 2nd ed. Philadelphia, PA: Temple University Press.

– 2000b. 'Legal Storytelling: Storytelling for Oppositionists and Others: A Plea for the Narrative.' In R. Delgado and J. Stefancic, eds. *Critical Race Theory: The Cutting Edge.*

DiManno, R. 2004. 'Scandal Makes Case for Civilian Oversight.' *Toronto Star.* 23 January.

Dodd, Vikram. 2003. 'Black People 27 Times More Likely to Be Stopped.' *Guardian Unlimited,* 21 April.

Duffy, D. 2004. 'Why Police Go Bad.' *Globe and Mail.* 4 May.

Dulude, L. 2000. *Justice and the Poor.* Ottawa: National Council of Welfare.

Dyer, R. 1997. *White.* London: Routledge.

Edwards, P. 2001. *One Dead Indian: The Premier, The Police and the Ipperwash Crisis.* Toronto: McClelland & Stewart.

Ehrenreich, B. 1990. 'The Usual Suspects.' *Mother Jones,* September–October.

Engel, R., J. Calnon, and T. Bernard. 2002.'Theory and Racial Profiling: Shortcomings and Future Directions in Research.' *Justice Quarterly* 19(2):249–73.

Entman, R., and A. Rojecki. 2000. *The Black Images in the White Mind: Media and Race in America*. Chicago: University of Chicago Press.

Erez, E., J.O. Finckenauer, and P.R. Ibarra. 2003. 'Introduction: Policing a Multicultural Society.' *Police and Society* 7 (April):5–12.

Essed, P. 2000. 'Everyday Racism.' In P. Essed and D.T. Goldberg, eds., *Race Critical Theories*. Malden, MA: Blackwell.

Ewick, P., and S. Silbey. 1995. 'Subversive Stories and Hegemonic Tales: Towards a Sociology of Narrative.' *Law and Society Review* 29(2):197–226.

Fairclough, N. 1992. *Discourses and Social Change*. Cambridge: Polity Press.

– 1995. *Media Discourse*. London: Arnold.

Fanon, F. 1967. *Black Skin, White Masks*. New York: Grove Press

Fantino, J. 2002. 'We Do Not Do Racial Profiling.' *Toronto Star*, 19 October.

Feeley, M., and J. Simon. 1994. 'Actuarial Justice: The Emerging New Criminal Law.' In David Nelken, ed. *The Futures of Criminology*. London: Sage.

Ferguson, G. 2003. *Review and Recommendations Concerning Various Aspects of Police Misconduct Commissioned by Chief Julian Fantino*. Toronto: Toronto Police Service.

Fielding, N. 1988. *Joining Forces: Police Training, Socialization, and Occupational Competence*. London and New York: Routledge.

Fiske, J. 1994. *Media Matters: Everyday Culture and Political Change*. London: Routledge; and Minneapolis: University of Minnesota Press.

– 1999. *Television Culture*. 10th ed. London and New York: Routledge.

– 2000. 'White Watch.' In S. Cottle, ed., *Ethnic Minorities and the Media*. Buckingham, UK, and Philadelphia, PA: Open University Press.

Fitzgerald, M. 1999. 'Final Report on Stop & Search.' Police Research Series (December). London: Home Office.

Fleras, A., and J. Kunz. 2001. *Media and Minorities: Representing Diversity in a Multicultural Canada*. Toronto: Thomson Nelson.

Foucault, M. 1977. *Discipline and Punish*. London: Tavistock.

– 1980. *Power/Knowledge: Selected Interviews and Other Writings, 1972–1977*, ed. C. Gordon. New York: Pantheon.

Fowlie, J., and G. Abate. 2003. 'Teenager Could Feel the Anger from Fantino.' *Globe and Mail*. 9 January.

Francis, D. 2002. *Immigration: The Economic Case*. Toronto: Key Porter.

Frankenberg, R. 1993. *White Women, Race Matters: The Social Construction of Whiteness*. Minneapolis: University of Minnesota Press.

Frideres, J., and R. Gadacz. 2001. *Aboriginal People in Canada: Contemporary Conflicts*. 6th ed. Scarborough, ON: Prentice-Hall.

Gabriel, J. 1998. *Whitewash: Racialized Politics and the Media*. London: Routledge.

Gandy, O. 1998. *Communication and Race: A Structured Perspective.* London: Arnold.

Garland, D. 1996. 'The Limits of the Sovereign State: Strategies of Crime Control in Contemporary Society.' *British Journal of Criminology* 36: 445–71.

Gilroy, P. 1991. *There Ain't No Black in the Union Jack: The Cultural Politics of Race and Nation.* Chicago: University of Chicago Press.

Girard, P. 2003. '*Kirk Johnson v. Michael Sanford and the Halifax Regional Police Service.*' Report to Board of Inquiry, Nova Scotia Human Rights Commission, Halifax, 22 December.

Giroux, H. 1995. 'Racism and the Aesthetic of Hyperreal Violence: Pulp Fiction and Other Visual Tragedies.' In *Fugitive Cultures: Race, Violence, and Youth.* London and New York: Routledge.

Gittens, M., and D. Cole. 1996. 'Systemic Racism in the Ontario Criminal Justice System.' Toronto: Queen's Printer.

Glasser, I. 1999. 'American Drug Laws: The New Jim Crow.' The 1999 Edward C. Sobota Lecture, Albany Law School.

– 2001. *Racial Profiling and Selective Law Enforcement: The New Jim Crow.* Chicago: American Bar Association.

Godfrey, T. 2004. 'Jamaica's Bloodbath May Spread to T.O. Cops Say.' *Toronto Sun.* 24 November.

Gold, A. 2003. 'Media Hype, Racial Profiling, and Good Science.' *Canadian Journal Of Criminology And Criminal Justice* 45(3):391–400.

Gordon, Y. 2004. 'Fantino Wants OHRC's Racial Profiling Information.' *Canada Extra*, 15–21 January.

Gray, H. 1995a. *Watching Race: Television and the Struggle for Blackness.* Minneapolis: University of Minnesota Press.

– 1995b. 'Black Masculinity and Visual Culture.' *Callaloo* 18(2):401–5.

Gray, J. 2004. 'Police Union Boss to Ignore Political Ban.' *Globe and Mail.* 15 December.

Habermas, J. 1974. *Theory and Practice.* London: Heinemann.

Hall, S. 1980. 'Encoding and Decoding.' In S. Hall, D. Hobson, A. Lowe, and P. Willis., eds., *Culture, Media, Language.* London: Hutchinson.

– 1997. 'The Work of Representation.' In S. Hall, ed., *Representation: Cultural Reresentations and Signifying Practices.* London: Sage.

Hall, S., C. Critcher, T. Jefferson, J. Clarke, and B. Roberts. 1978. *Policing the Crisis: Mugging, the State, and Law and Order.* London: Methuen.

Harper, T. 2003. 'Ottawa Police Chief Muzzles His Deputy.' *Toronto Star.* 4 March.

Harris, A. 2000. 'Gender, Violence, Race, and Criminal Justice.' *Stanford Law Review* 52(777):803.

Harris, D. 2002. *Profiles in Injustice: Why Racial Profiling Cannot Work.* New York: The New Press.

Harris, D.A. 2001. ' When Success Breeds Attack: The Coming Backlash against Racial Profiling Studies.' *Michigan Journal of Race and Law* 237(6):244–5.

Harrison, S.J. 1998. 'Police Organizational Culture: Using Ingrained Values to Build Positive Organizational Improvement.' Pennsylvania State University. http://www.thinbluelie.com/pamij.com/harrison.html.

Heidensohn, F. 1993. *Women in Control: The Role of Women in Law Enforcement.* London: Oxford University Press.

Hébert, Y. 2001. 'Identity, Diversity, and Education: A Critical Review of the Literature.' *Canadian Ethic Studies Journal* 33(3):155–85.

Hecker, S. 1997. 'Race and Pretextual Traffic Stops: An Expanded Role for Civilian Review Board. *Columbia Human Rights Law Review* 28:551.

Henry, F., P. Hastings, and B. Freer. 1996. 'Perceptions of Race and Crime in Ontario: Empirical Evidence from Toronto and the Durham Region.' *Canadian Journal of Criminology* 38(4):419–76.

Henry, F., and C. Tator. 2002. *Discourses of Domination: Racial Bias in the Canadian English-Language Press.* Toronto: University of Toronto Press.

– 2005. *The Colour of Democracy: Racism in Canadian Society.* 3rd ed. Toronto: Thomson Nelson.

Hier, S., and J. Greenberg. 2002. 'News Discourse and the Problematization of Chinese Migration to Canada.' In F. Henry and C. Tator, *Discourses of Domination*.

Holdaway, S. 1997. 'Constructing and Sustaining "Race" in the Police Work Force.' *British Journal of Sociology* 48(1):19–34.

– 2001. 'Police Race Relations,' Consultative paper written for Commission on the Future of Multi-Ethnic Britain.

– 2003. 'Police Race Relations in England and Wales: Theory, Policy, and Practice.' *Police and Society* 7(1):49–75.

Holland, B. 2000. 'Safeguarding Equal Protection Rights: The Search for an Exclusionary Rule under the Equal Protection Clause.' *American Criminal Law Review* 37:1107.

Honderich, J. 2003. 'Star's Statistics Analysis Holds Up to Fair Scrutiny.' *Toronto Star.* 1 March.

hooks, b. 1990a. *Yearning: Race, Gender, and Cultural Politics.* Toronto: Between the Lines.

– 1990b. 'Postmodern Blackness.' *Postmodern Culture* 1(1):1–15.

Independent Race and Refugee News Network. 2002. www.irr.org.uk/2002/november/ak0000006.html

Institute on Race and Poverty. 2000. 'Components of Racial Profiling Legislation.' Minneapolis: University of Minnesota Law School.

Hylton, J. 2002. 'The Justice System and Canada's Aboriginal Peoples: The
Persistence of Racial Discrimination.' In W. Chan and K. Mirchandani, eds.,
Crimes of Colour.

Jakubowski, L.M. 1997. *Immigration and the Legalization of Racism.* Halifax: Fernwood.

James, C. 1998. 'Up to No Good': Black on the Streets and Encountering Police.'
In V. Satzewich, ed., *Racism and Social Inequality in Canada: Concepts, Controversies, and Strategies of Resistance.* Toronto: Thompson.

– 2002. 'Armed and Dangerous! Racializing Suspects, Suspecting Race.' In B.
Schissel and C. Brooks, eds., *Marginality and Condemnation: An Introduction to
Critical Criminology.*

– 2003. 'It Can't Be Just Sports! Schooling, Academics and Athletic Scholarship
Expectations.' *Orbit* 33(3):33–5.

– 2005. *Race in Play: Understanding the Socio-cultural Worlds of Student Athletes.*
Toronto: Canadian Scholars' Press.

James, R. 2002. 'Why I Fear for My Sons.' *Toronto Star,* 21 October.

– 2003. 'Chief His Own Worst Enemy.' *Toronto Star.* 6 August.

Jernigan, A.S. 2000. 'Driving while Black: Racial Profiling in America.' *Law and
Psychology Review* 24:127–38.

Jiwani, Y. 2002. 'The Criminalization of "Race," the Racialization of Crime.' In
W. Chan and K. Mirchandani, eds., *Crimes of Colour.*

Johnson, K. 2000. 'The Case against Race Profiling in Immigration Law
Enforcement.' *Washington University Law Quarterly* 78(3):675–736.

Johnson, P. 1999. 'Reflections on Critical White(ness) Studies.' In T.K.
Nakayama and J.N. Martin, eds., *Whiteness: The Communication of Social Identity.* London: Sage.

Jordan, G., and C. Weedon. 1995. *Cultural Politics: Class, Gender, Race, and the
Postmodern World.* Oxford: Blackwell.

Jull, S. 2000. 'Youth Violence, Schools, and the Management Question: A Discussion of Zero Tolerance and Equity in Public Schooling.' *Canadian Journal
of Educational Administration and Policy* 17 (November).

Kappeler, V., R. Sluder, and G. Albert. 1994. *Forces of Deviance: Understanding
the Dark Side of Policing.* Long Grove, IL: Waveland Press.

Karim, K. 1993. 'Constructions, Deconstructions, and Reconstructions: Competing Canadian Discourses on Ethnocultural Terminology.' *Canadian Journal
of Communications* 18(2):197–218.

Kearney, J. 2001. 'Racial Profiling: A Disgrace at the Intersection of Race and
the Criminal Justice System.' Guest editorial. *Arkansas Lawyer.* Spring.

Kelly, J. 1998. *Under the Gaze: Learning to be Black in White Society.* Halifax: Fernwood.

Kennedy, R. 1997. *Race, Crime and the Law.* New York: Vintage Books.

Knight, E., and W. Kurnik. 2002. *The Defense Perspective on Civil Rights Litigation,* Chicago: American Bar Association.

Knowles, C. 1996. 'Racism, Biography, and Psychiatry.' In V. Amit-Talai and C. Knowles, eds., *Re-Situating Identities: The Politics of Race, Ethnicity, and Culture.* Peterborough, ON: Broadview Press.

Kobayashi, Audrey. 1990. 'Racism and the Law.' *Urban Geography* 11(5): 447–73.

Korstanje, C. 2003. 'Attacking Rights Concerns Very Unseemly in Ontario.' *Hamilton Spectator.* 24 February.

Law Reform Commission of Canada. 1992. 'Consultation Document.' Ottawa: Author.

Lawrence, E. 1982. 'Just Plain Common Sense: The Roots of Racism.' In Centre for Contemporary Cultural Studies, ed., *The Empire Strikes Back: Race and Racism in 70's Britain.* London: Hutchinson.

Lawson, E. 2003. 'Reassessing Safety and Discipline in Our Schools: Opportunities for Growth, Opportunities for Change.' *Orbit* 3(3):23–5.

Lejtenyi, P. 2002. 'Police on Their Back,' *Montreal Mirror.* www.montrealmirror.com

Lentricchia, F., and T. McLaughlin. 1995. *Critical Terms for Literary Study.* 2nd ed. Chicago: University of Chicago Press.

Leong, M. 2003. 'Chief Fails to Mollify Youth.' *Toronto Star.* 9 January.

LeSage, P. 2005. *Report of the Police Complaints System in Ontario.* Toronto: Ministry of the Attorney General of Ontario. http://www.attorneygeneral.ohrc.on.ca.

Levine-Rasky, C., ed. *Working through Whiteness: International Perspectives.* Albany: Albany State University Press.

Lewis, C. 1989. *Report of the Race Relations and Policing Task Force* (April). Toronto: Queen's Printer.

Lewis, S. 1992. Letter to Premier Bob Rae, 9 June.

Li, P. 2003. *Destination Canada: Immigration Debates and Issues.* Don Mills, ON: Oxford University Press.

Lipper, G.M. 2001. 'Racial Profiling.' *Harvard Journal on Legislation* 38:551.

Lyotard, J.-F. 1984. *The Postmodern Condition.* Manchester: Manchester University Press.

Mahtani, M. 2001. 'Representing Minorities: Canadian Media and Minority Identities.' *Canadian Ethnic Studies* 33(3):99–134.

Mackie, R. 2003a. 'Fantino Slams Critics of Police.' *Globe and Mail.* 23 January.

– 2003b. 'Anger Greets Runciman Comment.' *Globe and Mail*. 7 August.

Makin, K. 2003. 'Police Engage in Profiling, Chief Counsel Tells Court.' *Globe and Mail*. 18 January.

Mallan, C. 2003. 'Runciman Ignites Furor.' *Toronto Star*. 7 August.

Manning, P.K. 1977. *Police Work: The Social Organization of Policing*. Cambridge: MIT Press.

– 1993. 'Towards a Theory of Policing Organizations, Polarities and Change.' Paper presented at the International Conference in Social Change in Policing. 19 August.

Martinot, S. 2003. *The Rule of Racialization: Class, Identity, Governance*. Philadelphia: Temple University Press.

Mascoll, P., and J. Rankin. 2005. 'Black Officers Confirmed Profiling.' *Toronto Star*. 31 March.

McCabe-Lokos, N. 2002. 'Police Can't Be "Politically Correct": Bromell.' *Toronto Star*. 11 November.

McCarthy, B., and J. Hagan. 1995. 'Getting into Street Crime: The Structure and Process of Criminal Embeddedness.' *Social Science Review* 24(1):63–95.

McPherson, Sir W. 1999. The Stephen Lawrence Inquiry Report. Presented to Parliament by the Secretary of State, February, Home Office, U.K.

Mercer, K. 1994. *Welcome to the Jungle*. London. Routledge.

Mercer K., and Issac Julien. 1988. 'Race, Sexual Politics, and Black Masculinity: A Dossier.' In J. Rutherford and R. Chapman, eds., *Male Order: Unwrapping Masculinity*. London: Lawrence and Wishart.

Metropolitan Police Authority. 2003. 'Stop and Search Scrutiny MPA Status Report.' Report. London, U.K.

Miller, J. 2000. 'Profiling Populations Available for Stops and Searches.' Police Research Series, paper no. 131. London: Home Office.

Miller, J., N. Bland, and P. Quinton. 2000. 'Upping the Pace? An Evaluation of the Recommendations of the Stephen Lawrence Inquiry on Stops and Searches.' Home Office, Police Research Series Paper 128.

Morales, A.L. 1998. *Medicine Stories: History, Culture and the Politics of Integrity*. Cambridge, MA: South End Press.

Morris, M.V. 2001. 'Racial Profiling and International Human Rights Law: Illegal Discrimination in the United States.' *Emory International Law Review* 15:207–65.

Morrison, T. 1992. *Playing in the Dark: Whiteness and the Literary Imagination*. Cambridge, MA: Harvard University Press.

– 1997. Introduction. In T. Morrison and C. Brodsky Lacour, eds., *Birth of a Nation'hood: Gaze, Script, and Spectacle in the O.J. Simpson Case*.

Morrison, T., and C. Brodsky Lacour. 1997. *Birth of a Nation'hood: Gaze, Script, and Spectacle in the O.J. Simpson Case.* New York: Pantheon.

✷ Mosher, C. 1998. *Discrimination and Denial: Systemic Racism in Ontario's Legal and Criminal Justice Systems, 1892–1961.* Toronto: University of Toronto Press.

Murji, K., and J. Solomos, eds. 2005. *Racialization: Studies in Theory and Practice.* New York: Oxford University Press.

Murray, C. 2002. 'Silent on the Set: Cultural Diversity and Race in English-Canadian TV Drama.' Report prepared for Department of Canadian Heritage, Hull, Quebec.

Neiderhoffer, A. 1969. *Behind the Shield.* New York: Anchor.

Neugebauer, R. 2000. *Kids, Cops, and Colour: The Social Organization of Police-Minority Youth Relations.* In R. Neugebauer, ed., *Criminal Injustice: Racism in the Criminal Justice System.* Toronto: Canadian Scholars Press.

Nunan, R. 1999. 'Critical Race Theory: An Overview.' *Newsletter on Philosophy, Law, and the Black Experience* 98(2):1–18.

OCAP (Ontario Coalition Against Poverty). 2000. *Handbook to Surviving Bad Policing.* Toronto: Committee to Stop Targeted Policing.

Olsen, D. 2000. 'Justice in Black and White: The Justice Gap.' *MPR News,* 13 April.

Oman, K. 2003. *Racial Profiling and the Cultural Life of the Stereotype.* Paper presented at meeting of Southern Sociological Society, New Orleans, 20 March.

Omi, M., and H. Winant. 1986. *Racial Formation in the United States.* New York: Routledge.

Ontario Commission on Systemic Racism in the Criminal Justice System. 1995. *Report.* Toronto: Queen's Printer.

Ontario Human Rights Commission. 2003. *Paying the Price: The Human Cost of Racial Profiling.* Inquiry Report. Toronto: Ministry of the Attorney General.

– 2005. 'Policy Guidelines on Racism and Racial Discrimination.' http://www.ohrc.on.ca.

Ontario Human Rights Commission (Aboriginal Section). 2003. *Paying the Price: The Human Cost of Racial Profiling.* Inquiry Report. Toronto: OHRC.

Pedicelli, G. 1998. *When Police Kill: Police Use of Force in Montreal and Toronto.* Montreal: Véhicule Press.

Ponting, R. ed. 1997. *First Nations in Canada: Perspectives on Opportunity, Empowerment, and Self-Determination.* Toronto: McGraw–Hill Ryerson.

– 1998. 'Racism and Stereotyping of First Nations. In V. Satzewich, ed., *Racism and Social Inequality in Canada.* Toronto: Thompson Educational Publishing.

Porter, C. 2002. 'Police Union Blasts Star.' *Toronto Star*. 22 October.

Randall, A. 'Racial Profiling Allegations Bring Calls for Statewide Data Collection.' *MPR News*, 15 June.

Rankin, J., M. Quinn, S. Sheppard, and J. Duncanson. 2002. 'Singled Out.' *Toronto Star*. 19 October.

Razack, S. 1998. *Looking White People in the Eye: Gender, Race, and Culture in Courtrooms and Classrooms*. Toronto: University of Toronto Press.

– 1999a. 'Making Canada White: Law and Policing of Bodies of Colour in the 1990s.' *Journal of Law and Society* 14(1):159–84.

– 1999b. 'R.D.S. v. Her Majesty The Queen: A Case about Home.' In E. Dua and A. Robertson, eds., *Scratching the Surface*. Toronto: Women's Press.

Reiner, R. 2000. *The Politics of the Police*. 3rd ed. Hemel Hempstead: Harvester Wheatsheaf.

Reuss–Ianni, E. 1983. *Two Cultures of Policing*. New Brunswick, NJ: Transaction Books.

Riga, A. 2005. 'A Passion for Justice.' *The Gazette* (Montreal). 5 February.

Rocha, R. 2005. 'Police Admit to Racial Profiling.' *The Gazette* (Montreal). 29 January.

Rose, W. 2002. 'Crimes of Color: Risk, Profiling, and the Contemporary Racialization of Social Control.' *International Journal of Politics, Culture, and Society* 16(2):179–201.

Royal Commission on Aboriginal Peoples. 1996. *Report of the Royal Commission on Aboriginal Peoples*. 5 vols. Ottawa: Minister of Supply and Services. http://www.inac.gc.ca/ch/recap.

Royal Commission into the Donald Marshall, Jr. Prosecution. 1990. *Report of the Royal Commission into the Donald Marchall, Jr. Prosecution*. Halifax: Government of Nova Scotia.

Ruck, M., and S. Wortley. 2002. 'Racial and Ethnic Minority High School Students' Perceptions of School Disciplinary Practices: A Look at Some Canadian Findings.' *Journal of Youth and Adolescence* 31(3):185–95.

Russell, K. 1998. *The Color of Crime: Racial Hoaxes, White Fear, Black Protectionism, Police Harassment, and Other Macroagressions*. New York and London: New York University Press.

Russell–Brown, K. 2004. *Underground Codes: Race, Crime, and Related Fires*. New York and London: New York University Press.

Rutherford, J. 1988. 'Who's That Man?' In R. Chapman and J. Rutherford, eds., *Male Order: Unwrapping Masculinity*. London: Lawrence and Wishart.

St Lewis, J. 1996. 'Identity and Black Consciousness in North America.' In J. Littleton, ed., *Clash of Identities: Essays on Media, Manipulation and Politics of Self*. Englewood Cliffs, NJ: Prentice-Hall.

Samuelson, L., and P. Monture–Angus. 2002. 'Aboriginal People and Social Control.' In B. Schissel and C. Brooks, eds., *Marginality and Condemnation*.

Satzewich, V., and T. Wotherspoon. 1993. *First Nations: Race, Class, and Gender Relations*. Toronto: Nelson.

Scarman, Rt. Hon. Lord, OBE. 1981. *The Brixton Disorders*, 10–12 April 1981. Inquiry Report. London: HM Stationery Office.

Schissel, B., and C. Brooks. Eds. *Marginality and Condemnation: An Introduction to Critical Criminology*. Halifax: Fernwood.

Scott, J. 1990. *Domination and the Arts of Resistance: Hidden Transcripts*. New Haven, CT: Yale University Press.

Silverberg, C. 2004a. 'Can This Badge Shine Again?' *Globe and Mail*. 27 January.

– 2004b. 'After Stonechild: Rebuilding Trust.' *Globe and Mail*. 29 October.

Simmie, S. 2002. 'Understanding Jamaica: Digging Up the Roots of Violence.' *Toronto Star*. 24 November.

Skolnick, J. 1966. *Justice without Trial: Law Enforcement in a Democratic Society*. New York: John Wiley and Sons.

– 1996. 'A Sketch of the Police Officer's Working Personality?' In *Criminal Justice in America: Theory, Practice, and Policy*. Upper Saddle River, NJ: Prentice-Hall.

Slinger, J. 2003a. 'Police Union Sues *Star* over Race-Crime Series.' *Toronto Star*. 18 January.

– 2003b. 'Chief Fantino Takes a Swing and Misses Miller by a Mile.' *Toronto Star*. 13 November.

Small, P. 2004a. 'Judge Raps Police in Profiling Case.' *Toronto Star*. 17 September.

– 2004b. "Officers Acquitted of Beating Deaf Man.' *Toronto Star*, 15 October.

Small, S. 1999. 'The Contours of Racialization: Private Structures, Representation, and Resistance in the U.S.' In R. Torres, J. Inda, and L. Miron, eds., *Race, Identity, and Citizenship: A Reader*. Malden, MA: Blackwell.

Smith, C. 2003. *Borders and Exclusions: Racial Profiling and Canada's Immigration, Refugee, and Security Laws*. Paper commissioned by the Canadian Court Challenges Program, Winnipeg.

Smith, C., and E. Lawson, 2002. *Anti-Black Racism in Canada: A Report on the Canadian Government's Compliance with the International Convention on the Elimination of All Forms of Racial Discrimination*. Toronto: African Canadian Legal Clinic.

Smitherman-Donaldson, G., and T. van Dijk, eds. 1998. *Discourse and Discrimination*. Detroit: Wayne State University Press.

Solomon, P. 1992. *Black Resistance in High School: Forging a Separatist Culture*. Albany: State University of New York Press.

Solomon, P., and H. Palmer. 2004. 'Schooling in Babylon, Babylon in School: When "Racial Profiling" and "Zero Tolerance" Converge.' *Journal of Education Administration and Policy* 33 (September).

Solomos, J. 1988. *Black Youth, Racism, and the State: The Politics of Ideology and Policy.* Cambridge: Cambridge University Press.

Sorensen, C. 'Ottawa Police, Deputy Chief at Odds over Racial Profiling.' *Toronto Star.* 2 March.

Spence, C. 1999. *The Skin I'm In: Racism, Sports, and Education.* Halifax: Fernwood.

Stenning, P. 1994. *Police Use of Force and Violence against Members of Visible Minority Groups in Canada.* Ottawa: Canadian Centre for Police and Race Relations.

– 2003. 'Policing the Cultural Kaleidoscope: Recent Canadian Experience.' *Police and Society* 7:21–87.

Stoffman, D. 2002. *Who Gets In: What's Wrong with Canada's Immigration Program and How to Fix It.* Toronto: McFarlane Walter & Ross.

Sunahara, A. 1981. *The Politics of Racism: The Uprooting of Japanese Canadians during the Second World War.* Toronto: James Lorimer.

Symons, G. 2002. 'Police Constructions of Race and Gender in Street Gangs.' In W. Chan and K. Mirchandani, eds., *Crimes of Colour.*

Tanovich, D. 2002. 'Operation Pipeline and Racial Profiling.' *Criminal Reports* 1 C.R. (6th).

'Using the Charter to Stop Racial Profiling: The Development of an Equality-Based Conception of Arbitrary Detention.' *Osgoode Hall Law Journal* 40(2):145–88.

– 2004. 'Why Race Matters on Sentencing.' *Toronto Star*, 25 February.

Tator, C., F. Henry, and W. Mattis. 1998. *Challenging Racism in the Arts: Case Studies of Controversy and Conflict.* Toronto: University of Toronto Press.

Thompson, A.C. 1999. 'Stopping the Usual Suspects: Race and the Fourth Amendment.' *NYU Law Review* 74:956–1012.

Thorsell, W. 2002. "When We Fear to Speak Our Minds on Black and White.' *Globe and Mail.* 18 November.

Tyler, T. 2003. 'Judge Dismisses Suit against the *Star.' Toronto Star.* 25 January.

Ungerleider, C. 1992. 'Intercultural Awareness and Sensitivity of Canadian Police Officers.' *Canadian Public Administration* 32(4):612–22.

Van Dijk, T. 1988. 'How They Hit the Headlines: Ethnic Minorities in the Press.' In G. Smitherman–Donaldson and T. van Dijk, eds., *Discourse and Discrimination.*

– 1991. *Racism and the Press.* London: Routledge.

– 1993. *Elite Discourse and Racism.* Newbury Park, CA: Sage.

– 1998. *Ideology: A Multidisciplinary Approach.* London: Sage.

– 1999. 'Discourse and the Denial of Racism.' In A. Jaworski and N. Copeland, eds., *The Discourse Reader.* London: Routledge.

Vasil, A. 2003. 'Point of No Return.' *Now Magazine.* 1–7 May.

Verniero, P., and P.H. Zoubek. 1999. 'Interim Report of the State Police Review Team Regarding Allegations of Racial Profiling' 20 April. Report, State of New Jersey.

Visano, L. 2002. 'The Impact of Whiteness on the Culture of Law: From Theory and Practice.' In C. Levine-Rasky, ed., *Working through Whiteness.*

Waddington, P. 1999. 'Police (Canteen) Sub-Culture.' *British Journal of Criminology* 39(2):287–302.

Walker, J.W. 1997. *'Race,' Rights, and the Law in the Supreme Court of Canada.* Toronto and Waterloo, ON: Osgoode Society for Canadian Legal History and Wilfrid Laurier University Press.

Wallace, B. 2000. *The Taboo of Subjectivity: Towards a New Science of Consciousness.* New York: Oxford University Press.

Ware, V. 2001. 'Perfidious Albion.' In B.B. Rasmussen, E. Klineberg, I.J. Nexica, and M. Wary, eds., *The Making and Unmaking of Whitenesss.* Chapel Hill, NC: Duke University Press.

Wente, M. 2002 'Death, Guns and the Last Taboo.' *Globe and Mail.* 29 October.

Wetherell, M., and J. Potter. 1992. *Mapping the Language of Racism.* New York: Columbia University Press.

Wieviorka, M. 1992. *La France Raciste.* Paris: Seuil.

Wilkes, J. 2002. 'Chief Fantino Blasts the Media.' *Toronto Star.* 9 January.

– 2003. 'Chief Fantino Blasts Media.' *Toronto Star.* 9 January.

Williams, P. 1991. *The Alchemy of Race and Rights.* Cambridge, MA: Harvard University Press.

Wilson, B. 1997. 'Good Blacks and Bad Blacks: Media Constructions of African-American Athletes in Canadian Basketball.' *International Review of Sociology of Sport* 32(2):177–89.

Wilson, J.Q. 1995. 'Crime and Public Policy.' In J. Wilson and J. Petersilia, eds., *Crime.* San Francisco: ICS Press.

Wodak, R., and B. Matouschek. 1993. '"We Are Dealing with People Whose Origins One Can Clearly Tell Just by Looking": Critical Discourse Analysis and the Study of Neo-Racism in Contemporary Australia.' *Discourse and Society* 4(2):225–48.

Worthington, P. 2002. 'Profiling Essential to Fighting Crime.' *Toronto Sun.* 31 October.

Wortley, S. 1997. 'The Usual Suspects: Race, Police Stops and Perceptions of Criminal Injustice.' Paper presented to the 48th Annual Conference of the American Society of Criminology, Chicago.

– 1999. 'A Northern Taboo: Research on Race, Crime, and Criminal Justice in Canada.' *Canadian Journal of Criminology* 41(2):261–74.

– 2002. 'Misrepresentation or Reality: The Depiction of Race and Crime in Toronto Print Media.' In B. Schissel and C. Brooks, eds., *Marginality and Condemnation*.

– 2003. 'Civilian Governance and Policing in a Multicultural Society.' Discussion paper prepared for the Multicultural Directorate. Ottawa: Canadian Heritage.

Wortley, S., and L. Marshall. 2005. 'Race and Police Stops in Kingston, Ontario: Results of a Pilot Project.' Kingston, ON: Kingston Police Services Board.

Wortley, S., and J. Tanner. 2003. 'Data, Denials and Confusion: The Racial Profiling Debate in Toronto.' *Canadian Journal of Criminology and Criminal Justice* 45(3):367–90.

Yon, D. 2000. *Elusive Culture: Schooling, Race and Identity in Global Times.* Albany: State University of New York Press.

York, D. 1994. *Cross-Cultural Training Programs.* Westport, CT: Bergin and Garvey.

Yourk, D. 2003. 'Toronto Police Chief Slams Racial Profiling Report.' *Globe and Mail.* 9 December.

Index